# THE LEGAL HISTORY OF
# PIRATES &
# PRIVATEERS

# THOMAS J. SHAW

# THE LEGAL HISTORY OF
# PIRATES &
# PRIVATEERS

Cover images:

Left column: George Hay, Edward Ward, Samuel Sewall.
Middle column: Execution of Stede Bonnet.
Right column: Joseph Story, Nicholas Trott, John Marshall.

The materials contained herein represent the opinions of the author and should not be construed to be the views or opinions of the companies with whom the author is associated with or employed by.

Nothing contained in this book is to be considered as the rendering of legal advice for specific cases, and readers are responsible for obtaining such advice from their own legal counsel. This book is intended for educational and informational purposes only.

Printed in the United States of America.

ISBN 979-8-58680-010-7

# Contents

# *Dedication*

I would like to express gratitude for the ongoing support of my wife and daughter during the writing of this book amidst the pandemic of 2020, and my daughter's help with the proofreading.

# *Foreword*

This book is the fourth in a series of books on legal history, covering the legal issues that arose during certain significant periods in American, European, and global history. I started this series of books by looking at the Second World War. This was the war my father had fought in. Next, I wrote about the First World War, the war that my grandfather had fought in. The third, the American Revolutionary War, continued to go back further in time, to cover the first major global war the United States was involved in, before there was officially a United States of America. This fourth book partially arose out of research on the latter book, as privateers played a material role in the American Revolution. A later fifth book in this series looks at the 125-year period of the American Frontier, focusing on the four categories of actors who played the most significant roles on that frontier.

Like these three books on America during wartime, what hopefully makes this new book unique is it bringing a legal perspective to oft-told stories. It presents a look at the legal actions undertaken from both sides of the line delineating the criminality of piracy, in America and its legal ancestor, Great Britain. This book brings together in a single volume, and highlights, the major legal issues surrounding piracy and privateering. It also introduces many lawyers and judges involved with these issues, some well-known and some less recognizable today or long forgotten.

This book is neither a general history of the piracy and privateering nor a legal treatise but a legal history somewhere in between. There are literally hundreds of books on piracy and many more on privateering, which focus mostly on telling the story of a certain pirate or ship. This book instead looks at those stories only briefly, to find the legal issues presented through statutes, clarifying cases, crew agreements, ship's papers, court documents, and the many court trials of pirates, and captured ships and cargo. Nearly 200 legal issues are identified across the chapters of this book.

Geographically, the events in this book takes place almost entirely in the Atlantic Ocean and the varied bodies of water connected to it. The period presented spans from the era known as the golden age of piracy in the early 18th century to the American Civil War in the mid-19th century, and the effective end of privateering. Given the age of some of the legal materials available, they are often deficient in recording details and may be physically missing parts of documents. The trustworthiness of other documents, such as pirate articles, is uncertain. From these fragmentary and disparate sources come significant legal issues worth presenting.

The book is organized around three sections: the public crimes of piracy; the private agreements used onboard ships to regulate the voyage; and the public agreements between governments and privateers. The first and third sections are further broken into individual chapters covering first Great Britain, and America as a colony under British rule, and second the United States as a republic. Each of those four chapters is subdivided into two parts: a section on the statutes enacted to either suppress piracy or support privateering and a section on trials held to convict pirates or to condemn or acquit captured privateering prize ships and cargo.

The trials chosen may be of more famous or less famous pirates, privateers, or prizes. What is presented are not necessarily the complete stories of the pirates' adventures or the privateers' cruises, but the acts that illuminate legal issues. However, the trial records and sources used were of varying degrees of robustness. With the adequacy of court records often elusive, and to help facilitate the understanding of the reader, each trial writeup has a box with three of the main legal points found in that trial. Some trial records, especially for privateering cases, were rather brief, so three separate trials are presented in one trial group. The four pirate trial sections, across two chapters, each has five pirate trials. The four privateering trial sections, across two chapters, each has ten groups of trials, which may contain up to three trials each. The book presents more than 20 pirate trials and nearly 100 privateering trials.

Also, I must note that, for the quotations used within the book, I have endeavored to leave in their original wording. This often means use of words spelled differently than they are modernly, or words that are misspelled due to errors made by the original writer or transcriber. I believe this provides a much more realistic feel for the historical setting. This carries over into two other areas. The statutes cited are often based on very archaic spellings or usages and I have tried to preserve these as much as possible.

And proper names appear to have been recorded with several different proper (or possibly improper) spellings and it is not uncommon to see names spelled two or three different ways, in the same case or document. I do not consider any of these as errors needing correction but more as differences to be enjoyed. The reader should, in almost all cases, be able to easily substitute the proper spellings in their mind. Finally, some materials are quoted extensively, especially in the chapter on articles of agreement, ship's papers, and court documents. While paraphrasing may lower the word count, I believe reading the actual texts will better enhance the reader's understanding.

I have included a list of all the legal issues, the principal focus of the book, in the appendix, summarized by each chapter. My attempts to create an index were unsatisfactory, which properly would require a re-listing of the names of statutes and cases already in the footnotes, as well as a long list of defendants and plaintiffs involved in the trials and of all the varied ships involved, both those being libeled and those doing the capturing. I have chosen then to omit this reference at this time. I have also included Additional Writings that I have authored outside this book.

My intent with this book, as always, is to entertain, educate and inform readers, which I can only wish that I have achieved in some measure. While my target audience with this type of book is lawyers who enjoy legal history, hopefully the book's materials are at a level that can be read easily by those generally interested in this topic, or this period of history. Unlike my prior legal history books, this book is not presented to provide a foundation for the legal issues in the future, but more to capture a snapshot of a period in time, during the era of sail, which will never return, and to enjoy looking at it from a legal angle. My goal then is to have a single source to reinterpret often told tales of pirates and less often told tales of privateers, viewing them through the prism only of the governing legalities, while making the topics light enough to easily read for fun. I again hope that I have accomplished this in some small measure.

*Thomas J. Shaw, Esq.*
July 2024

# About the Author

**Thomas J. Shaw, Esq., Author, Lawyer, CPA, DPO**

Thomas J. Shaw is an EU-based lawyer and the author of a dozen books on legal history and on technology and privacy law, including books describing the legalities involved with pirates and privateers, global wars and wartimes, and the adventurers, speculators, settlers, and natives who populated the American frontier.

He can be reached at thomas@tshawlaw.com.

# Chapter 1

# PIRACY – BRITAIN,
# HENRY VIII TO VICTORIA

The history of piracy first began in the ancient world, around the Mediterranean Sea, with Egyptian, Phoenician, Greek, and Roman rulers and merchants suffering attacks on their towns and ships. The effects on commerce and security and therefore the wealth and prosperity of emerging city-states and nations led to laws addressing piracy. One such Roman law, in the first century B.C., was *lex de piratis persequendis*, which deprived pirates of land bases and gave Pompey the Great powers to tackle piracy. Illegal piracy continued to plague seaside towns and merchant ships over the centuries, and different rulers, including Alexander, Julius Caesar, Justinian, and Charlemagne and later, Louis IX, Ferdinand and Isabella, and Süleyman the Magnificent, all looked for effective ways to stop piracy's drain on their nations' water-borne commerce.

It was in the reign of Henry VIII that the first significant English law was enacted addressing piracy. Attacks by local pirates at that time occurred around the coasts and major rivers of the British Isles, so the law addressed only English courts. Yet the laws prohibiting piracy would need to expand as British commerce grew, following the flag. On the back of a burgeoning empire, the pleas of colonial governors and overseas traders to stamp out piracy committed by these *enemies of mankind* brought new legislation. A statute enacted in the reign of William III gave the British colonies overseas the same types of judicial tools to address piracy.

The incidents of piracy often came in waves, tending to wax after military conflicts ended, as now unemployed former privateers, with ships and crews available, needed to earn a living. It was from 1714, after the conclusion of the War of Spanish Succession, that illegal piracy saw perhaps its biggest boom. The first section of this chapter reviews the laws enacted in England/Great Britain, from the time of Henry VIII to Victoria. These statutes addressed piracy both within England and its overseas empire. This was to create an unfortunate dichotomy in the rules governing pirate trials based on the location of the trial, which would persist through this whole period. This dichotomy often found Parliament and courts trying to reconcile the differing rules for different locations.

The second section addresses the trials of captured pirates. Many of the more infamous pirates, such as Henry Avery, Blackbeard Edward Teach, Edward Low, Bartholomew Roberts, and Edward England, were never captured alive and their trials do not appear here. The trials presented are not based on the notoriety of the pirate, although many are well-known, but on the legal issues that their cases raised. These legal issues discussed include the extraterritorial jurisdiction of English law, the intention to turn pirate, acting piratically under color of a privateering commission, pirate crew members who were acting under compulsion and constraint, excusing those found on pirate ships, use of fellow pirates as witnesses, and the culpability of women pirates, ship's surgeons, and minor children.

## 1.1 STATUTES

English maritime law is of ancient origin but laws addressing piracy and the admiralty courts to try pirates were in a loose form by the reign of Edward III, in the 14th century.[1] Courts of admiralty, in dealing with international trade, were based on French, and therefore Roman, civil law. The laws used initially had originated with the Rolls of Oleron, a maritime trading island off the French coast, in the 12th century. The English admiralty courts were not created under any specific statute. Instead, they operated under the oversight of the respective admiral assigned to a specific region of the country.

This uncertainty caused overlapping jurisdictional problems with the existing common law courts. There were unclear geographic boundaries (e.g. how far up a waterway connected to the sea belonged to the admiral), and imprecise subject matter scope (e.g. which court had responsibility for wrecks, issues of seamen on land, or contracts about the sea). The ongoing tension between these two courts systems led, for example, in the reign of Richard II, to statutes that restricted the role of the admiralty courts[2] and later those in the reign of Elizabeth I that would expand it.[3] Sir Edward Coke described this tension in significant detail in one of his Institutes[4] and it would underlie the first two English significant piracy statutes, passed during the reigns of Henry VIII and William III.

### A.  16th and 17th Century

*1.  Henry VIII*

Replacing a similar statute from the previous year,[5] the Offenses at Sea Act of 1536 was enacted in the reign of Henry VIII, because "Traytors, Pirates, Thieves, Robbers, Murtherers and Confederates upon the Sea, many Times

---

[1] A Remedy where a Merchant's Good be robbed or perished on the Sea, 27 Edw. III stat. 2, c. 13.

[2] What Things the Admiral and his deputy shall meddle, 13 Rich. II c. 5; In what Places the Admiral's Jurisdiction doth lie, 15 Rich. II c. 3.

[3] An Act for Preservation of Spawn and Fry of Fish, 1 Eliz. I c. 17.

[4] The Fourth Part of the Institutes of the Laws of England, Concerning the Jurisdiction of Courts, ch. 22.

[5] An Act for Pirates and Robbers on the Sea, 27 Hen. VIII c. 4.

escaped unpunished."[6] This was because the civil law trials held before admirals, which had been used up till now, required that either the pirates confess, which was said that "they will never do without Torture or Pains," or required disinterested witnesses (not fellow pirates) to testify against them. However, as these witnesses were often killed by the pirates during the commission of their crimes or were ordinary sailors who had to return to the sea and could not stay around to testify, successful prosecution was difficult.

The changes that this statute brought was the ability to try these offenses at sea ("Treasons, Felonies, Robberies, Murthers and Confederacies") as if they occurred upon the land. This meant that defendants could be tried in any county in England, under the related common law provision for the offense, before courts operating under commission from the king (which were directed to the admiral and others appointed by the Lord Chancellor). This allowed for indictments and then jury trials on land for offenses at sea and the use of interested witnesses (fellow pirates) testifying for the crown. Those found guilty could not only be condemned to death without the benefit of clergy (which signified possible clemency, not clergy being available at the execution), but their lands, goods, and chattels could be ordered seized. The act did not extend to those who acquired "victual, cables, ropes, anchors or sails" from ships, either from necessity, when paying money for them, or if buying them on credit.

William Blackstone's comment on this statute's impact on the common and civil law was,

> "this statute did not alter the offence, or make the offence felony, but leaveth the offence as it was before this Act, viz. felony only by the Civill law, but giveth a man of triall by the Common law, and inflicteth such pains of death, as if they had been attainted of any felony, etc. done upon the land. But yet (as hath been said) the offence is not altered, for in the indictment upon this statute, the offence must be alledged upon the sea; so as this Act inflicteth punishment for that,

---

[6] An Act for Pirates, 28 Hen. VIII c. 15.

which is a felony by the Civill law, and no felony, whereof the Common law taketh knowledge."[7]

## 2.　Charles II

The law to Prevent the Delivering Up of Merchant Ships of 1670[8] was enacted because of the common practice of merchant ships' crews not defending their cargos against pirates. This had serious effects,

> "hereby not only the Merchants are much prejudiced, but the Honour of the English Navigation is thereby much diminished, and Merchants discouraged from lading their Goods on Board English Ships, to the Decay of Shipping; in the Preservation of which the 'Wealth, Honour and Safety of this Nation is so much concerned."

Ships of at least 200 tons and with at least 16 guns were required to fight, as were those of lesser size and armaments, if the pirate ship did not have at least twice as many guns. Failure to do so saw the commander banished from further command of English ships, under threat of imprisonment. Any monies or goods paid to the commander, by pirates taking the goods, was forfeited to the owners of the goods by a court of admiralty. Commanders were not to desert their ships for any reason when confronted by pirates.

Seamen were also required to fight, if ordered to, and not to discourage their shipmates, or to suffer a loss of wages and up to six months' imprisonment at hard labor. If seamen laid "violent hands" on the commander to keep him from defending the ship, he was relieved of penalties under this statute but the seamen who did so would then suffer death, considered to be felons. Up to two percent of the value of the ship and cargo defended could be used to compensate the crew who defended a ship, for those injured or maimed, and the widows and children of those killed defending the ship. Those crews who were successful in capturing their attacker were to share in the prize money.

---

[7] The Third Part of the Institutes of the Laws of England, Concerning High Treason, and Other Pleas of the Crown, and Criminal Causes, ch. 49.
[8] An Act to prevent the Delivery up of Merchant Ships, and for the Increase of good and serviceable Shipping, 22 & 23 Car. II c. 11.

*3. William III*

The Suppression of Piracy Act of 1698 was enacted in the reign of William III, to address the fact that piracy was occurring in places far from England and so it had become impractical to bring pirates all the way back to the British Isles for trial. The concern was not only for the cost of shipping pirates back home for trial but also for the impacts on commerce in the West Indies and India, which had recently become significant. Specifically,

> "that many idle and profligate Persons have beene thereby encouraged to turne Pirates and betake themselves to that sort of wicked Life trusting that they shall not or at least cannot easily be questioned for such their Piracies and Robberies by reason of the great Trouble and Expence that will necessarily fall upon such as shall attempt to apprehend and prosecute them for the same And whereas the Numbers of them are of late very much increased and their Insolencies soe great that unless some speedy Remedy be provided to suppresse them by a strict and more easie way for putting the ancient Laws in that behalfe in Execution the Trade and Navigation into remote Parts will very much suffer thereby."[9]

To address this problem, trials could now be undertaken on sea or on land, in "any of His Majesty's Islands, Plantations, Colonies, Dominions, Forts, or Factories." By a king's commission or commissions under the great seal of England or the seal of the Admiralty, any three of admirals, ship commanders, and colonial governors could call for courts of admiralty. Trials in these courts of admiralty were to be before a panel of seven persons, made up of known merchants, naval officers, and officers of other English ships. They could issue warrants for the arrest of the accused, to summon and examine witnesses, make a final determination, and then sentence the convicted to death.

Being available to courts outside England and the common law, trials were to be done "according to the Civill Law and the Methods and Rules of the Admiralty." It was no longer a jury trial, as it would be under the

---

[9] An Act for the more effectuall Supressions of Piracy, 11 & 12 Will. III c. 7.

common law. However, tying it to the previous statute, anyone convicted and,

> "attainted of Piracy or Robbery shall have and suffer such Losses of Lands Goods and Chattells as if they had beene attainted and convicted of any Piracies Felonies and Robberies according to the aforementioned Statute made in the Reigne of King Henry the Eighth."[10]

The procedure for trial was detailed, starting with the reading of charges against the accused and his plea. The witnesses for and against the accused were questioned in open court by the president of the court, and the defendant could then speak in his own defense before the court adjourned to consider the case before it. With a plurality of votes, the defendant would be convicted and sentenced to death and loss of lands, goods, and chattels, as per the statute of Henry VIII. There was no other sentence allowed for those convicted of piracy, felony, and robberies on the seas.

Those English citizens or residents acting under a commission from any foreign power against English ships or subjects were also subject to this statute. Any commander or seaman that turned pirate by "run[ning] away" with his ship or cargo, gave the ship or cargo to a pirate or conspired to do so, relayed "seducing Messages" from a pirate, laid hands on or confined the commander to prevent defense of a ship, or encouraged a revolt, were considered to be pirates. Informers who halted such a conspiracy were paid ten or fifteen pounds.

To prevent people who were not pirates from benefiting from the acts of piracy, those convicted of aiding, abetting, and counseling pirates were deemed an accessory to the crime of piracy. Those who, after the act of piracy, entertained or concealed such pirates, or knowing of their actions, received the ships, chattels, or good illegally gained, were also considered to be accessories. Accessories of either type were to be tried and judged as if they were pirates themselves.

---

[10] *Id.*

To encourage the defense of English ships, officers and crew were to be compensated, at a rate "not exceeding Two Pounds per Cent[um] of the Freight and of the Shipp and Goods soe defended."[11]   A reasonable compensation was to be determined by the admiralty court judge, advised by four disinterested merchants. It was to be levied on the owners of the ship and goods, and special compensation was to be paid to the widows and children of those slain in defense of the ship and cargo, and to those maimed or wounded.

To discourage merchant seamen from joining pirates, their wages earned would be lost if they deserted. To ferret out pirates hiding in America, the statute specified that only appointed commissioners, under this statute or the statute of Henry VIII, could call a court and try pirates in the American colonies and plantations. They could also issue warrants for the arrest of pirates, confederates, and accessories. Colonial governors and plantation proprietors were required to assist in the execution of these warrants and to deliver up these individuals located in their colonies. Failure to do so meant that the colony could lose its charter or propriety.

## B.   18th and 19th Century

### 1.   George I

There were several piracy statutes passed during the reign of George I. The first, in 1717, was the An Act for... declaring the Law on some Points relating to Pirates.[12]   It principally concerned the transportation of criminals to colonies, but it also allowed colonial courts trying pirates to follow, at their discretion, either the civil law rules under the statute of William III or the common law rules under the statute of Henry VIII. As there were few lawyers learned on the civil law in the colonies, they would be more familiar following their usual common law rules. It also clarified that those convicted as pirates under the statute of William III were to be denied the benefit of clergy (possible clemency), as stated in the statute of Henry VIII.

---

[11] *Id.*

[12] An Act for the further preventing Robbery, Burglary, and other felonies, and the more effectuall Transportation of Felons, and unlawful Exporters of Wooll; and for declaring the Law upon some Points relating to Pirates, 4 Geo. I c. 11.

A proclamation that same year from the king granted pardons to pirates who turned themselves in within a year, and offered rewards for pirates or others who turned in other pirates who had refused to surrender.[13] James II had issued a pirate pardon proclamation in 1687 and William III in 1697. A statute in 1719[14] made the act of William III, which had been set to expire, perpetual. An Act for the more effectual Suppressing of Piracy[15] was enacted in 1721. This required any commanders of vessels or others person who traded with pirates, supplied them with ammunition, stores, or provisions, or corresponded with them, to be treated as a pirate.

Those entering a merchant ship and throwing its cargo overboard or destroying it were likewise to be considered pirates. The ship and cargo of any vessel fitted out to trade with pirates was to be considered forfeit, with half going to the crown and half to the discover of the ship. Trying accessories to piracy, defined in the statute of William III, no longer required the trying of the principal pirate. Accessories could now be subject to the same punishments as if they were a principal pirate. Commanders and seamen were required to defend their merchant ship with arms and guns when pirates attacked it. If they did not, or discouraged others from doing so, and the ship was taken by pirates, they would lose their wages earned, and face six months' imprisonment.

Seamen maimed in defending their ships would be compensated, as under the statute of Charles II, and given preferential admittance to the Greenwich Hospital. To further address the desertion of seamen to pirate ships, ship owners were not allowed to pay seamen more than one-half of their wages in advance, until such time as the ship returned to Britain or one of the king's dominions. Any owner who was found to be doing so

---

[13] Royal Proclamation for Suppressing of Pirates (Sept. 5, 1717).
[14] An Act for making perpetual so much of an Act made in the tenth Year of the Reign of Queen Anne, for the reviving and continuing several Acts therein mentioned, as relates to the building and repairing County Gaols; And also an Act of the eleventh and twelfth Years of the Reign of King William the Third, for the more effectual Suppression of Piracy; and for making more effectual the Act of the thirteenth Year of the Reign of King Charles the Second, intituled, An Act for establishing Articles and Orders for the Regulating and better Government of his Majesty's Ships of War and Forces by Sea, 6 Geo. I c. 19.
[15] 8 Geo. I c. 24.

would be fined twice the amount of the money paid to the seamen, and these amounts paid in part to the informer.

## 2. George II

In 1744, the statute of William III was revised,[16] during hostilities between Britain and its current enemies Spain and France. That statute had required that British citizens or residents who took up a commission for a foreign power be deemed a pirate and subject to those punishments. This raised the question that, with these citizens and denizens already guilty of high treason, were they also guilty under this statute and subject to be tried in a court of admiralty? This revision to the statute addressed that question by definitively stating that these people who entered hostilities against their own country or host country could indeed be tried under this statute and convicted of being a pirate. However, anyone either found guilty or innocent under this statute could not then be tried for treason for the same acts. They could, however, be tried for treason if they had not been tried under the statute of William III.

## 3. George III

In 1799, the act of Henry VIII was revised to add more crimes.[17] This revision stated that all other offenses committed on the high seas, beyond "treasons, felonies, murthers and confederacies," could now be tried and judged in a similar manner. The punishments would be the same as if they committed the act upon land. The possibility of being convicted of manslaughter instead of murder was now also permitted, with those convicted of manslaughter instead of murder being given the benefit of clergy.

In 1806, a new statute addressed the fact that maritime murders, treason, and other felonies and misdemeanors which would be triable in England, under the statute of Henry VIII, were not triable under the statute

---

[16] An Act to amend an Act made in the eleventh Year of the Reign of king William the Third, intituled, An Act for the more effectual Suppression of Piracy, 18 Geo. II c. 30.

[17] An Act for remedying certain Defects in the Law respecting Offences committed upon the High Seas, 39 Geo. III c. 37.

of William III and those defendants had to be sent to England.[18] To diminish the cost and inconvenience of doing so, all offenses committed on the sea under admiralty jurisdiction could now be tried in the overseas colonies and plantations, "according to the common course of the laws of this realm used for offenses committed upon the land."[19]

### 4.  George IV

In 1825, a bounty act for the capture of pirates was passed by Parliament, "to give Encouragement to the Commanders, Officers, and Crews of His Majesty's Ships of War and hired armed Ships to attack and destroy any Ships, Vessels, or Boats, manned by Pirates or Persons engaged in Acts of Piracy."[20] This act provided rewards to the crews of privateers and naval ships for the capture or deaths of pirates, on ships manned by pirates or engaged in acts of piracy.

A sum of £20 was to be paid for every pirate either taken and secured or every pirate killed in an attack on a pirate ship, leading to the taking sinking, burning, or destroying the ship. A further £5 was to be paid for every other person either not secured or killed who was alive on the pirate ship at the beginning of the attack. The number of pirates onboard had to be proven by the ship's papers. This act also required that any British ship re-taken from the pirates be restored to the original owners, upon a salvage payment equal to 1/8 the value of the ship, cargo, merchandise, and other personal property onboard.

### 5.  Victoria I

In 1837, many of the provisions of the piracy acts of Henry VII, William III, George I, and George II were repealed and replaced by a new statute.[21] This act made assault with intent to murder or wounding that endangered the life of a victim, either committed immediately before or after an act of piracy, a crime punishable by death.  Those convicted of piracy could now

---

[18] An Act for the more speedy trial of offenses committed in distant parts upon the sea, 46 Geo. III c. 54.
[19] Id.
[20] An Act for encouraging the Capture or Destruction of piratical Ships and Vessels, 6 Geo. IV c. 49.
[21] An Act to amend certain Acts relating to the Crime of Piracy, 7 Will. IV & 1 Vict. c. 88.

be transported "beyond the Seas" for the life of the defendant or at least fifteen years or be imprisoned for not more than three years. Principals in the second degree and accessories before the fact would receive the same punishment as principals in the first degree, including death, while accessories after the fact could be punished by up to two years' imprisonment.

## 1.2 TRIALS

Trials of pirates under these English and British statutes would occur in various locations across the world, including in American courts before the American Revolution. However, not everyone tried for piracy was a pirate, as some were who happened to be aboard a pirate ship when it was seized. In 1724, John Fillmore, a fisherman and the grandfather of future U.S. president Millard Fillmore, was taken off his fishing boat by real pirates, but would later rise against them, leading to their capture. Separating the true pirates from the innocents was a key role of the courts in piracy trials. The following trials occurred during the years beginning after the Glorious Revolution in England, at the end of the 17th century, until the start of the American Revolution in the later 18th century.

Many well-known pirates and their crews, including Henry Avery's crew, William Kidd, Stede Bonnet, Jack Rackham, and William Fly and many lesser-known pirates would come to trial. One of the biggest problems for the judges in these trials was determining which type of law they were supposed to follow. Was it the English common law, or the civil law historically used in admiralty because of the trade connections with the European continent? The statutes of Henry VIII and William III were both employed by courts in trying to determine the rights available to those accused of piracy and the proper procedural rules to employ.

### A.   Trials under the Statute of Henry VIII

*1. Henry Avery's Crew*

| Legal issues to watch for |
|---|
| ❖   Scope of the crime of piracy |
| ❖   Importance of the intention to turn pirate |
| ❖   Extraterritorial jurisdiction of English law |

In October 1696, the trial of some of the men belonging to the crew of Henry Avery began at the Old Bailey in London. Avery's career as a pirate started in Spain aboard his purported privateer, the *Charles the Second*, in which he was first mate. However, the ship did not receive an expected privateering commission and the crew had not been paid their wages for several months. Part of a four-ship group sailing from England, the seamen on Every's ship and another ship mutinied, in May 1694, off Coruña, Spain, and took over the ship from Capt. Gibson. Renaming their ship the *Fancy*, so began one of the most profitable pirate cruises on record. When these successful pirates later split up, some returned to the British Isles, were captured, and brought to trial.

According to the statute of Henry VIII, a commission was chosen to hear this matter as part of the Admiralty Sessions (criminal court). It consisted of Charles Hedges of the High Court of Admiralty as president of the court, John Holt, chief justice of the King's Bench, George Treby, chief justice of the Common Pleas, Edward Ward, chief baron of the Exchequer, three more justices from the King's Bench, one from Common Pleas, one from the Exchequer, two from the Admiralty, and three Doctors of Law. These courts represented the various major branches of English law: admiralty civil law, common law (King's Bench and Common Pleas), and equity (Exchequer).

A grand jury was called and returned a true bill against Henry Every (who was not in custody), Joseph Dawson, Edward Foreseith, William May, William Bishop, James Lewis, and John Sparkes (as was common at the time, their last names were spelled variously in different usages). The crimes charged were for feloniously and piratically taking, on the high seas off Surat, India, the ship of Aurengzeb, the Grand Mughal of India, *Gunsway* [*Ganj-i-sawai*] and its cargo, including "100000 Pieces of Eight, and 100000 Chequins."[22] Dawson pled guilty, but the others pled not guilty. Surprisingly, (or not, considering the victims were all foreigners in a faraway place), the petty jury went against the prosecution's summation and found the defendants not guilty. Chief Justice Holt later described the verdict as "a dishonour to the Justice of the Nation."[23]

Another grand jury was called and to this jury, Justice Hedges defined the crime of piracy.

---

[22] The Tryals of Joseph Dawson, et al. for several Piracies and Robberies by them committed in the Company of Every the Grand Pirate (1696), p. 3.
[23] *Id.* p. 11.

"Piracy is only a Sea term for Robbery, Piracy being a Robbery committed within the Jurisdiction of the Admiralty; if any man be assaulted within that Jurisdiction, and his Ship or Goods violently taken away without a Legal Authority, this is Robbery and Piracy. If the Mariners of any Ship shall violently dispossess the Master and afterwards carry away the Ship itself, or any of the Goods, or Tackle, Apparel, or Furniture, with a felonious Intention, in any place where the Lord Admiral hath, or pretends to have Jurisdiction; this is also Robbery and Piracy."[24]

He next described the Admiralty's jurisdiction as,

"extended throughout all Seas, and the Ports, Havens, Creeks, and Rivers beneath the first Bridges next the Sea, even unto the higher Water-mark... also an undoubted Jurisdiction, and Power, in concurrency with other Princes, and States, for the punishment of all Piracies and Robberies at Sea, in the most remote parts of the World."[25]

This meant that the court could hear cases on acts by pirates of any nationality that took place all over the world, including for attacks on ships of countries with which it was at peace, such as those of the Great Mughal of India. Pirates were described as *hostis humani generi*, literally, enemies of the human race.

The grand jury returned an indictment against the same six men, this time for the theft of the ship they used in pirating, the English merchant vessel *Charles the Second*, charging them with piratically and feloniously taking this ship, its chattels, and cargo. The statute of Henry VIII allowed indictments to consist of "any treasons, felonies, robberies, murthers, manslaughters, or such other offences, being committed or done in or upon the sea."[26] Hedges definition of piracy had possibly expanded its normal meaning of taking another's ship and cargo to taking one's own ship and cargo, instead of just labelling it mutiny.

---

[24] *Id.* p. 6.
[25] *Id.*
[26] 28 Henry VIII c. 15.

Witnesses testifying included fellow pirates turning King's evidence, like seamen John Dann and Philip Middleton, and former shipmates who did not turn pirate, like second mate Joseph Gravet and second officer David Creagh. They placed Dawson, May, and Sparkes as crew on the *Charles the Second* before it was taken, while Foreseith, Bishop, and Lewis were part of a group of seamen who departed the *James* on orders of its captain to prevent the takeover but instead remained onboard the *Charles the Second* after the takeover. All who did not wish to join the pirate cruise were able to depart, so anyone staying on board, except the ship's surgeon, did so willingly. More damningly, none of the defendants departed the newly pirated ship when it soon stopped to take on provisions on the Isle of May, in the Cape Verde Islands.

The witnesses also testified to the ships and humans taken, the goods plundered, and the sinking of ships no longer required during their cruise and importantly, that all members shared in the plunder. The defendants were all allowed to interrogate witnesses or otherwise plead their case. Some claimed they were forced to pirate against their will, they knew nothing in advance of the intent to take over the ship and go on a pirate cruise, or that they intended to report to the authorities but were arrested before doing so. The prosecution believed the case against the defendants had been proved, saying,

> "These are Crimes against the Laws of Nations, and worse than Robbery on the Land; For in Case of a Robbery on the Land, we know who is to pay it; but in a Robbery by Sea, it often happens that innocent Persons bear the loss of what these Men do."[27]

Holt said that even though the men were not part of the original plan to turn pirate, because they took part in the pirating and received shares of the plunder, they would equally be guilty of piracy. He concluded by saying,

> "If you are not satisfied in your Consciences that the Evidence is sufficient to find these Men Guilty, in God's Name, acquit them. But if

---

[27] *Id.* p. 25.

you are satisfied in the sufficiency of the Evidence to convict them, you must find them Guilty."[28]

The jury asked a question of the court regarding the proof of consent for defendant Sparkes, whom they believed was tried for his consent to running away with the ship. Holt replied,

"What do you mean by Consenting? If a Ship be carried away with force from her Captain, diverse Piracies are committed with her, one continues aboard and receives a Share of the Profit of the several Piracies; Is not that an Evidence of Consent to the piratical Design? Was it not proved that many went out of the Ship, that were not willing to go on that Design? And that was with the leave of the rest that remained."[29]

The jury found the five guilty (Dawson had already pled guilty). The same defendants were subsequently tried and found guilty on two further indictments, for robbing and stealing two Danish ships and plundering a "Moorish" ship (the *Fateh Muhammed*, the escort of the *Ganj-i-sawai*). Thomas Newton, the admiralty advocate general, had told the jury that global piracy,

"disturbs the Commerce and Friendship betwixt different Nations; and if left unpunished, involves them in War end Blood... all the World is concerned in this Tryal, and expects and demands justice of them, if they are Guilty, at your Hands."[30]

Having been found guilty of piracy over three indictments (four for Dawson, who pled guilty to all), the court sentenced all six to the same punishment, saying that,

"you be taken from hence to the Place from whence you came, and from thence to the Place of Execution, and that there you and every one of you be Hanged by the Necks, until you and every one of you be Dead; And the Lord have Mercy upon you."[31]

---

[28] *Id.* p. 26.
[29] *Id.* p. 27.
[30] *Id.* p. 27-28.
[31] *Id.* p. 28.

They were all executed at Execution Dock, on the River Thames, later that month.

Other men in Every's crew went to America and either disappeared or were found innocent when tried for piracy. One, John Devin, was found innocent of pirating with Every in a court in the Bahamas and then had the local chief justice create a certificate proclaiming "the sd John Devins Innocency relating to the supposed piracy of Capt. Every als Bridgeman in the ship *Charles* als *Fancy*."[32]    Devin later used this certificate of proclamation to escape piracy charges when he was arrested shortly afterwards, in Massachusetts.

### 2. William Kidd – Murder

| Legal issues to watch for |
| --- |
| ❖  Pleading without benefit of counsel |
| ❖  Use of fellow defendants as witnesses |
| ❖  Implied malice |

In May 1701, the trial of William Kidd and his crew began at the Old Bailey in London. William Kidd had started his career as an honest seaman with a good reputation. This reputation led him to being recommended to the Earl of Bellomont by Robert Livingston of New York. The three made an agreement for Kidd to go on a privateering mission against pirates, with Bellomont putting up four-fifths of the cost of buying, fitting out, and provisioning a ship and Livingston and Kidd the other one-fifth. Bellomont in turn found five other men to subscribe to his portion, including John Somers, the highest legal officer in the land. Kidd was required to find the seamen for the ship and Bellomont to acquire the commissions for Kidd as a privateer.

Kidd was to seize the goods, merchandize, and treasure from pirates and to capture prizes (ships and cargo) of England's enemies. The crew was entitled to no more than one-quarter of the prize money, with Kidd and Livingston receiving one-fifth and Bellomont receiving four-fifths of what remained after the crew's take. If Kidd did not capture enough treasure

---

[32] Certificate of John Devin, by Bahamas Chief Justice Ellis Lightwood Esq. (Sept. 1696).

and prizes, excepting in the case of his death or a maritime disaster, he and Livingston would be required to pay back and so buy out Bellomont's share in the ship. If he brought back £100,000 or more of treasure and prizes, he would be given the ship as reward. So, there was significant financial pressure on Kidd from the start, to gather as much treasure as he could, to pay his crew, himself, and Bellomont.

Kidd started his cruise in the ship *Adventure Galley* from Portsmouth England, in May 1696, proceeded to New York, then to Madeira, sailed around the Cape of Good Hope to Madagascar, and then eventually on to the Red Sea, to await the Grand Moghul's fleet (ala Every). That fleet turned out to be too strong, as it was now also guarded by the English and Dutch, as penance for Every's attack. Kidd and crew moved to the southeastern coast of India, where they encountered the *Quedagh Merchant*. The indictments against Kidd and his crew were for piracy of this ship, with an additional indictment against Kidd only for murder.

Members of his crew indicted were Nicholas Churchill, James Howe, Robert Lamley (servant), William Jenkins (servant), Gabriel Losse, Hugh Parrot, Richard Barlicorn (servant to Kidd), Abel Owens, and Darby Mullins. The arraignment was held at the Old Bailey, before a court that included admiralty justice and London recorder (criminal judge) Salathiel Lovell. The trial judges would also include justice John Powell of Common Pleas, justices John Turton and Henry Gould of the King's Bench, Edward Ward, chief baron of the Exchequer, and Henry Hatsell, baron of the Exchequer. The prosecutors were many and varied, including the solicitor general John Hawles, John Conyers, William Cowpers, Mr. Knapp, and chief admiralty advocate Thomas Newton.

Assisting the defendants but not able to perform cross-examinations (which were done through questions asked by the defendants) were William Oldys, Mr. Lemmon, and Mr. Moxon. The commissions for the court were under the great seals of both England and the Admiralty. After the grand jury brought in an indictment, the defendants were asked to plead, which led to a series of matters being raised by Kidd, including his right to have his counsel speak, the right to delay the trial until his evidence arrived, and a request to extend the two-week time allowed for preparation. Prosecutor John Conyers was opposed to delaying the trial or allowing counsel before pleading.

Before the men pled, Nicholas Churchill insisted that he had come in on the king's proclamation of clemency, as did Owens and Mullins. Lovell said that if they did not plead, that was the same as a confession of guilt, leading all of them to then plead. The statute of William III stated,

> "And then each Prisoner shall be asked whether he be guilty of the said Piracy and Robbery or Felony or not Guilty whereupon every such Prisoner shall immediately plead thereunto guilty or not guilty or else it shall be taken as confessed and he shall suffer such Pains of Death Losse of Lands Goods and Chattells and in like manner as if he or they had beene attainted or convicted upon the Oath of Witnesses or his owne Confession."[33]

The first indictment tried was for murder and this only applied to Kidd, not his fellow crew members on the *Adventure Galley*. Although not stated, murder on the high seas was in violation of the statute of Henry VIII. It was alleged that he had violently, voluntarily, and with malice aforethought smashed a bucket ringed with iron hoops onto the head of gunner William Moore, a member of his crew, while sailing off the coast of India. This location in the high seas was considered within the jurisdiction of the admiralty. Moore lingered for a time then died. Kidd pled not guilty.

Kidd again requested and was granted the use of his counsel to speak on matters of law. William Oldys, an admiralty advocate for Kidd, requested a delay to the trial, as a witness was needed, and there to retrieve two French privateering commissions Kidd claimed he operated under, justifying his actions. The court agreed to send for the witness, but in the interim, would proceed with the murder charge. Witness Joseph Palmer said that Kidd struck Moore after insulting him, while Moore was busy filing a chisel. One of the prosecutors, William Cowpers, asked if Kidd struck Moore immediately after they had clashed over not taking a Dutch

---

[33] An Act for the more effectuall Supressions of Piracy, 11 & 12 Will. III c. 7, § 5.

ship they had recently encountered, or whether "he made a turn or two on the Deck."[34]

Palmer replied it was the latter and that Moore was in good health before he was hit and died. Kidd then asked questions of Palmer, trying to get him to admit a mutiny was afoot and his action stopped it. Palmer did not agree. The jury then inquired as to why Kidd had struck Moore. Palmer explained that two weeks' prior they had met the Dutch ship *Loyal Captain* and the two captains had boarded each other's ships. Some of the men had wanted to take her, but Kidd would not have it, leading to further resentment from the seamen. Witness Robert Bradinham, the ship's surgeon, was then called and he stated that Moore had a fracture skull and died of the wound given him by Kidd. The prosecution rested and turned it over to Kidd to put on a defense to the murder charges.

Kidd called three witnesses, all members of his crew who would shortly be on trial with him for piracy. Court president Ward ruled that the other pirates, no matter their guilt on that crime, could testify on this murder charge. First was Abel Owens, who said there was a mutiny on board when Kidd told those who wanted to take the Dutch ship that they would not be allowed back on to the *Adventure Galley*. This occurred weeks prior when Kidd refused to attack the *Loyal Captain*. Moore complained to Kidd that "You have brought us to ruin, and we are desolate."[35] Richard Barlicorn was next and related the near mutiny that occurred, "there was a Mutiny in the Ship, and the Men said, *If you will not take her, we will.*"[36] He identified Moore as one of the mutineers.

He also contradicted the surgeon, claiming that Moore had been sick for some time and the doctor had stated that it was not the blow from the bucket that killed him. Hugh Parrot then testified that right before the incident, Moore told Kidd "I could have put you in a way to have taken this Ship, and been never the worse for it."[37] Ward then summarized the charges and evidence for the jury. He explained that murder required

[34] The Arraignment, Tryal, and Condemnation of Captain William for Murther and Piracy, Upon Six Several Indictments (1701), p. 8.
[35] *Id.* p. 10.
[36] *Id.*
[37] *Id.* p. 12.

malice, either express or implied. "The Law implies Malice, when one man, without any reasonable Cause or Provocation, kills another."[38]

The jury had to determine if there was reasonable provocation from Moore's words immediately preceding the blow, or from the aborted mutiny of a few weeks prior. Given there was no mutiny present at the time of the blow, the court suggested there may be no valid defense for Kidd. The jury quickly found him guilty of murder.

*3. William Kidd and Crew – Piracy*

| Legal issues to watch for |
|---|
| ❖ Qualifying for a royal pardon |
| ❖ Acting under color of a privateering commission |
| ❖ Withholding evidence |

The trial for piracy for Kidd and his crew then started for robbery and plunder of the *Quedagh Merchant*, owned by Armenian merchants, and commanded by an Englishman. They were charged with piratically and felonious stealing the ship, and its tackle, apparel, and cargo. After the jury was sworn, the same three defendants raised the issue of the king's pardon, under which they said they surrendered. This proclamation from the king was then presented in court. Targeted at pirates operating in the East Indies, it read,

> "Requiring and Commanding all persons who have been guilty of any Act of Piracy… in any place Eastward of the Cape of Good Hope, to surrender themselves with the several Respective Times herein… to Captain Thomas Warren… and to Israel Hayes, Peter Dellanoye, and Christopher Pollard, Esquires, Commissioners appointed by us… to give Assurance of our most gracious Pardon unto all such Pirates in the East-Indies… who shall so surrender themselves for Piracies or Robberies committed by them upon the Sea or Land."[39]

The court asked whether the prisoners had surrendered themselves within the specified time limits. Mr. Moxon, acting for the prisoners,

[38] *Id.* p. 13.
[39] A Royal Proclamation (Dec. 1697).

introduced a document that stated they had done so, by surrendering to Jerimiah Basse, the governor of the province of West Jersey in America, in May 1699. The court ruled that this was a special proclamation with certain restrictions, including that those surrendering only do so to the four named people in it. As Governor Basse was not one of those so named, the court refused to allow the proclamation to exempt the three defendants and moved on to the trial for piracy.

Thomas Newton, again acting as an advocate for the Admiralty, described how Kidd had been giving a commission to catch pirates but instead had turned pirate himself, taking ships around India before returning to Madagascar. There the loot was shared out among the pirate crew of the *Adventure Galley*. Kidd also declined to fulfill his commission and seize the pirate Capt. Culliford of the *Resolution* when meeting him in Madagascar, instead befriending him. The prosecution again called as witnesses Joseph Palmer and surgeon Robert Bradinham.

Justice Powell made clear the issue was that if Kidd were sailing under a privateering commission and acting according to it, he would not be liable for piracy. If, however, he was acting under the color of the commission and acting outside of it, then that would be piracy. Bradinham and Palmer both testified to the piracy cruise, the ships and cargoes that were taken, the men who either signed on or were forced on, the tortures of captured crews, and the actions against the *Quedagh Merchant*. They also described how each of the defendants shared in the plunder and how Kidd befriended the captain of the pirate ship *Resolution* (renamed as *Mocha Frigate*).

The court had queried the witnesses several times on whose ships and whose cargo was taken. This was because of the commission issued to Kidd, which partly said it would,

"grant Commission to, and do Licence and Authorize the said William Kid to set forth in warlike manner the said Ship called, *The Adventure Gally*, under his own Command, and therewith by force of Arms to Apprehend, Seize and take the Ships, Vessels, and Goods belonging to the French King and his Subjects, or Inhabitants within the Dominions of the said French King."[40]

Kidd, on his way to New York, had taken a French ship as prize, which his privateering commission authorized but the *Quedagh Merchant* was not authorized by the commission. The goods he took from aboard that latter ship were owned by Armenians, who were not enemies of England like the French, so the seizures were not authorized by this commission. Further, there was a second commission, this one to cruise for pirates. This one gave Kidd,

> "full Power and Authority, to Apprehend, Seize, and Take into your Custody, as well the said Capt. *Thomas Too, John Ireland,* Capt. *Thomas Wake,* and Capt. *William Maze,* or *Mace,* as all such Pirates, freebooters, and Sea-Revers, being either Our own Subjects, or of other Nations associated with them, which you shall meet with upon the Coasts or Seas of America, or in any other Seas, or Ports, with their Ships and Vessels, and also such Merchandizes, Money, Goods and Wares, as shall be found on board, or with them, in case they shall willingly yield themselves. But if they will not submit without fighting; then you are by force to compel them to yield: And we do also require you to bring, or cause to be brought such Pirates, Freebooters, and Sea-Rovers as you shall seize to a legal Tryal... And We do hereby strictly charge, and command you, as you will answer the fame at your utmost peril, that you do not in any manner offend, or molest any of Our Friends Or Allies, their Ships, or Subjects."[41]

Upon query from the court, Kidd claimed he seized the *Quedagh Merchant* legally, because she had a French master (he was actually the master gunner) and had French passes, although he did not follow the required process to condemn such a prize. These French passes were claimed to exist on this ship by Kidd but were not seen by anyone else and they were never produced at the trial (perhaps they were withheld by an embarrassed Bellomont). For the pirate ship *Resolution,* he claimed that he did not seize it because too many of her crew were ashore.

---

[40] *Id.* p. 26.
[41] *Id.* p. 27-28.

Justice Ward summarized the case for the jury as being about whether they believed there were French passes, otherwise it was piracy. For the three servants,

> "if these Men did go under the Compulsion of their Masters, to whom they were Servants, and not voluntarily, and upon their own Accounts, it may difference their Case from others."[42]

The court also asked the jury to consider whether the three who came in on the proclamation for the king's pardon and whether the seamen thought they were operating under Kidd's valid commission. The jury returned with guilty verdicts on piracy for all except the three servants. The same men were indicted for four other piracies on their cruise, by two new juries. The trial repeated the witnesses from the first piracy trial and the verdicts were the same, guilty for the seven but not guilty for the three servants. Those found guilty of piracy and murder (Kidd) were sentenced to hang and were executed later that month.

*4.  Stede Bonnet and Crew – Piracy*

| Legal issues to watch for |
| --- |
| ❖   Choosing common law instead of civil law |
| ❖   Joining a pirate crew after being marooned |
| ❖   Crew member who was constrained |

The trial of Stede Bonnet and his crew began in Charleston, South Carolina in October 1718. He had started as a self-made pirate out of Barbados, building his own ship the *Revenge*, and paying his men wages, instead of the usual spoils of piracy. He would soon fall under the influence of the pirate Blackbeard, who would take many of his men and supplies, after the two had done much pirating together. Bonnet then applied for a pardon, which was received and sought a privateering commission to sail against the Spanish but as often happened, returned instead to piracy, and was eventually captured and sent for trial in South Carolina.

The vice-admiralty court was headed by Nicholas Trott, who was the chief justice of South Carolina. It was also comprised of ten more members

---

[42] *Id.* p. 34.

from local society. Trott gave the charge to the grand jury of 23 men, by instructing them on the statute of Henry VIII, ignoring the more recent statute of William III. In taking advantage of the statute passed the previous year in England which allowed colonies to choose to use either statute, Trott was attempting to use more familiar to both lawyers and civilians in South Carolina. The jurisdiction claimed was that within the court of vice-admiralty for that colony.

In defining piracy, Trott referred to the statute of Henry VIII and quoted from the usual legal scholars, including Coke, before veering over to the civil law and its scholars, concluding by noting that piracy was a felony under civil law and so piracy and felony were both used in the indictment. The grand jury returned an indictment, which charged "Stede Bonnet, Robert Tucker, Edward Robinson, Neal Paterson, William Scot, and Job Bayley, for feloniously and piratically taking the Sloop *Francis*."[43] Its retuned indictments against the same men regarding the sloop *Fortune* and their cargo, and against the rest of the crew for the same two ships.

Richard Allien, the colony's attorney general and lead prosecutor, introduced the case to the petty jury and Thomas Hepworth, a future chief justice, took over from there. Boatswain Ignatius Pell was the first to testify, describing all the varied ships and their cargo that the pirates had taken, including the *Francis*. Then Thomas Read, the captain of the *Fortune*, and a prisoner on the *Revenge*, testified to the men gathering their share and to the removal of the *Francis'* cargo. The captain of the *Francis*, Peter Manwareing, testified to the taking of the cargo and that he himself was required to remain a prisoner on the *Revenge*.

When it was the defendants' turn, the crew members testified that they were marooned, by Blackbeard, on Maroon Island after being robbed of their goods, arms, and money. When they were told by Bonnet that they could join his depleted crew and would be going to St. Thomas to get a commission to sail against the Spanish, they took the chance, instead of heading inland, as they had no money. The ships they took were just to get provisions, which were insufficient on the *Revenge*, to keep themselves from perishing. And many of them claimed no wish to go pirating but had

---

[43] The Tryals of Major Stede Bonnet, and Other Pirates (1719), p. 5.

no good answer when the court pointed out that they got a share of the loot.

The prisoners were tried before different juries in groups of six to ten at a time, for the piracies of the *Francis* and the *Fortune*. The same witnesses furnished their testimony, with the only differences the individual cases of certain defendants. One, Thomas Nicholas, claimed he took not part in the piracy and wished to leave the ship, but Bonnet would not allow him to do so. The witnesses confirmed this. The court termed him as being "under Constraint and Fear."[44] Three others who were taken aboard the *Revenge* were also found not guilty but 29 of the crew were found guilty of piracy and sentenced to hang, of which 22 were executed shortly thereafter.

Then Bonnet was sent to trial himself for piracy of the two ships whose captive captains were there to testify against him. Among his defenses to piracy of the *Francis* was that quartermaster Robert Tucker often overruled him when engaging in piracies and Blackbeard also did so when they sailed together. After being convicted of this piracy, Bonnet changed his plea regarding the piracy on the *Fortune* and pled guilty. Saying that he could easily have been convicted of a further eleven recent cases of piracy, He noted all the men who died either resisting his piracies or the attempts to capture him. The court then sentenced him to death, for which he was hung the following month, after several delays.

5.   *Edward Johnson – Revolt and Murder* and *William Lawrence – Piracy*

| Legal issues to watch for |
|---|
| ❖   Aiding and abetting in a murder on the high seas |
| ❖   Proving revolt on a ship from pirate's articles |
| ❖   Piracy when only receiving pirated goods |

In February 1737, Edward Johnson and five other members of the crew of the *Dove*, Nicholas Williams, Lawrence Senett, Nicholas Wolf, Pierce Butler, and John Bryan, went on trial in the Admiralty Sessions at the Old Bailey. They were charged with murder and revolt on their ship in September

---

[44] *Id.* p. 20.

1736, off the coast of Italy. They were accused of assaulting, and Johnson of murdering, Benjamin Hawes, who was the master of the ship. The other five seamen were accused of aiding and abetting in the murder of Hawes. Both crimes were accused of being done with "feloniously, wilfully, and of your Malice aforethought."[45]

Richard Walker, a captain's apprentice, testified first that Williams was hauling up the anchor to sail, even though there was not enough wind to depart. After hearing a noise "Like the Groans of a dying Man,"[46] he went to see the master but found Johnson coming up, with a knife in his bloody hand. Walker accused Johnson in front of other crew members, but when they did nothing to apprehend the killer, Johnson heard what was said and told Walker, "I'll kill you too." Freeing himself from Johnson's grasp, Walker jumped into the sea and swam to other ships, which eventually sent boats to catch the pirates.

William O'Mara, who was lying near to Hawes at the time he was killed, testified next. He said he was sleeping until hearing the noise from Hawes. Then he noted that Williams gave up trying to raise the anchor and instead cut the cable. O'Mara said that when he had first joined the crew, he was told that the ship was full of valuable cargo and the crew intended to take both the ship and the cargo and sell them. In a tavern, Williams, O'Bryan, Butler, Andrew Downing, Senett, and O'Mara made an agreement, assigning each of them post-mutiny roles, respectively, of captain, mate, supercargo, second mate, boatswain, and doctor.

However, the crew fell into dissention and decided to burn the agreement they had signed. Then Williams, Senett, Johnson, and O'Mara signed a second agreement, assigning themselves roles, after taking the ship, of captain, mate, boatswain, and supercargo. Butler and O'Bryan had read this second set of articles and were upset to have lost their original positions. Johnson also agreed to be tasked with handling the captain in any manner he wished. There was a disagreement whether to maroon the

---

[45] The Proceedings of the Old Bailey, London's Central Criminal Court, 1674-1913, t17370224-2.
[46] Id.

captain or kill him but on the night prior to his death, the crew met to load weapons and discussed the number of balls to load to kill the captain.

O'Mara finally claimed that Johnson admitted the killing in front of his crewmates. The prosecution rested, and the defendants asked no questions nor put on any witnesses. The court found Johnson and Williams guilty of the murder, as principal and accomplice. Senett, Wolfe, Butler and Bryant were found not guilty of the murder. Johnson, Williams, and Senett were also indicted for "for feloniously and piratically endeavouring to make, and causing to be made, a Revolt in the said Ship, and running away with the same,"[47] based on the second agreement. Those found guilty were sentenced to death.

In October 1759, William Lawrence, Samuel Dring, William Goff, and Hendric Muller, of the privateer *Pluto*, were indicted for piracy. They had been captured when one of their crew was impressed into the Royal Navy and decided to testify against his old crew to gain his freedom. The trial took place before the Admiralty Sessions at the Old Bailey, before Thomas Salisbury of the High Court of Admiralty, Edward Clive and Henry Bathurst of Common Pleas, and other commissioners.

The defendants were indicted for

"for piratically and feloniously boarding a ship called the *Enighadt*... upon the high seas, within the jurisdiction of the admiralty of England... in the county of Kent, in this kingdom, and assaulting Christian Van Asten, then master thereof, and robbing him"[48]

of various goods and monies. Van Asten, his mate, a passenger on the *Enighadt*, and Thomas Seal of the *Pluto* testified that Lawrence or some of his men demanded money and that Lawrence left some men on board and sent more men over, with the implicit understanding that they should take the cargo from the ship. Lawrence claimed he was in his cabin when the goods were taken off the *Enighadt* and further,

---

[47] *Id.*

[48] The Ordinary of Newgate's Account of the Behaviour, Confession, and Dying Words of Three Malefactors, viz. Captain William Lawrence, Who was Executed on Wednesday the Nineteenth of December 1759, for Piracy, at Execution Dock. (1760).

"that it was not he, but Hendrick Muller, who demanded the papers, and looked at them, and that one of his crew demanded and took the shot-money; owned that he fired a two pounder three or four times to bring him too; denied that he had any of those liquors to drink, which the Dutch captain said he gave him, or that he blacked his face, or otherwise disguised himself, or that he struck Van Asten, or any of his men, when on board him; or that he was present when four guineas more, besides the first two, were demanded and taken, or when the captain and crew were locked up in the cabbin...

[later] again denied he ever struck Van Asten, or saw any one strike him; but if he had been so struck, it must be after he had left the ship *Enighadt*, on which he had not been aboard above fifteen minutes... he denied that the six guineas therein charges, were taken by him, or one Doit, nor did he ask for any, but believes they were taken by lieutenant Seal and his company, as also the several other goods therein charged; and that the cambricks therein laid at 700 l. were by them brought aboard him, and quickly after sold by the said lieutenant, and another man, and then shared, among the ship's crew, to the amount of 225 l. or thereabouts, of which he declared he had no part; but the other men sold the bed-ticks, charged 100 l. value, and brought the price, and threw it down to him, which he kept to pay the charges of sitting out and victualling the vessel."[49]

According to Lawrence, he had been shortchanged wages in the last several sailing cruises he had been on, then turned to privateering, first about the *Lark*, then about the Pluto. Unfortunately, these privateers either did not capture any enemy ships or the ships that they did capture were not valid prizes. This long draught led to the situation on the *Enighadt*, where the crew fell into piracy. The Lawrence, Muller, and Dring were all found guilty of piracy but Muller and Dring were later reprieved. Lawrence, having "acknowledged however the justice of his sentence,"[50] was executed in December.

---

[49] *Id.*
[50] *Id.*

## B.   Trials under the Statute of William III

*1.  John Quelch and Crew – Piracy and Murder*

| Legal issues to watch for |
| --- |
| ❖   Use of common or civil law in colonial piracy trials |
| ❖   Accomplice testimony |
| ❖   Cross-examining witnesses |

In June 1704, the trial of John Quelch and his crew for piracy and murder began in Boston. Quelch was the lieutenant on the privateer *Charles*, commanded by Daniel Plowman, which was commissioned by colonial governor Joseph Dudley to sail against the shipping of the enemies of England, which were currently France and Spain. Upon departing in August 1703, Plowman became ill and the crew, not countermanded by Quelch, locked him in his cabin, where he subsequently died. Quelch and others then took over the ship and ignoring the privateering commission, turned pirate in the waters off the coast of Brazil.

Upon returning to New England, they were eventually captured and brought to trial locally, instead of being returned to England like William Kidd. The indictment for Quelch and 24 of his crew was for piratically and feloniously assaulting nine different ships belonging to the king of Portugal (an ally of England), killing crew members, and stealing various items of cargo, between the months of November 1702 and February 1703. To present the evidence, the prosecution pardoned three members of the crew, Matthew Pimer, John Clifford, and James Parrot, to use as witnesses. John Menzies was appointed attorney to help Quelch, upon matters of law only. The court had somewhat condescendingly pointed out, upon his request for counsel, that "The Articles upon which you are Arraigned, are plain Matters of Fact."[51]

Those judges commissioned for this vice-admiralty trial included Joseph Dudley, the colonial governor of the Massachusetts and New Hampshire colonies and the man who had sponsored the voyage, and his

---

[51] The Arraignment, Tryal, and Condemnation of Capt. John Quelch, and the Others of his Company, &c., for Sundry Piracies, Robberies, and Murder, Committed upon the Subjects of the King of *Portugal,* Her Majesty's Allie, on the Coast of Brasil, &c. (1705).

lieutenant governors of Massachusetts, Thomas Povey, and of New Hampshire, John Usher. Nathaniel Byfield was the vice-admiralty judge for both provinces. Samuel Sewall was an associate justice of superior court of Massachusetts (and a former court member in the Salem witchcraft trials). Over a dozen members of the respective colonial councils were also included as commissioners.

The trial started after two short postponements requested by the defense. The defense unsuccessfully requested that the prosecution witnesses be sequestered from each other before trial, but the court did agree to separate them during their testimony. Thomas Newton (former attorney general of New York, not the English admiralty advocate of the same name) opened the case for the prosecution and was followed by Paul Dudley, the attorney general of Massachusetts and son of the colonial governor and court president. He stated that this trial was to be conducted under the statute of William III. He also reflected upon local sentiment, saying that "though it may be thought by some a pretty severe thing, to put an Englishman to Death without a Jury,"[52] the commissioned judges were there to strike a balance of justice between the defendants and the prosecution, speaking for England's ally Portugal.

The prosecution opened the trial against Quelch by introducing samples of the many goods and coins the crew had taken during their piratical cruise and took pains to describe each as being Portuguese (or Brazilian) in origin. Pimer testified on what happened during the seizing of each ship, plus how Quelch had taken his journal pages describing the piratical acts. Two small boy captives taken from the Portuguese ships were interviewed in Spanish and French but did not speak those languages, just Portuguese. One of the boys testified that he was told to say he spoke Spanish by the pirate crew, if interviewed after arriving in New England. The other two witnesses soon followed, testifying to the same actions.

Things became more interesting when the defense counsel Menzies raised several objections to the evidence presented. The first was that the prosecution had quoted the use of the *London Gazette* to prove the alliance between Portugal and England. The court said the alliance did not

---

[52] *Id.* p. 6.

PIRACY – BRITAIN | 33

have to be proved, only that the two countries were not at war. He then offered a goldsmith's testimony that he could not tell between Spanish and Portuguese gold, which the court ignored calling it "very vain thing",[53] asking for an explanation from the defense for the Portuguese gold coins seized.

Menzies then noted the differences in the testimony of the three prosecution witnesses as to the locations of the ships attacked and the number of people on them, which the court termed "immaterial." He also pointed out that none of the witnesses spoke Portuguese and addressed the use of civil law versus common law. He said that Quelch could not be charged with murder under civil law, as that charge only applied to someone who strikes or wounds another. It was one of the crew, not Quelch, who killed the captain of one of the vessels they took.

Newton's response was contradictory to the civil law basis of the trial under the statute of William III,

> "That if the Common Law have Jurisdiction of the cause, all that are present, and assisting at such a Murder are principals. Now the Statute 28 Henry VIII makes all Felonies, Robberies and Murders upon the high Sea, Tryable according to the Rules of the Common Law, as if they had been committed upon the Land."[54]

Menzies then objected to the competence of the witnesses, as they had not yet received their pardons, which was typically only done after a conviction. After getting Newton to admit they were not pardoned, Menzies then reiterated that this trial was done according to civil law and under civil law, accomplishes could not be witnesses. Paul Dudley stated that under the common law, accomplishes could be witnesses, but Menzies protested he had not answered his objection, that the statute of William the III applied in the colonies to piracy trials, not the statute of Henry VIII.

---

[53] *Id.* p. 13.
[54] *Id.*

Further, if it was common law rules being used, then there should be a jury of local citizens, not appointed commissioners, deciding the fate of the defendants. Menzies said that,

> "the Statute seems to design an equivalent to a Jury, by directing the Commissioners of such Courts, to proceed according to the Civil Law, and method of the Court of Admiralty."[55]

Paul Dudley's weak retort was that the admiralty courts had used the common law since the statute of Henry VIII and the new statute should not change that, as "The second Aft of Parliament should be reconciled to that Method, to restore and set it up in the Plantations."[56] The court did not allow these well-founded objections.

Then, Quelch was asked if he had anything else to say, upon which he began to ask the witnesses specific questions. Joseph Dudley interrupted this line of questioning, saying that "This is not cross examining the Witness, but rather examining him over again."[57] This left the defense with little else to do and the commissioners then deliberated for just an hour, returning with a guilty verdict against Quelch. The remainder of the crew was then tried.

Three slaves, named Caesar Pompey, Charles, and Mingo, were found not guilty. Two members of the crew were found not guilty, one due to illness and the other was a young servant. Other defendants attempted to change their not-guilty pleas to guilty to receive the queen's pardon, but this was rejected by the court. Of the remaining 17 members of the crew, all were found guilty of piracy, either through guilty pleas or being judged guilty of piracy. Quelch and several members of his crew were executed at the end of the month, with the others eventually pardoned and pressed into service in the Royal Navy.

---

[55] *Id.* p. 14.
[56] *Id.*
[57] *Id.*

## 2.  Jack Rackham and Crew – Piracy

---

### Legal issues to watch for

❖  Charged with conspiracy to commit piracy
❖  Special proofs needed for women pirates
❖  Charged with piracy for socializing with pirates

---

The trial of John "Calico Jack" Rackham and his crew began in Jamaica, in November 1720. Rackham was a crew member of pirate Charles Vane's *Ranger* but eventually supplanted Vane as captain. He continued in piracy then sailed to the Bahamas to take advantage of a general amnesty by governor Woodes Rogers. He then returned to piracy, stealing a ship in August 1720, negating his pardon. Rogers issued a proclamation declaring,

> "that the said John Rackam and his said Company [including 'two Women, by Name, Ann Fulford alias Bonny & Mary Read'] are hereby proclaimed Pirates and Enemies to the Crown of Great Britain and are to be so treated and deemed by all his Majesty's Subjects."[58]

This led to their eventual capture and trial. The court was led by Nicholas Lawes, the governor of the Bahamas. The panel included William Nedham, the chief justice of the island, two navy captains, and ten other commissioners from the island's council and government posts, appointed under the statute of William III. The indictment charged John Rackham, George Fetherston, Richard Corner, John Davies, John Howell, Patrick Carty, Thomas Earl, James Dobbin, and Noah Harwood, with "Piracies, Felonies, and Robberies, committed on the high Seas within the Jurisdiction of this Court."[59]

They were charged with attacking and taking the ships and/or cargo, apparel, and tackle from eleven ships, including seven fishing vessels, two merchant sloops, commander Thomas Spenlow's unnamed schooner, and commander Thomas Dillon's *Mary*. Various witnesses on those ships came forward to testify to the piracies, including Spenlow, who testified to the piracy on his own ship and the *Mary*. The first charge was different than

---

[58] Proclamation by Woodes Rogers, Govenour of New Providence, &c. (Sept. 5, 1720).
[59] The Tryals of Captain John Rackham, and Other Pirates (1721), p. 8.

the others, in that it charged them with conspiring to commit piracy, as banned by the statute of Henry VIII,

> "upon the high Sea, in a certain Sloop of an unknown Name, being; did Solemnly and Wickedly consult, and agree together, to Rob, Plunder, and Take all such Persons, as well Subjects of our said Lord the King that now is, as others in Peace and Amity with His said Majesty, which they should meet with on the high Sea, and in execution of their Evil Designs, afterwards,,, did Piratically, Feloniously, and in a Hostile Manner, Attack, Engage, and Take, seven certain Fishing Boats."[60]

The defendants did not really put in any defense, except to claim that they were sailing against the Spanish, despite most of the ships attacked being English. The court took little time to find all of them guilty of piracy of Spenlow's and Dillon's ships and sentenced them to death. The next day, a smaller group of commissioners tried two more pirates for the attack on the *Neptune*, commanded again by Spenlow, who testified against both. They were found guilty and sentenced to hang. All eleven of these men were quickly executed and their bodies hung in gibbets and chains for public display.

A week later began a more interesting trial, that of the women pirates Ann Bonny and Mary Read. The two women were charged with the same four charges as the men on their ship, except that their indictments for conspiracy included not only themselves but also included their nine pirate comrades who had just been convicted of piracy and already executed. The witnesses against them included Spenlow, Dillon, and a woman named Dorothy Thomas, who encountered the pirates when she was in a canoe, testifying,

> "the Two Women, Prisoners at the Bar, were then on Board the said Sloop, and wore Men's Jackets, and long Trousers, and Handkerchiefs tied about their Heads; and each of them had a Machet and Pistol in their Hands, and cursed and swore at the Men, to murder the Deponent; and that they should kill her, to prevent her coming against them, and the Deponent further said, That the Reason of her knowing

---

[60] *Id.* p. 8.

and believing them to be Women then was, by the largeness of their Breasts."[61]

Two Frenchmen testified, through an interpreter, that the two women were on board Rackam's ship when Dillon's and Spenlow's ships were attacked and that they were very active, including handing gunpowder to the men. They sometimes wore men's clothes and other times, women's clothes. Importantly, "they did not seem to be kept or detain'd by Force, but of their own Free Will and Consent."[62] Dillon testified that Bonny was carrying a gun and "That they were both very profligate, cursing and swearing much, and very ready and willing to do any Thing on Board."[63]

When the prosecution finished presenting its evidence, the court asked the defendants if they had any questions for the witnesses or if they had any witnesses of their own to put on, but they declined. The court then found them both guilty of piracy against Dillon's and Spenlow's ships and sentenced them to death. Upon hearing the judgment, both women stated they were pregnant ("quick with Child") and asked for a delay in carrying out the sentences. The court ordered a stay of execution and an inspection of the women to determine if their claims were true. Their ultimate fates are unknown, but Read is said to have died in prison.

In January 1721, nine fishermen, John Eaton, Edward Warner, Thomas Baker, Thomas Quick, John Cole, Benjamin Palmer, Walter Rouse, John Hanson, and John Howard, were also indicted for piracy before the court of admiralty in Jamaica. The prosecution accused them, through two witnesses of going over to Rackam's ship, drinking on it, carrying arms, and while eventual captor Lt. Barnet was pursuing Rackham, some of the fishermen rowed the ship to help it escape.

The defendants told a different story, that they were approached by Rackam's crew to come over and drink with fellow Englishmen. They first hid and then refused the offer but were finally persuaded. Just after they had come on board Rackam's ship, Barnet attacked it. Rackam ordered them to help weigh his ship's anchor but when they all refused, he turned

---

[61] *Id.* p. 18.
[62] *Id.*
[63] *Id.*

violent, compelling them. When Barnet later boarded that ship, they immediately surrendered themselves. Despite their protests of innocence, most of the court voted to find them guilty, and all nine were sentenced to hang.

3.  *Charles Harris and Crew – Piracy*

---

Legal issues to watch for

❖ Piracy by attacking a warship believing it was a merchant ship
❖ Proof against a physician pirate
❖ Various reasons for excusing those found on pirate ships

---

The trial of Charles Harris, and his crew of 35, charged with piracy, began in Newport, Rhode Island, in July 1723. Harris was part of a pirate fleet along with pirate captains Edward Low and George Lowther. He sailed either onboard their ships or on his own ship, sailing in tandem with the others. Harris and Low then separated from Lowther and, while sailing along the eastern seaboard of North America and in the Caribbean, engaged in many instances of piracy and acts of cruelty to captured seamen. Off Delaware, the Royal Navy man-of-war *Greyhound* engaged them in a battle, capturing Harris' ship *Revenge* and his crew, while Low escaped.

The nine-man court for their trial, which would consist of several separate trials over three days, consisted of court president William Dummer, lieutenant governor of Massachusetts, Samuel Cranston, governor of Rhode Island (who had himself been captured by pirates when younger), Addington Davenport, justice from Massachusetts' superior court of judicature, John Menzies, judge of vice admiralty (and defense counsel in Quelch's trial), and five other government officials, such as members of the Massachusetts colonial council. Although the trial took place in Rhode Island, that colony had a troubled relationship with pirates, so it was deemed better to involve another colony's officials.

The long list of the pirates who would be found guilty included Charles Harris, Thomas Linnicar, Daniel Hyde, Stephen Mundon, Abraham Lacy, Edward Lawson, John Tomkins, Francis Laughton, John Fitz-Gerrald, William Studfield, Owen Rice, William Read, William Blades, Thomas Hugget, Peter Cues, William Jones, Edward Eaton, John Brown ("the tallest"), James Sprinkly, Joseph Sound, Charles Church, John Waters, Thomas Powell, Joseph Libbey, Thomas Hazel, John Bright, John Brown ("the shortest"), and Patrick Cunningham. Those who would be found not guilty included John Wilson, John Fletcher, Thomas Child, Henry Barns, Joseph Swetser, Thomas Jones, Thomas Mumford, and John Kencate.

John Valentine led the prosecution but there was no defense counsel. The charges were for piracy, robbery, and felony, including sinking the ship *Amsterdam Merchant*, off Cuba in May 1722, stealing its cargo, and cutting off the ear of its commander and, in June 1722, attacking the warship *Greyhound*, believing it was a merchant ship, and wounding seven of its men. Over several trials, John Welland, the commander of the *Amsterdam Merchant*, testified to the attack on his ship, and on him personally, by Harris in the *Ranger* and Low in the *Fortune*. He said that all pirates had their weapons harnessed (i.e. were armed with guns), except Thomas Jones, and that Henry Barns was sick and had tried to hide from the pirates.

The mate and the carpenter from the *Amsterdam Merchant* testified to the same facts. Capt. Peter Solgard of the *Greyhound* testified, upon a tip from a merchant ship attacked by the pirates, went towards their location and the *Ranger* and *Fortune* had chased him and fired upon his ship, mistaking it for a merchant vessel and running up the pirate's flags. He ran up the Royal Navy colors and engaged the two ships, eventually getting the better of them and capturing the *Ranger*. The *Greyhound's* lieutenant confirmed this account and the ship's surgeon confirmed their casualties. A sailor also testified that he had been asked to join the pirates, after being captured by them, showing their intent to go pirating.

The ship's surgeon, John Kencate, was tried separately, and several witnesses had varied perspectives:

"he seem'd not to rejoyce when he was taken but solitary... walking forwards and backwards disconsolately on board... the Doctor, who drank and was merry with some of the Pyrates... he never signed

Articles as they knew or heard, but used to spend great part of his Time in reading, and was very courteous to the Prisoners take."[64]

The surgeon aboard the *Greyhound* testified that when captured, "he searched his [Kencate's] Medicaments, and the Instruments, and found but very few Medicaments, and the Instruments very mean and bad."[65]

Some of those already found not guilty testified that Swetser had not used arms, did not board other ships when taken, and tried to be released from the ship, that Thomas Child had only been aboard the pirate ship a few days before they were taken, after he had been forced off his own ship, and that John Fletcher was just a boy on the ships. There was no defense put on, except the usual claims of being forced, so the court found 28 defendants guilty of piracy and sentenced them to hang.

Eight were found not guilty, with their ages and the reasons for acquittal as follows. Thomas Jones (17, servant, not armed), Henry Barns (22, ill and tried to escape), Thomas Mumford (21, Native American taken as a servant), John Kencate (22, surgeon who did not partake in the piracy), Joseph Swetser (24, had been forced and tried to leave), Thomas Child (15, taken by force and had not used his weapons), John Fletcher (17, boy), and John Wilson (23, reason unclear). Two others who had been convicted, Patrick Cunningham, age 25, who had assisted Welland after he had been wounded and John Brown ("the shortest"), age 17, were recommended for the king's mercy. The other 26 convicted pirates, ranging in ages from 20 to 50 years old, were executed a week after the final trial completed.

---

[64] Tryals of thirty-six persons for piracy in Rhode Island (1723).
[65] *Id.*

4. *William Fly and Crew – Piracy* and *John Baptist and Crew – Piracy*

---

<u>Legal issues to watch for</u>

❖ Accusing all men on a pirate ship to find the actual pirates
❖ Convicting and condemning minors for piracy
❖ Allowing piracy if the victims are enemies

---

The trial of William Fly and fifteen of his crew began in Boston in July 1726. Fly was the boatswain on a ship type called a snow, and named the *Elizabeth*, in April 1726. The *Elizabeth* was on a cruise to Africa, when Fly seized control by throwing the master and mate overboard to their deaths. He then renamed the ship *Fames' Revenge* and started on his pirate cruise, taking several ships and their crews. He was captured within a few months, after he had sent most of his crew off to man a prize ship to chase another potential prize ship, and some of his captives rose up and put him into irons. This led to his appearance in court, with members of his crew.

The court looked like that in Harris' trial three years' before. William Dummer, lieutenant governor of Massachusetts, was again the president of the court, and many members of the provincial council, were appointed commissioners. Also included was Samuel Sewall, now the chief justice of the superior court of judicature, Benjamin Lynde, Sr. and Addington Davenport, associate justices on that court, John Menzies, judge of the vice-admiralty court, a navy commander, the secretary of the colony, and the surveyor-general of North America. The prosecution was led by Robert Auchmuty, who would have a long career in vice admiralty, and whose loyalist son of the same name would serve on the vice admiralty bench, to the annoyance of American patriots.[66] There was no defense counsel.

The indictment was for the piracies, felonies, and robberies of the ships the *John & Betty*, the *Rachel*, and the *James*, in June 1725, by William Fly's crew in the *Fames' Revenge*. The first pirate tried was William Atkinson. The prosecution called the mate and two mariners, George Girdler, Joseph Marshall, and William Ferguson, from the *James*, who testified that Fly's ship hoisted a black flag and fired a great gun at them. When they were taken off the *James* to the *Fames' Revenge*, they did not

---

[66] *See* THOMAS J. SHAW, THE LEGAL HISTORY OF THE REVOLUTIONARY WAR.

see Atkinson armed. Then, Fly put six men on the *James* and went off to chase another prize. This gave Atkinson and three others on board the opportunity to clamp Fly into irons, seize the other three pirates still on board, and take the *Fames' Revenge* into Boston. The court voted Atkinson not guilty.

The same result ensued for Samuel Walker and Thomas Streaton, who were judged to be forced captives on the *Fames' Revenge*, taken from the *John & Hannah*, like Atkinson, who testified to that effect. Girdler, Marshall, and Ferguson testified that Walker and Streaton were forced men, and they were two of the men who had helped subdue Fly and lock him in chains. The court pronounced them both not guilty. Then John Cole, John Brown, Robert Dauling, John Daw, James Blair, Edward Lawrence, Edward Apthorp, and James Benbrooke were brought before the court. By the testimony of same three witnesses and the three men who were previously found not guilty, these men were said to be forced prisoners from the *John & Hannah*, the *John & Betty*, or the *Rachel*. Further, one of them, Benbrooke, had been the fourth man in seizing Fly. Again, the court voted all eight of them not guilty.

Fly was then tried, being charged with violently assaulting and causing the felonious murders of the master and mate of the *Elizabeth*, and taking the ship and its cargo; piratically and feloniously seizing the *John & Hannah* and keeping Atkinson and the master captive; piratically and feloniously seizing the *John & Hannah* and stealing some of its sails and apparel; piratically and feloniously seizing the *Rachel* and James Benbrooke; and piratically and feloniously seizing the *James*, taking the master and two mariners captive, and sending it off to pursue other victims.

As a precursor to the evidence against Fly, Auchmuty asked the court to ignore,

> "that Hackney Defence made by every Pirate upon Trial, namely, That he was a forced Man... what dangers they encounter'd, at the Risque of having their Brains blow'd, and what Severities they underwent... before they departed from their native Integrity. All which, if prov'd, will not, strictly speaking, amount to an Exemption from Punishment; For neither Necessary... or Self-Preservation, can legally justify the

Commission of an Act... But unmask these Dreggs of Mankind, and then they will appear Blaspheming their Creator, Coursing of Oaths, Embrewing their Hands in Innocent Blood, and checking their Hellish Inventions for unheard of Barbarities."[67]

One other sailor on the *Elizabeth*, Morrice Cundon, having been found not guilty of these charges for not being a willing pirate, testified, along with Thomas Streaton, against Fly. They said that just before the captain of the *Elizabeth* was thrown overboard, he said,

> "For God's sake, Boatswain, don't throw me overboard, for if you do I shall go to Hell: Then the said Fly bid the Captain say after him these words, viz. "Lord have Mercy upon my Soul. And soon after he was thrown overboard."[68]

Many of the prior witnesses testified to Fly's many acts of piracy described above and the court found him guilty of all the charges and sentenced him to hang.

His three crew members were tried next. Henry Greenvill was found guilty on all charges, George Condick on all but the murder charge, which occurred while he was sleeping, and Samuel Cole was guilty of all but the charges for the taking the *Rachel* and the *James*, as he had been put in irons for mutiny and did not participate. The court sentenced Cole and Greenvill to hang but,

> "in Consideration that the beforenamed George Condick was commonly Intoxicated with Liquor, and an Ignorant Man, about Twenty Years of Age, having no hand (as appeared) in the Murther of the Captain, or Mate, and seldom taking up Arms at the Caption of any of the Vessels, but mostly was imployed as Cook on board the Snow; The Court Voted, That the said George Condick be Recommended... for a Reprieve for Twelve Months."[69]

---

[67] The Tryals of sixteen persons for piracy, &c. Four of which were found guilty, and the rest acquitted (1726).
[68] *Id.*
[69] *Id.*

The trial of John Baptist and his crew of four began in Boston in October 1726. Baptist, his son of the same name, and three Native Americans: James Mews, Philip Mews, and John Missel, were charged with piracy on the ship *Tryal*, in August 1726. William Dummer again led the court, with significant numbers of the colonial council as members. Auchmuty was again the prosecutor but this time, there was a defense counsel, George Hughes. There were also interpreters for the two Frenchmen and for the Native Americans. Baptist had been on trial for piracy just two years before but was found not guilty.

The charges against Baptist and the other four were for feloniously and piratically taking the ship *Tryal* off Nova Scotia, holding the crew captive, plundering stores, provisions, and other valuable items, and then used the ship to sail about looking for other vessels to rob. Samuel *Doty*, master of the *Tryal*, testified that Baptist had originally come on aboard to drink but stayed to take over the ship and prepared to attack another ship, "loaded them [their weapon] with design (as they said) to take the said Scooner, if she had been an English Vessel."[70] But it turned out to be French. They continued to hold the crew on the ship, until they were finally overpowered.

Four other members of the crew also testified to these acts of taking over the ship, searching for other ships to take, eating, and drinking the provisions, and stealing items belonging to the crew. They also said that on coming onboard, that Baptist had noted that there was now peace between the English and Native American tribes, but this attitude changed when they turned piratical, including striking the English colors, with the son wearing it about his waist. They testified to the animosity the French and Indians had toward the English.

Hughes then raised two legal objections. The first had to do with the fact that this took place in a harbor and quoting from Giles Jacob's *Lex Mercatoria*,

---

[70] The Trials of five persons for piracy, felony and robbery, who were found guilty and condemned (1726).

"If a Pirate enter a Port or Haven, and Assaults and Robs a Merchant-Ship at Anchor there, this is no Piracy, because it is not done Super Altum Mare, but it is a downright Robbery at the Common Law, the Act being infra Corpus Comitatus."[71]

His second objection was that the son, at the age of 14, could not be charged with a crime resulting in a sentence of death. Auchmuty's response to the first point is that the principal statute of George I determined this, quoting,

"if Any Person belonging to any Ship or Vessel whatsoever, upon meeting any Merchant-Ship upon the High Seas, or in any Port, Haven or Creek whatsoever, shall forcibly Board and Enter into such Ship, and... destroy any part of the Goods or Merchandizes belonging to such Ship, the Persons guilty thereof, shall be deemed and punished as Pirates."[72]

As to the son, he quoted Lord Hale saying, "if by Circumstances it appeareth he could distinguish between Good and Evil, it is Felony."[73] The court judged both guilty of piracy.

The court then turned to the trial of the three Native Americans. Doty testified that James Mews had proclaimed himself captain and that he would burn the ship and keep the goods, until the English in Boston released his brother. Doty told him that there was now peace between the English and his tribe, but Mews said he would never make peace with the English. Doty also testified that all three were abusive and threatening to the ship's mate. The other members of the crew also testified to these acts and the thefts. The previous interviews with the three were introduced, where they blamed much on the French, who told them there was no peace, gave them rum, and encouraged them to attack the English.

The peace treaty between the Indian tribes (Penobscot, Narridgwalk, Saint John's, Cape Sables, and other Nova Scotia tribes) and the English was also introduced. Hughes objected, claiming that the peace treaty

---

[71] *Id.*
[72] *Id.*
[73] *Id.*

affecting their province was only ratified less than three weeks before the incident, and the men lived far away and could not have known of it. Further, they were told that there was no peace by both the French and English. Auchmuty disputed both that they were not at peace, based on an early treaty, and that the men should be ignorant of it. The court agreed with him and found all three, James Mews, Philip Mews, and John Missel, guilty and sentenced them to hang.

5.   *Ansell Nickerson – Piracy*

| Legal issues to watch for |
| --- |
| ❖   Use of circumstantial evidence to prove piracy |
| ❖   Using piracy as a front for a murder charge |
| ❖   Colonies' ability to prosecute murder on the high seas |

The trials of Ansell Nickerson began in Boston, in July 1773, before the special court of vice-admiralty. Nickerson was a passenger on a small fishing schooner sailing out of Boston, captained by his cousin, and crewed by the captain's brother and brother-in-law. He was found by another ship, which noted the distress signal flying. On the ship, it was discovered that the three men except Nickerson and the cabin boy were all missing, there was blood on the ship, and money from the sale of the last fishing catch and goods, including rum. had been stolen.

Nickerson was soon arrested and charged with piracy but pled not guilty at his arrangement. The trial was delayed until the following year, due to the need to obtain claimed evidence from another ship that had sailed around the same time. When the matter came up from trial the following July, the court was comprised of eight members, including Governor Thomas Hutchinson, Lt. Governor Andrew Oliver, Adm. John Montagu, and Secretary Thomas Flucker. Advocate Samuel Fitch led the prosecution. The defense was led by future U.S. president John Adams and James Otis, Jr.

Nickerson, who said he only made the trip to retrieve his clothes, explained that pirates had come on board from a twelve-oared boat, killed the three other men, thrown their bodies overboard, and kidnapped the cabin boy. Fearing impressment by the Royal Navy (a common problem for sailors in those days), he had slipped over the side of the boat, holding on to the stern. Fitch asserted that although Nickerson was accused of committing a murder, the murder and the taking of the ship from its captain and its money and goods were what made piracy the actual charge, under the statute of William III.

Fitch made many references to the civil law, often quoting from Jean Domat's *The Civil Law in its Natural Order*. As there were no witnesses, presumptions needed to be made from the circumstances, shown by the evidence. He said that there were many improbable things about Nickerson's explanation, including not being discovered by the pirates while hanging on under the ship. His whereabouts on land were unknown for some time, meaning he may have been hiding the stolen money. Not all the goods onboard had been taken, unusual for pirates. And despite an armed warship being sent out to look, no pirates were found nearby.

Adams's defense included that the interviews done with Nickerson by the original justice of the peace and some of the commissioners, were extrajudicial confessions and so should be thrown out. Being a trial under the civil law, guilt could only be proven a confession or by two witnesses (there were none), so it was important to get the confessions from the interviews discarded or discredited. Adams asserted that the entire interviews, not selected parts, had to be introduced. He also said that murder needs a body to be proved, that manslaughter was not a capital crime under the civil law, and cited examples from the *Quelch* and *Bonnet* cases.

The court deliberated, split 4-4, and ruled that the evidence was not sufficient, finding Nickerson not guilty. Hutchinson later explained the court's judgment was due to the statute of William III addressing only piracy, not murder, and although the charge was piracy, the prosecution was trying to prove this through a murder. To try him for murder would require sending him and all the evidence to England. If the local court convicted Nickerson in this manner, they would be exceeding their remit. This interpretation was likely based upon a 1761 opinion from the King's advocate, attorney general, and solicitor general, which said, "[is there] any sufficient authority for the trial and punishment of murder, committed upon the seas, within the admiralty jurisdiction, in the said colonies... upon the following questions... Question 1st - Does the act of the 28th of Henry VIII cap. 15... (being passed before the establishment of any of the British colonies,) extend to the said colonies; and if it does, how are the regulations therein set down to be executed? We are of opinion, that the statute 28 Henry VIII, does extend to the case of murder committed anywhere on the high seas; and, consequently, that a commission might issue, in the present case, into any county, within the realm of England, to try the offenders, who might be brought over, for that purpose, and the witnesses examined, and a jury sworn before such commissioners, unless that mode of inquiry and trial should be deemed inconvenient.

Question 2d — Does the act of the 11th and 12th of William III cap. 7th... or the 7th section of the act of the 4th of George I cap. 11th... contain sufficient authority for the trial and punishment of persons guilty of murder upon the seas, or waters, within the admiralty jurisdiction, in the plantations? We are of opinion, that neither of the acts of parliament mentioned, in this quære, were intended to affect the case of murders. They relate merely to such felonies as are equal, or inferior, to the species particularly expressed."[74]

---

[74] The opinion of the King's advocate George Hay, attorney general Charles Yorke, and solicitor general Fletcher Norton (Nov. 5, 1761).

## Chapter 2

# PIRACY – AMERICA,
# HUNTINGTON TO LINCOLN

There was illegal piracy in the Americas before the United States came into existence. The sea-borne transfer of gold and silver extracted from the Latin American colonies of Spain and Portugal attracted many pirates, as did the exports of sugar, coffee, and other produce from the French and British colonies in the West Indies. It was the armed ships of the British, French, and Spanish that tried to defend their country's commerce against pirates operating in the region. The British colonies in the future United States created their own navies to protect local merchant shipping. The dynamics changed when American independence was declared in 1776. Now only a small American navy and assorted privateers could protect American merchant ships, if they had the time and interest to do so. The Continental Congress tried to encourage this protection, passing ordinances against piracy, locally supplanting the British statutes discussed in Chapter 1.

With the founding of the republic in 1789, the United States enacted its own laws, under a constitutional power to define piracy. Congress tried several times to enhance the definition of what piracy encompassed. The overlap between the English common law, the law of nations, and American statutes would cause a fair amount of confusion in pirate trials. When these statutes were applied to the definitions and scope of the term "piracy," many courts ended up certifying questions to the Supreme Court for interpretation. The results were not always consistent, as different voices on the court espoused different world views on piracy, especially

Joseph Story and John Marshall. Around those interpreting cases, many pirates were brought to trial in federal courts, from the start of the 19th century until the American Civil War, with courts refining the boundaries of illegal piracy in the United States.

The first section of this chapter starts with the Continental Congress and its attempts to address piracy, before moving on to the constitutional power given to the U.S. Congress and the statutes that ensued from those powers to define and punish piracy. In enacting these laws, the courts were commonly asked to interpret the statutory meanings in various contexts, including who was a pirate and what acts were to be considered piratical. The second section deals with pirates as defendants before American courts. While long past the Golden Age of piracy in the early 18th century, piracy continued into the 19th century in many forms, especially around the War of 1812 and the wars for independence from Spain in Latin America in the 1820s.

The issues raised in these trials included trying pirates from other nations, the definition of piracy under American law, the mental state necessary to commit piracy, having foreign citizens on juries for non-American defendants, the difficulty in identifying pirates at trial, the culpability of those captured aboard a pirate ship, proving the ownership of a ship used by or captured by pirates, forced compulsion to commit piracy, trying Black pirates, the use of expert testimony in locating the likely location of a piratical attack, the jurisdiction of courts over piratical defendants, and whether Confederate privateers should be considered pirates.

## 2.1 STATUTES

Before independence, the thirteen American colonies had varied piracy statutes which were in essence just copies of the British statutes.[1] After declaring independence, no longer under the legal regime of Great Britain, both the confederated states together and the individual states, between 1776 and 1788, passed laws prohibiting piracy. The Articles of Confederation, passed by the Continental Congress, specified that individual states could not appoint their own courts for the trial of maritime pirates. States had previously created courts of admiralty which could try pirates, but that power now was reserved for the United States in confederation.

These powers were replaced in 1789 by the U.S. Constitution, which in article 1, section 8, gave Congress the power to "define and punish Piracies and Felonies committed on the high Seas, and Offences against the Law of Nations." Article 3 section 2 gave the United States the judicial power extending "to all Cases of admiralty and maritime Jurisdiction." With these powers, Congress enacted statutes banning piracy and the federal courts took on the exclusive jurisdiction for trying piracy cases. State-sponsored piracy leading to tribute, treaties, and war, like that waged by the Barbary States against the United States, in the late 18th and early 19th centuries, is not discussed in this chapter. However, those treaties' privateering provisions are discussed in Chapter 5.

### A.   18th Century

*1.   Confederation Period*

The Articles of Confederation, passed by the Continental Congress in 1777 but not ratified until 1781, included provisions that addressed piracy. In section 9, it stated that "The United States in Congress assembled, shall have the sole and exclusive right and power of... appointing courts for the trial of piracies and felonies committed on the high seas."[2] It took a while

---

[1] *E.g.,* S.C., An Act to put in force in this Province the several Statutes of the Kingdom of England and South Britain, therein particularly mentioned, c. 322 (Dec. 1712).
[2] Articles of Confederation and perpetual Union between the states of New Hampshire, Massachusetts-bay, Rhode Island and Providence Plantations, Connecticut, New York, New

but in March 1781, while lawyer Samuel Huntington was the president of Congress, a committee was formed. The committee reported back the following month, resulting in a new ordinance being enacted.[3] This law specified that those guilty of piracy on the high seas, either as a principal or as an accessory, before or after the fact, could be tried by grand and petit juries,

> "according to the course of the common law, in like manner as if the piracy or felony were committed upon the land, and within some county, district or precinct in one of these United States. And the justices of the supreme or superior courts of judicature, and judge of the Court of Admiralty of the several and respective states, or any two or more of them, are hereby constituted and appointed judges for hearing and trying such offenders."[4]

Those indicted of piracy or felony on the high seas would be treated the same as,

> "robbers, murderers, or other felons for robbery, murder, or other felony done upon the land within such county, district, or precinct, as by the laws of the said State is accustomed; and the trial of such offence or offences, if it be denied by the offender or offenders, shall be had by twelve lawful men of the said county, district, or precinct."[5]

This meant that piracy in the new nation would be under the common law rules, including the use of juries. Those convicted were to suffer death, loss of land, goods, and chattels, which would become property of the states, and convicted pirates could not receive the benefit of clergy (possible clemency) if this were not allowed for the same offense on land. To further clarify this meaning, a revision to the first ordinance on piracy was enacted by Congress two years later.[6] This further specified that the

---

Jersey, Pennsylvania, Delaware, Maryland, Virginia, North Carolina, South Carolina, and Georgia.

[3] Ordinance for establishing courts for the trial of piracies and felonies committed on the high seas (Apr. 1781).

[4] Journals of the Continental Congress, p. 355 (Apr. 5, 1781).

[55] *Id.*

[66] An Ordinance to amend an ordinance, entitled "An Ordinance for establishing courts for the trial of piracies and felonies committed on the high seas" (Mar. 1783).

courts for piracy trials could be comprised of a combination of the state admiralty judges and justices from the supreme or superior courts (common law judges), requiring at least two of them, one of whom must be an admiralty judge.

The use of the common law in admiralty proceedings may have caused some confusion to the states, as two years later, a resolution spoke to the need to make all states' piracy laws similar,

> "Whereas it has been the policy of all civilized nations to punish crimes so dangerous to the welfare and destructive to the intercourse and Confidence of Society with death in an exemplary manner. And it being consistent with that uniform system of legislation which should pervade the Confederacy in all subjects committed to the care and administration of Congress, That similar crimes should be punished in a similar manner, And as the Ordinance of April 1781, respecting the punishment of piracies and felonies has a different operation in some of the States."[7]

This proposal called upon the secretary of foreign affairs, who was lawyer. and future chief justice of the Supreme Court, John Jay, to respond, which he did with a detailed plan on conducting trials of pirates. He noted the limitations by,

> "the Power given to Congress by the Confederation, is not to declare what is or shall be Felony or Piracy, nor to declare what Shall be the Punishment of either, but merely to appoint Courts for the Trial of Piracies and Felonies committed on the high Seas."[8]

A year later, Congress tried to correct this deficiency, as part of an effort to amend the Articles of Confederation,

> "necessary to recommend to the several states for the purpose of obtaining from them such powers as will render the federal government adequate to the ends for which it was instituted."[9]

---

[7] Journals of the Continental Congress, p. 682 (Sept. 6, 1785).
[8] Journals of the Continental Congress, p. 797 (Oct. 3, 1785).
[9] Journals of the Continental Congress, p. 494 (Aug. 7, 1786).

Seven new articles were proposed, one of which would have given Congress the power to declare what is piracy and felony on the high seas, define appropriate punishments, and create a federal judicial court for trying those accused of these crimes. These revisions were not enacted, and the different treatments were not resolved until the Constitution came into force in 1789.

During the time between independence in 1776 and the start of the republic thirteen years later, several states created their own laws on how to try illegal piracy. These included the states containing most of the major seaports at that time: Charleston, Newport, Philadelphia, and Boston. The first was South Carolina, which passed a new statute even before independence, in April 1776,[10] revised it two years later,[11] and passed a new law in 1788, in conformance with the revised 1781 ordinance from the Continental Congress.[12] In September 1778, Pennsylvania passed its act regarding admiralty jurisdiction.[13] This was repealed by a new act, in March 1780, which started by describing the type of law it would follow in admiralty,

"in all cases of prize, capture or re-capture upon the water from enemies, or by way of reprisal, or from pirates, the same shall be tried, adjudged and determined, as well as to the question whether prize or not, as to the claims of the parties interested or pretending to be interested in the same, by the law of nations and the acts and ordinances of the honorable the Congress of the United States of America, before the said judge, by witnesses according to the course of the civil law."[14]

[10] S.C., An Act to impower the Court of Admiralty to have jurisdiction in all cases of capture of the ships and other vessels of the inhabitants of Great Britain, Ireland, the British West Indies, Nova Scotia, East and West Florida; to establish the trial by jury, in the Court of Admiralty, in cases of capture; and for the other purposes therein mentioned, no. 1019 (Apr. 1776).
[11] S.C., No. 1091 (Mar. 1778).
[12] S.C., An Act to carry into effect the Ordinances of Congress for establishing Court for Trial of Piracy and Felonies committed on the High Seas, no. 1396 (Feb. 1788).
[13] Penn., An Act for Establishing a Court of Admiralty, c. 811 (Sept. 1778).
[14] Penn., An Act for Regulating and Establishing Admiralty Jurisdiction, c. 887 (Mar. 1780).

However, when dealing with piracy, the act differentiated how the court would proceed, including that justices of the supreme court and the judge of admiralty would comprise the court and,

"And whereas the trial of pirates and other sea felons in the late British colonies, now the United States of America, hath been heretofore without a jury, and in a method much conformed to the civil law, the exercise of which jurisdiction in criminal cases was contrary to the spirit of the common law, although the legislature of England had, by a statute passed in the reign of King Henry the Eighth, entitled "For Pirates," relieved the subjects within the realm from this grievance. And whereas the constitution of this state provideth that in all prosecutions for criminal offenses no man can be found guilty without the unanimous consent of a jury. Be it therefore enacted by the authority aforesaid, That all traitors, pirates, felons and criminals who shall offend upon the sea or within the admiralty jurisdiction, shall be enquired of, tried and judged by grand and petit juries, according to the course of the common law, in like manner as if the treason or felony or crime were committed within one of the counties of this state."[15]

The act was revised[16] six months later, by including as acts of piracy: accessories before and act the fact; murder and manslaughter; acting against Americans under color of a foreign privateering commission; and any commanders or seaman who turned pirate. Other states followed, such as Rhode Island in September 1779,[17] and Connecticut one month later, giving its superior courts the power to try piracies, felonies, or robberies occurring on the high seas or within the admiralty jurisdiction "in the same manner as in case of felonies committed on the land within the jurisdiction of the State.[18]

---

[15] Id.

[16] Penn., A Supplement to the Act entitled "An Act for Regulating and Establishing Admiralty Jurisdiction," c. 915 (Sept. 1780)."

[17] R.I., An Act empowering the superior court of judicature, court of assize and general jail delivery, to take cognizance of all acts of piracy and felony committed on the high sea (Sept. 1779).

[18] Conn., An Act to impowering the Superior Court to try and determine Piracies, Felonies and Robberies committed on the High Sea &c. (Oct. 1779).

New Jersey passed admiralty statutes in 1776 and 1778, then again in 1781[19] and 1782, similar to Pennsylvania's statutes. Massachusetts passed an act in 1783 following from the congressional ordinance,[20] but other states did not implement this ordinance, instead passing varied statutes dealing with certain aspects as admiralty, according to the current needs of that state.[21]

## 2. Early Republic

The Judiciary Act of 1789[22] gave federal district courts jurisdiction over federal crimes on the high seas. In 1790, as the previous resolution of the Continental Congress had called for, Congress passed a statute was specifying the various crimes and the punishments thereof.[23] These criminal acts had to occur on the high seas, or in rivers or bays outside the jurisdiction of any state. The acts included murder, robbery, and any other crimes that would receive a death sentence if done on land. Any commander or mariner who "piratically and feloniously run away"[24] with their ship and cargo or yield the ship to pirates, or seaman who prevented a commander from defending a ship against pirates by violently laying his hands upon him, or who caused a revolt, were all considered pirates and felons and subject to death, if convicted.

Any American citizen committing piracy or robbery against the United States or its citizens under a commission from a foreign power was to be considered a pirate, felon, and robber, subject to death. Anyone aiding and abetting, on land or sea, "murder or robbery, or other piracy"[25] on the seas before the fact would also be subject to death. Those aiding after "any

---

[19] N. J., An Act for Regulating and Establishing Admiralty Jurisdiction, c. 7 (Mar. 1781).

[20] Mass., An Act for Carrying into Execution an Ordinance of Congress for Establishing Courts for the Trial of Felonies and Piracies Committed on the High Seas, c. 43 (Feb. 1783).

[21] *E.g.*, Va., An Act to prevent losses by pirates, enemies, and others, on the high seas, c. 69 (Oct. 1785); N.H., An Act for Extending the Powers and Authority of the Maritime Court in this State, c. 27 (Jan. 1787); N.Y., An Act to prevent encroachments on the court of admiralty, c. 24 (Feb. 1787).

[22] An Act to establish the Judicial Courts of the United States, c. 1, s 1, ch. 20, §§ 9.

[23] An Act for the Punishment of certain Crimes against the United States, c. 1, s. 2, ch. 9, §§ 8-12.

[24] *Id.*

[25] *Id.*

murder, felony, robbery, or other piracy,"[26] such as by entertaining, concealing, or receiving the stolen ship or cargo, were subject to up to three years' imprisonment and a $500 fine. The term "piracy" was used elastically to mean specifically robbery on the high seas or more generally all violent crimes committed on the high seas, including murder, robbery, and other serious felonies.

A series of offenses were subject to up to three years' imprisonment and a $1,000 fine. These included manslaughter on the high seas, attempting to corrupt a commander or others to yield up or run away with a ship, turning pirate, entering into a confederacy with pirates, communicating, trading with, or supplying ammunition, stores, or provisions to known pirates, fitting out a vessel to trade with or supply pirates, and a seaman confining a commander or attempting to cause a revolt. Maiming or disfiguring an American or anyone on an American ship was punished by imprisonment for seven years and a $1,000 fine.

## B. 19th Century

### 1. Revisions

Starting in March 1819, revisions to the original statute were made. The first[27] allowed armed U.S. warships to capture armed pirates or re-take any vessel that the pirates had captured and bring ship and pirate to trial before federal courts. Merchant ships were given the same powers to fend off pirates. Convicted pirates, with piracy on the high seas defined by the law of nations, were subject to death. In May of the following year, a statute was passed[28] that specified not only was any robber at sea, or in bays or roadsteads considered a pirate and subject to death but any robbery on land done from a pirate ship was also considered piracy. Those engaged in the international slave trade were also to be considered pirates.

---

[26] Id.

[27] An Act to protect the commerce of the United States, and punish the crime of piracy, c. 15, s. 2, ch. 77.

[28] An Act to continue in force "An act to protect the commerce of the United States, and punish the crime of piracy," and also to make further provisions for punishing the crime of piracy, c. 16, s. 1, ch. 113.

One further revision two years later reaffirmed death sentences for those convicted of certain offenses "upon the high seas, or in any arm of the sea, or in any river, haven, creek, basin, or bay, within the admiralty and maritime jurisdiction of the United States and out of the jurisdiction of any particular state."[29] These offenses included murder, rape, and striking, stabbing, shooting, or poisoning causing death. Their aiders and abettors received the same punishment. Those attempting but not succeeding in these crimes, or aiding and abetting the attempts, and other felonies, such as robbery, brought sentences of up to five years' imprisonment at hard labor and fines up to $1,000.

Those convicted of violently attacking another ship, including ships in distress, intending to plunder it, and their aiders and abettors, were to subject to ten years' imprisonment at hard labor and fined up to $5,000. In 1847, an additional provision was added[30] that allowed foreign citizens of a country in treaty with United States, who cruised against U.S. vessels or citizens, to be tried for piracy in U.S. courts. In 1861, after the outbreak of the U.S. Civil War, President Lincoln issued a proclamation[31] that made ships of the Confederacy attacking U.S. ships, their cargo, or U.S. citizens, subject to the laws on piracy.

*2. Case Interpretation*

There were many cases which interpreted the various provisions of the piracy statute in the early decades of the republic, especially with the wars of independence against Spain raging in South America. In *U.S. v. William Bevans*,[32] the defendant, a marine sentry, was charged with the murder of cook's mate Peter Leinstrum, under the 1790 act. They were both posted on a U.S. warship *Independence* in November 1816, which was in Boston Harbor, at nearest one quarter of a mile from the shore of the state. The closest federal land was one and three-quarters miles away. After being convicted, Bevans appealed on the question of whether the federal courts had jurisdiction. The Supreme Court ruled that Boston harbor was within

---

[29] An Act more effectually to provide for the punishment of certain crimes against the United States, and for other purposes, c. 18, s. 2, ch. 65.
[30] An Act to provide for the Punishment of Piracy in certain Cases, c. 29, s. 2, ch. 51.
[31] Proclamation 81—Declaring a Blockade of Ports in Rebellious States (Apr. 19, 1861).
[32] 16 U.S. 336 (Feb. 1818).

the jurisdiction of the state, having not been ceded, so the federal conviction could not stand.

In *U.S. v. Palmer*,[33] American citizens John Palmer, Thomas Wilson, and Barney Calloghan were indicted for attacking a Spanish ship, *Industria Raffaelli*, and stealing sugar, rum, honey, hides, coffee, silver, and gold, valued at nearly $100,000. These three were apprehended in Massachusetts, and after being indicted, appealed several questions from the circuit court to the Supreme Court. These included whether the statute could stipulate a death sentence for robbery on the seas when robbery on land was not a capital crime, whether the statute prohibited piracy against non-U.S. ships and nationals, and whether operating under a commission of privateering was sufficient to avoid being charged. The Court ruled that Congress had made robbery on the high seas punishable by death but that the statute was intended to protect against crimes against the United States and its citizens, not piracy launched from a foreign ship against foreign victims. This ruling led to revisions in the statute.

In *U.S. v. Klintock*, Ralph Klintock, an American citizen, was found guilty of piracy and appealed on several points, including whether his privateering commission excused the charge of piracy and because the victimized ship was foreign with foreign nationals aboard. The Court first ruled that, because he was under a commission from a non-recognized country, he could not have a proper privateering commission. On the second issue, the Court differentiated its opinion in *Palmer*, where the victimized ship was Spanish, with this case, where the victimized ship was not flying under a recognized flag. Because it was a U.S. citizen committing the piracy using the flag of a non-recognized entity, he was properly charged and convicted under U.S. law, as "offences committed against all nations, including the United States."[34]

In *U.S. v. Smith*, Thomas Smith was a member of a privateer commissioned by the government of Buenos Aires in its war for independence from Spain. The crew mutinied, left their privateer, and stole the warship *Irresistible* to cruise without commission, and soon

---

[33] 16 U.S. 610 (Mar. 1818).
[34] 18 U.S. 144 (Feb. 1820).

robbed and plundered a Spanish ship, in April 1819. Smith was found guilty in Virginia federal court of piracy under the 1819 statute, if his acts fell within that statute. Upon certification of that question to the Supreme Court, one issue raised was the lack of a specific definition of piracy in the 1819 statute, as required by the Constitution. The Court refuted that assertion, quoting many sources from the laws of nations, maritime law, and the common law, ruling "that piracy, by the law of nations, is robbery upon the sea, [*anima furandi*,] and that it is sufficiently and constitutionally defined by the fifth section of the act of 1819."[35]

In *U.S. v. Wiltberger*, the defendant master Peter Wiltberger was charged and convicted with manslaughter of a crewman named Peters. The death occurred while the ship *Benjamin Rush* was at anchor in the River Tigris in China, 35 miles from the mouth of the river. A confrontation between Wiltberger and two crewmen, Peters, and another name Clark, led the master to strike Peters with a stave. He was convicted on manslaughter, but the question of jurisdiction was certified to the Supreme Court. The Court noted that the act of 1790 had provided jurisdiction for "manslaughter upon the high seas," as opposed to murder occurring "upon the high seas, or in any river, haven, basin or bay, out of the jurisdiction of any particular state."[36] Because the ship was located quite a distance inland, it could not be considered to be on the high seas, so the Court ruled that there was no American jurisdiction over a charge of manslaughter.

In *U.S. v. Furlong*,[37] several pirates were variously charged with and found guilty of piracy and murder in different incidents. In Georgia federal court, John Furlong was charged with: the murders of master Thomas Sunley and mate David May, who had refused to join the pirates after an attack on their merchant ship; for the piratical seizure of an unknown ship; and for piratical robbery on an American ship. Benjamin Brailsford and James Griffin were charged in federal court in South Carolina for piracy. David Bowers and Henry Mathews were charged in federal court in Georgia for piratical robbery.

---

[35] 18 U.S. 153 (Feb. 1820).
[36] 18 U.S. 76 (Feb. 1820).
[37] 18 U.S. 184 (Mar. 1820).

The issue with Furlong was whether he could be charged under the statute of 1790, as the victims of his murder were not American citizens (they were all English) and the ship on which they sailed, *Anne of Scarborough*, was not American. Further, he was Irish, not American. The Court ruled that, as the pirate ship from which he launched the attack, *Mary of Mobile*, although registered to American owners before taken over piratically, had become aligned with no country. As such, the court had jurisdiction over such acts of piracy, and Furlong could properly be charged under the statutes for the piracy crimes against him. The murder charge, against a foreigner for killing a foreigner on the high seas, could be sustained under American jurisdiction if the killings had happened from or on the *Mary of Mobile* or her boat, as American ships. However, it could not if carried out on the *Anne of Scarborough*, an English ship.

Brailsford and Griffin objected to their convictions because, although they were American citizens sailing on an American ship, they had a privateer commission to cruise against ships of a country at peace with the United States. The court rejected the claim that such a commission could cover up acts of piracy. Bowers and Mathews were American citizens convicted of piratical robbery against the American ship *Asia* and the British ship *Sir Thomas Hardy*. They were part of a crew that turned pirate on the privateer *Louisa*, fighting in the wars of independence from Spain. Among their objections were that the act of 1790 did not apply to crew of a foreign vessel attacking a foreign vessel (in the attack on the British ship), but the Court rejected that, as American court jurisdiction over piracy applied to American citizens anywhere.

In *U.S. v. Holmes*,[38] William Holmes, Thomas Warrington, and Edward Rosewain, only one of whom was American, were accused of killing master Reed, by stabbing and throwing him overboard. Reed was the master of a prize ship captured by privateers commissioned by Buenos Aires. Upon certification, the Court reaffirmed American jurisdiction over any piratical ship where murder or robbery occurred, unless it was definitively owned and controlled by a recognized foreign state. It also reaffirmed that murder or robbery done by those on an American ship (both privateer

---

[38] 18 U.S. 412 (Mar. 1820).

commanders had ties to America), or a pirate ship, were both subject to American jurisdiction, and the citizenships of the perpetrators and the victim were not relevant.

In *The Marianna Flora*, Lt. Stockton of the U.S. warship *Alligator* believed, based on the actions by the Portuguese ship *Marianna Flora,* first that she needed assistance and then, after that ship opened fire, she was either a pirate or slaver. He returned fire and the merchant ship surrendered. On being libeled, one of the questions raised before the Supreme Court was whether the attack by the merchant ship was piratical. The Court answered negatively, ruling that there was no piratical intent to plunder. The Court also ruled that "Pirates may, without doubt, be lawfully captured on the ocean by the public or private ships of every nation, for they are... the common enemies of all mankind... But every hostile attack in a time of peace is not necessarily piratical. It may be by mistake, or in necessary self-defense, or to repel a supposed meditated attack by pirates. It may be justifiable."[39]

In *U.S. v. Kelly*, Kelly and others were charged and convicted of making a revolt on the high seas on the U.S. merchant vessel *Lancaster*, in violation of the 1790 act. The definition of revolt was not stated in the statute, so upon certification, the Court defined that it "consists in the endeavour of the crew of a vessel, or any one or more of them, to overthrow the legitimate authority of her commander, with intent to remove him from his command, or against his will to take possession of the vessel by assuming the government and navigation of her, or by transferring their obedience from the lawful commander to some other person."[40]

In *Peter Harmony v. U.S.*, the act of 1819 was used to charge the acts of the captain of the brig *Malek Adhel*. As testified by the crew, the captain Joseph Nunez, on a merchant voyage from New York to California, fired at several ships, demanded various items from their crews, and sometimes sent armed boarding parties and restrained members of the other crews. The ship was taken into custody by the U.S. warship *Enterprise* while in Brazil and returned to the United States for condemnation. The issues

---

[39] 24 U.S. 1 (Feb. 1826).
[40] 24 U.S. 417 (Feb. 1826).

raised included whether the brig was considered an armed vessel and if the "aggressions, restraints, and depredation"[41] were piratical.

The ship had a cannon and pistols and knives on board, which the Court considered sufficient to be an armed vessel,

> "No distinction is taken, or even suggested in the act, as to the objects, or purposes, or character of the armament, whether it be for offence or defence, legitimate or illegitimate."[42]

The Court also said piracy was more than just an intent to plunder and found the actions of the captain piratical,

> "Where the act uses the word "piratical," it does so in a general sense; importing that the aggression is unauthorized by the law of nations, hostile in its character, wanton and criminal in its commission, and utterly without any sanction from any public authority or sovereign power… It punishes any piratical aggression or piratical search, or piratical restraint, or piratical seizure, as well as a piratical depredation. Either is sufficient. The search or restraint may be piratical although no plunder follows."[43]

---

[41] 43 U.S. 210 (1844).
[42] *Id.*
[43] *Id.*

## 2.2 TRIALS

Trials of pirates under the American statutes began in the 1790s and continued until the American Civil War. In the period after independence but before the start of the republic, captured pirates like loyalist supporter Joseph Wheland, Jr., during the Revolutionary War, could be detained by the local committees of safety.[44] An early example of a trial under the new U.S. statutes was that of three pirates aboard the schooner *Eliza*. In 1799, they rose against their captain, murdered other members of the crew, and tried to steal the ship and its contents, only to finally be captured by their captain. They were tried before the U.S. circuit court in April 1800, convicted, and executed the following month.

There were also federal trials of pirates of many nationalities, like the *Eliza* pirates, who were of Scandinavian and French-Canadian origin, but were tried under American law. With piracy considered a crime against humanity, U.S. courts frequently dealt with pirates from different countries, when there may not have been either a U.S. ship or U.S. citizen involved. The largest number of trials presented occurred around the War of 1812 and the wars of independence against Spain in the 1820s, with several more trials at the beginning of the American Civil War.

### A. Adams to Adams

*1. William Brigstock and Jonathan Robbins – Piracy and Murder*

| Legal issues to watch for |
|---|
| ❖  Piracy on non-U.S. ships by non-U.S. nationals tried in U.S. courts |
| ❖  Prosecutorial discretion to not try piracy and murder |
| ❖  Concurrent jurisdiction for crimes on the high seas |

The first major federal piracy cases involved mutiny, murder, piracy, impressment, and international relations. These cases arose out of a mutiny aboard the British warship *Hermione*, in September 1797, off Puerto Rico. This was during the Napoleonic Wars, when the French and their Spanish allies were the enemies of the British. The ship's crew

---

[44] Journal and Correspondence of the Maryland Council of Safety, July 7-Dec. 31, 1776, p. 166.

revolted against a cruel captain, killed him and several other officers, sailed the ship into Spanish-controlled waters in Venezuela, and disposed of it. Several of the mutineers were subsequently captured, convicted at a British naval court martial, and executed. Three of the crew, William Brigstock, John Evans, and Johannes Williams, British nationals by birth, were later arrested in New Jersey, in March 1798.

They went on trial the following month, for murder and piracy, in the U.S. federal court in New Jersey. There were three separate indictments. First, the grand jury indicted Brigstock, Evans, and Williams for piracy under the statute, as the actions occurred "out of the jurisdiction of any particular state of the United States, and within the jurisdiction of this court."[45] Specifically, they were accused of stealing the ship, its tackle, and apparel, worth $50,000 and,

> "one silver tankard, of the value of fifty dollars like money, and one gold watch of the value of one hundred dollars of like money, and one silver spoon of the value of two dollars of like money, of the goods and chattels of certain subjects of the said king of Great Britain... piratically, and feloniously did run away with."[46]

Before district judge Robert Morris and Supreme Court justice Samuel Chase riding circuit, the three were brought to trial, prosecuted by U.S. district attorney Lucius Horatio Stockton, and defended by state attorney general Aaron Woodruff. The sole witness against them was Frances Martin, the wife of one of the seamen killed aboard the *Hermione*, who witnessed the mutiny and was victimized by it. She could not identify the piratical acts of Evans or Williams and with Brigstock claiming American citizenship, the jury quickly found all three not guilty of piracy. Brigstock alone was indicted for the murder of Lt. Henry Foreshaw, one of the officers who had been attacked on the *Hermione*, struck with a tomahawk,

---

[45] U.S. v. Henry Brigstock (Mid. Cir. Apr. 1798), from *The Trial of William Brigstock and Others for Murder and Piracy* (1800), p. 4-5.
[46] *Id.* p. 5.

"feloniously, piratically, wilfully, and of his malice aforethought, did kill and murder, against the peace of the United States, and against the form of the statute."[47]

Brigstock was also separately indicted for piracy under the statute, for betraying the trust of his position as boatswain's (bosun's) mate. For these charges, there was more evidence, as Mrs. Martin said Brigstock was active in the mutiny and murders. Before these two indictments could proceed to trial, an unusual event occurred, when prosecutor Stockton announced that U.S. president John Adams had ordered him to drop the charges against this British citizen,

"By the special command of the President of the United States, a *nolle prosequi* is entered on this indictment the twenty-eighth day of June, in the year of our Lord one thousand seven hundred and ninety-eight."[48]

The British had claimed, under the 1794 Jay Treaty,[49] that they had a right to try their own citizens for incidents on the high seas. Article 27 of that treaty required each country to deliver up any of other country's citizens charged with murder in either jurisdiction, if the evidence of the crime would justify a trial in the country where the fugitive was found. The Adams administration apparently did not believe there was sufficient evidence, as the British purportedly sent new evidence from the Royal Navy that Brigstock may not have been involved. There was also the matter that Brigstock claimed he was an American citizen who had been impressed by the British, a major source of diplomatic tension at that time. Rather than taking him to trial and risk a not guilty jury verdict, it was decided to not try him at all.

This may have been predicated on an opinion from the U.S. attorney general, Charles Lee. In this opinion, in March 1798, just before the trial, he had said that under the Jay Treaty, the United States was required to

---

[47] *Id.* p. 6.

[48] *Id.* p. 8.

[49] Treaty of Amity Commerce and Navigation, between His Britannick Majesty; and The United States of America, by Their President, with the advice and consent of Their Senate (Nov. 1794).

extradite British citizens fugitive in the United States only if the murder was committed in the territorial jurisdiction of Great Britain, not if it was committed on the high seas. Whether they were American citizens or foreigners,

> "as they are triable in the courts of the United States, and in the custody of our laws for trial, I deem it more becoming the justice, honor, and dignity of the United States, that the trial should be in our courts."[50]

This was not the end of the *Hermione* piracy trials in the United States. In February 1799, another mutineer was arrested, in South Carolina. Former bosun's mate Jonathan Robbins came before the district court, but he had not been indicted for piracy and murder before a grand jury. Instead, the British were asking for extradition under article 27 of the Jay Treaty, helped by a "request" from President Adams. Judge Thomas Bee heard Robbins' claim to be an impressed American sailor, proved by providing his own notarized affidavits of citizenship, but Bee ruled these to not be evidence (defendants could not testify for themselves at that time). This contrasted with an affidavit of Lt. John Forbes of the Royal Navy, who knew Robbins from his time on the *Hermione*. Forbes claimed, not from his own experience but from testimony in other courts martial, that he understood Robbins to be one of the principals in the mutiny.

Defense counsel Samuel Ker argued that he must have been impressed into service, as being an U.S. citizen, he could not voluntarily join the Royal Navy, due to American neutrality laws. Given that he was impressed, he had a right to forcibly resist this imprisonment. Additionally, as an American, he has the right to a jury trial. Among the many other arguments raised by Ker and co-counsel Alexander Moultrie, as summarized in the court's decision, were:

> "It is contended, that it is a question of magnitude whether a citizen of the United States shall be tried by a jury of his own country, or in a foreign one; that the 27th article of the treaty, on which this motion is

---

[50] Extradition, A requisition from the British minister is not authorized by the 27th article of the treaty of 1794, unless the persons demanded are charged with murder or forgery committed within the jurisdiction of Great Britain (Mar. 14, 1798).

founded, is contrary to the [C]onstitution of the United States, and is therefore void; that the treaty can only relate to foreigners; that the fact in this case being committed on the high seas, the courts of the United States have competent jurisdiction; that a grand jury ought to make inquest, before a party shall be sent away for trial;... this would strike at the root of the liberties of the people; that the [C]onstitution secured the right of trial by jury to the citizens and that treaties and laws altering that, were of subordinate authority and of course void; that the treaty making power may be abused and it could never give authority to seize a person and send him away for trial;... this is not an offence within the contemplation of the treaty; the word "jurisdiction," means "territorial jurisdiction" and that the act must be confined to offences committed within the territory of either; [and] that the sending a person in confinement to be tried in a foreign country, is a punishment not to be inflicted on a citizen."[51]

Rejecting all these arguments, and with unclear jurisdiction about holding a hearing on a treaty-based request from a foreign power, Bee ruled there was sufficient evidence of criminality, despite there being no direct proof of Robbins' involvement with any murder, as required by the treaty. He also said there was concurrent jurisdiction over the high seas, allowing U.S. courts to try this case of piracy aboard a British ship, but that the Jay Treaty article prevailed over American jurisdiction. Bee had Robbins handed over the British and he was swiftly moved to Jamaica, tried before a court martial for the murder of Lt. Foreshaw, mutiny, piracy, and desertion, convicted, and executed.

Reaction to the decision to give up an arguably American seaman to the British was highly politicized between Adams' Federalists and Thomas Jefferson's Democratic-Republicans. In the House of Representatives, two resolutions were passed in March 1800. These decried executive interference with judicial decisions, but shed light on the request of the president (encouraged by secretary of state Timothy Pickering), where Adams had declared, in a letter to Bee, that it was his opinion, subject to evidence of criminality,

---

[51] U.S. v. Robins, 27 Fed. Cas. 825 (D. S.C. Aug. 1799).

"an offence committed on board a public ship of war on the high seas, to have been committed within the jurisdiction of the nation to whom the ship belong and, in consequence of such opinion and construction, did advise and request the said Judge to deliver up the person so claimed, to the agent of Great Britain... without any presentment or trial by jury, or any investigation of his claim to be a citizen of the United States, [Robbins was] delivered up to an officer of his Britannic Majesty, and afterwards tried by a court martial and executed, on a charge of mutiny and murder."[52]

*2. Samuel Tulley – Piracy and Murder*

Legal issues to watch for

❖ Convicting a pirate on testimony of a single witness
❖ Differentiating piracy from larceny in feloniously running away
❖ Whether violence is necessary for piracy

American Samuel Tulley and Englishman John Dalton were brought to trial in Boston in October 1812, before district judge John Davis and Supreme Court justice Joseph Story, riding circuit. They were charged in three indictments under the statute of 1790, with running away with an American ship called the *George Washington* in the Cape Verde Islands, in January 1812, taken from its American master Uriah Phillips Levy, subsequently scuttling that ship, and murdering George Cummings, all on the high seas. The ship contained cargo and merchandize worth $5,000, that included "fourteen quarter casks of Teneriffe wine, and two thousand Spanish milled dollars."[53]

Levy testified that the two defendants, as mate and foremost hand, were part of a crew of six plus the commander. The ship had sailed from Delaware to Tenerife, intending to land its cargo, take on the wine and money, and then sail to the Cape Verde Islands. When Levy was off the ship visiting another captain, he found that his ship had disappeared, and the anchor cables had been cut. That meant that only seaman George

---

[52] Journal of the House of Representatives of the United States (Mar. 8, 1800), p. 618.
[53] U.S. v. Samuel Tulley (1st Cir. Oct. 1812), from *The Trial of Samuel Tulley and John Dalton on an Indictment for Piracy and Murder* (1813), p. 4.

Cummings, cook John Owen and the two defendants remained on board. Levy eventually received word that the defendants had been detained at St. Lucie and upon arrival there, he was able to recover some of his funds, with the remainder retained to cover the local expenses in detaining the defendants.

Owen testified that he was asleep and awoke to find that Tulley was trying to hoist the sail, with seamen Joseph Neal and Daniel Hopkins saying they would not help unless Tulley explained why the anchor lines had been cut. They were soon put into a boat, with Owen's request to join them denied. The four remaining men sailed for the next several weeks, when Owen saw the defendants throwing Cummings overboard, after a purported attack on Tulley by Cummings. The next day they made land and the defendants bored holes in the ship to sink it, with all three taking the long boat which held the stolen goods and their personal effects. Owen eventually confessed and all three were arrested. With this evidence, prosecutor George Blake rested his case.

The defense counsel, James T. Austin and Peter O. Thatcher, then called their witnesses. First were Capt. Benjamin Harris and Capt. Michael Tompkins, who testified that due to the weather in January in the Cape Verde Islands, it was not unusual for anchor cables to snap, and the proper response is to hoist sail, as the defendants had done. Counsel made the point to the jury that an accidental departure was consistent with what the prosecution witnesses had described, meaning the defendants did not feloniously and piratically running away with the vessel.

The defense labeled Owen as an accomplice who had received his share of the monies and so was an unreliable witness, and that it would not be proper to condemn two men on the testimony of one other. The counsel said that this was not a crime of piracy, which required the use of violence. As they had taken the ship without any violence, they could only be accused of larceny, which was not a capital crime. They also differentiated the two prongs of piratically and feloniously, along with larceny and robbery,

"The word *feloniously* referred to the disposition and temper of mind, what in law is called *animus furandi;* and the word *piratically,* to the manner in which this disposition was exercised; and that nothing could amount to the crime of *piratically* running away with the vessel, but a larceny of the property, TOGETHER WITH such personal violence or putting in fear, as would change the crime of larceny into the more aggravated crime of robbery, if it had been committed on shore."[54]

The prosecution closed by making several points, including that the cables had been cut, Tulley had been left in charge, and the captain's personal belongings were found when the defendants were captured, so there was no more reasonable explanation than that they had taken the ship. The testimony of Owen was not necessarily to prove the piracy but just corroborated Levy's testimony. Accomplice testimony was allowable if he was truly an accomplice and not just an unwilling victim. Feloniously running away with a ship was piratical and violence was not necessary, which the court agreed with, saying that every act of feloniously running away with a ship was considered piratical under the statute of 1790.

The jury at first could not agree that the acts amounted to piracy but upon further instruction from the court, returned with guilty verdicts for both men. The defense counsel then filed a motion for a new trial, based on two points: that the court misdirected the jury by saying that feloniously running away with a ship amounts to piracy, and that the verdict was against the weight of the evidence, which demonstrated that there was no violence or apprehension of any kind. The court considered the motion for some time, not reconvening for more than three weeks. Then Justice Davis provide the opinion of the court. On the first issue, Davis said that at common law, piracy was robbery and depredation on the high seas, which is part of the statute of 1790.

However, the statute also included other acts that were not crimes at common law, in accordance with the statute of William III, such as running away with a ship and its goods and merchandize. The unlawful depredation was the piracy and feloniously was the willfulness of the act. For a mariner at sea to feloniously plunder property is, under the statute, piratical. On the second issue, Davis said counsel was trying to analogize piracy to robbery on the land, which required putting the victim in fear.

---

[54] *Id*. p. 13.

Saying that attacking an empty ship and plundering her goods was still piracy, it ruled that violence was not a necessary component of piracy. The violation of trust by the mariners aboard the ship was sufficient for piracy. After dismissing a motion for a new trial, the court sentenced the defendants to hang, and they were soon executed. Before execution, Tulley admitted only to the first crime, saying it was Dalton and Owen who threw Cummings overboard, after he had attacked Tulley, and that he did not scuttle the ship.

*3. John H. Jones – Piracy*

### Legal issues to watch for

❖ Statutory definition of piratical robbery
❖ Whether commissioned privateers can be charged with piracy
❖ If privateering statutes shield privateers from civil courts

John H. Jones, first lieutenant of the American privateer *Revenge* during the War of 1812, was brought to trial in 1813 in Philadelphia before Supreme Court justice Bushrod Washington riding circuit and district judge Richard Peters. He was indicted for attacking, in November 1812, the Portuguese ship *Triumph of Mars*, a country that was at peace with the United States. He and second lieutenant Richard Pickle were accused of "piratically, feloniously, violently and unlawfully"[55] assaulting the ship, putting its crew in fear, and stealing money and its cargo. A true bill from the grand jury was only returned for Jones.

U.S. attorney Alexander J. Dallas opened for the prosecution by defining piracy as the "felonious taking of property from another by violence and against his will."[56] He then explained that Jones had been a crew member of the validly commissioned privateer *Revenge*, describing what such a privateer could lawfully do. Since the United States was now at war with Britain, commissioned privateers could not legally attack neutral ships, but they could stop and board them to ascertain their nationality. If they suspected the vessel contained cargo for their enemies,

---

[55] U.S. v. John. H. Jones (3rd Cir. Apr. 1813), from *The Trial of John H. Jones, First Lieutenant of the Privateer Schooner* Revenge, *of the Charge of Piracy* (1813), p. 4.
[56] *Id.* p. 7.

they were to send the vessel to port for condemnation but were not to plunder the ships. It was for the jury to determine if Jones intended to bring the ship and cargo in for adjudication.

Several witnesses testified. The Portuguese master of the ship, Simao da Rocha Munho, described how Jones and crew had boarded his ship while flying an English flag, asked for his papers, then pointed a pistol at him and proceeded to plunder monies, cargo, and various supplies from the ship. When the ship finally arrived in the United States, he had remained, but sent the ship and all its papers back to Lisbon. He was asked by Dallas if the ship and cargo were Portuguese property. The defense counsel objected, as the register, bills of lading, and invoices would prove that. The court overruled the objection, stating there were other ways to prove ownership, and without a suggestion of fraud, the witness had shown that there was a Portuguese owner, and the cargo was from a Portuguese merchant.

Third mate Bernardo Antonio also testified to the same events but defense counsel Charles Jared Ingersoll, a member of Congress, asked him very detailed questions about the boarding, such as the clothing worn by Jones, to expose any differences in his recollections and those of the master. Seaman Solomon Le Brun, from the *Revenge*, then testified but apparently gave an account different than the one he had previously given to a justice of the peace. The prosecution tried to call that magistrate, but the court would not allow him to discredit his own witness. With this, the prosecution rested.

The defense opened by making four assertions. The first is described below. The second was that a privateer has a right to seize a ship when they have suspicions it was enemy property, and if they had the intention to do so at the seizure, even if they later abandoned that plan, they cannot be guilty of felony. The third was that under their privateering commission, the men could only be tried for offenses under a naval court martial. The fourth was that Jones was second in command to Capt. Butler and was required to follow his commands. The first assertion was,

"That robbery on the high seas is not piracy by the laws of the United States; that the offence is not defined by the act of Congress, the word robbery being only made use of in the general, and that as there is no criminal common law in the United States, We cannot resort to that code for its definition."[57]

The witnesses for the defense then testified. James Goodwin was a seaman on the *Revenge*. He stated that, contrary to prior testimony, Jones had drawn his sword after discovering his men had taken small items, claiming he would run through any man who took something without orders. Upon returning to the boat, Capt. Butler told several seamen to go back to the Portuguese ship and take what they needed. Goodwin saw Jones at this time apparently ill or asleep on the privateer. Men, including bosun's mate Hancock, who looked like Jones, took back to the *Revenge* supplies, cargo including sugar, and money, according to Goodwin. He also said that Jones had left his pistols on the boat and never used them when boarding a vessel, only his sword.

Prosecutor Dallas asked Goodwin if, he was when arrested for piracy, had he spent time in jail with Jones, which Goodwin denied. A marine on the *Revenge*, Jacob Wonderley, was called to testify to the same. Several character witnesses were called to say that had known Jones for a long time and knew him to be honest. Dallas then called a witness, John Smith, to impugn the character of Goodwin, by saying that Goodwin had discussed with him, while both were in prison, another trial where Goodwin was also a defendant.

In closing for the defense, Ingersoll started by claiming "Mr. Jones, the prisoner, was not the guilty man, on board the *Revenge*, yet [the] public example."[58] He then went on to examine the four points of the defense argument, asking "what is piracy?"[59] and answered that the common law of England could not be used, no longer being the common law of the United States, so the answer had to be in the statute. He said that Constitution gave Congress the power to define and punish piracies, which it did in the statute of 1790, for piratical murder in section 8, and piratical larceny in section 16. He then inquired,

---

[57] *Id*. p. 23.
[58] *Id*. p. 31.
[59] *Id*. p. 34.

"But where shall we find the definition of piratical robbery? Where shall we find its punishment provided for? I look in vain, thro' all the sections of this elaborate act of congress, put together, I may be permitted to say, rather more accurately than acts of congress commonly are. I find in the constitution, a direction, an injunction to congress to define and punish piracies. But I cannot find that congress, who have met the cases of piratical murder and piratical larceny, have, as they were bound to do, provided for the crime of piratical robbery. If not, this prosecution falls."[60]

William Rawle also spoke for the defense, reiterating the point about the lack of a definition for piratical robbery in the statute but then went on to note that section 9 defines piracy as acting against the United States or its citizens under a foreign commission. He extended this to mean that section 8 could not apply to acts done under any commission, including a U.S. privateering commission. In closing for the prosecution, Dallas said that section 9 was created for the specific purpose of those with a foreign commission only, and that privateering rules mandating trial before a court martial were only for those acts committed aboard a privateer ship, which was not the case here.

He said that both the common law and the law of nations allowed piracy charges against privateers and then showed how the statute of 1790 defined robbery to be piracy,

"here is a plain definition of what shall constitute a piracy and felony on the high seas, under three forms of description: 1. *Murder* committed on the high seas. 2nd. *Robbery* committed on the high seas. 3d. *Any other offence* committed on the high seas, which would be capital, by the laws of the United States, if committed on land. *Murder* and *robbery* are both technical terms, and are here equally unexplained. Without reference to the degree of punishment inflicted upon murder or robbery if committed on shore, by a federal, or a state penal code, congress evidently meant, and have explicitly said, that murder and robbery, if committed on the high seas, shall be deemed piracy and felony, subject to the punishment of death.

---

[60] *Id.* p. 35.

But after selecting these crimes, for capital punishment, without any reservation or reference, congress proceeded to define *other* maritime offences, not by naming the offences, but in terms of reference, by declaring, that only such other offences, as were capital, if committed on land, should be adjudged piracy and felony, if committed at sea. The relative pronoun 'which,' must be connected with the next antecedent, 'any other offence.' If it is carried more remotely back, it would not only be a violation of the rules of grammar, but lead to this legislative absurdity, that congress after naming robbery on the high seas, with an evident view, to render it a capital piracy and felony, have in the same sentence, declared, in effect, that it shall be no offence at all."[61]

The court, per Justice Washington, agreed with Dallas that robbery on the high seas was definitely a crime under the statute of 1790. He also said that a privateering commission does not shield the privateer against a charge of piracy if felonious intent for robbery was formed. And he said that following an illegal order of a commander was not an allowable defense. He summed up the witnesses as describing a plunder, with perhaps the only issue being whether the two Portuguese witnesses, otherwise credible, had mistaken Hancock, whom all who testified claimed was a plunderer, for Jones. The jury evidently believed that to be the case, as they quickly returned to find Jones not guilty.

*4. Josef Perez – Piracy*

---

Legal issues to watch for

❖  Identifying pirates at trial
❖  Trying an indigent, non-citizen for piracy
❖  Double jeopardy in dismissing hung jury in piracy trial

---

Josef Perez, a native of Spain, went on trial in New York in September 1823, charged with piracy aboard the American schooner *Bee*, off Cuba, in August 1822. He appeared before district judge William Van Ness and Supreme Court justice Smith Thompson, riding circuit. Perez was indicted for piratically and feloniously stealing some of the cargo of this merchant

---

[61] *Id.* p. 52.

ship, putting the crew in fear of bodily harm or death. Two additional indictments were the same charges, except adding that the piracy occurred on the high seas or in a bay. The prosecutors were Robert L. Tillotson and C. G. Haines, while the defense counsel were Josiah Ogden Hoffman and George W. Niven. Niven immediately made a request to submit an affidavit from the defendant, who claimed this was a case of mistaken identity.

In this affidavit, Perez gave a detailed account, by the months, weeks, and days, of what he had been doing and where he was located over the prior nine years. He ended by stating that he arrived in New York as a supernumerary (not a member of the crew), so had departed the ship and was living onshore, until arrested. He claimed at the time of the incident, he was in the service of Don Bernard Ansuotige, working onshore in Buenos Aires. He further says that because he is indigent, he cannot afford to pay for bringing this man to New York for trial. The next day, the defense produced further affidavits from others that agreed with how he had arrived in New York, contrary to the assertions of the prosecution. The court ruled it would proceed to trial, as it was unlikely that the witness from Buenos Aires would be produced.

The defense challenged many of the jurors, exhausting the pool, so bystanders were drafted into the jury. The first prosecution witness was Capt. Edward Johnson of the *Bee,* commander and owner of the ship. He detailed the piracy, how the cargo of his ship was loaded on to several pirate vessels after the attack, how he and the crew were locked in the cabin, how he was regularly beaten, and his many interactions with Josef Perez during the week plus of captivity. After they were given a dilapidated boat, the *Bee* was run ashore and burned by the pirates. On cross-examination, he said he noticed no marks on Perez.

The next witness was seaman Joseph Porter of the *Bee*. He testified also to Perez's actions in threatening to hang the cook, finding a gold coin in the captain's quarters, and his involvement with breaking open the hatch. He said he had a scar on his left wrist, and he was the one who saw Perez on the streets of New York and had him arrested. The defense attempted to throw doubt on the identification, asking why he did not notice the scar on Perez's right wrist, when the pirates had their sleeves rolled up, playing cards, and dining together. The turnkey at the city prison, Richard Grant, testified that when Capt. Johnson first saw Perez there, he did not have an immediate outward response and did not remark.

The prosecution then tried to prove that Perez arrived aboard the *Esperanza* in July. Tillotson claimed it was the same pirate ship that attacked the *Bee*. He put on two witnesses who had seen the defendant on the ship or thought the manifest to be suspicious for so small a vessel. That ship departed quietly and quickly from New York the same day Perez was arrested. The Spanish consul for New York, Don Thomas Stoughton, claimed that the ship Perez said he arrived on, the *Tarantula*, had a Josef Perez listed as a supernumerary, but he was not sure that it was the defendant, as that name was quite common in Spain. The owner of the guest house where Perez stayed in New York, Nicholas Clemments, testified to his coming off the *Tarantula* to his house in June. Another mariner claimed that he sailed on that ship with Perez from Cadiz.

In closing, defense counsel Nivens talked again about cases of mistaken identification and the fact that the boarding house owner said Perez arrived at the boarding house before the supposed pirate ship *Esperanza* arrived in New York. Defense counsel Hoffman closed by discussing the differing testimony of the prosecution witnesses, such as who broke open the hatch, whether Perez could speak any English, the identifying marks on his arms, and that one witness was sure it was Perez, the other less certain. Finally, he said, "if he had been robbing Americans, would he come to America" Voluntarily run into the arms of danger—into the very jaws of death!'"[62]

Prosecutor Haines discussed how confederates can work together to make up a story to tell and how arriving on the ship from Cadiz was possible, given the piracy occurred nearly a year previous. He focused not so much on markings on his arms but upon his face as the distinguishing feature with which to identify Perez, saying,

---

[62] U.S. v. Josef Perez (2nd Cir. Sept. 1823), from *A Correct Report of the Trial of Josef Perez for Piracy committed on board the Schooner* Bee (1823), p. 26.

"Look at the prisoner! Was that a face easily to be forgotten? Was that a face, which any man living could not learn in eight days to recognize? Persons in danger of their lives, have all their senses animated by fear and resentment. Men under such circumstances, observe narrowly, and remember well. The faces, especially of those who have put them in fear for their life, are deeply fixed in their recollection."[63]

He also said there were no contradictions in the testimony of the prosecution witnesses, as "But they speak of two different acts at two different moments. When Johnson saw the action, he says Porter was not present; —when Porter saw it, he says Johnson was not present."[64] The jury retired but returned to say they were hopelessly deadlocked 6-6 and despite instructions from the judges and again retiring, they came to the same deadlock, 7-5 for acquittal. Over defense counsel objection that this should be recorded as an acquittal, the jury were dismissed.

The defense the next day entered a motion that the court did not have to power to dismiss the jurors except in extreme circumstances (i.e. days of deliberation without a result) and this should be treated the same as an acquittal. The two judges were themselves of different opinions on whether the defendant should be dismissed, or a new trial ordered. Under the Judiciary Act of 1802, such a differing opinion meant that the question of whether a new trial should occur had to be certified to the Supreme Court for clarification.

However, that court would not sit again until February, months away. So, the defense counsel reiterated that the 1802 Act,

"provided also, that imprisonment shall not be allowed, nor punishment in any case be inflicted, where the judges of the said court are divided in opinion upon the question touching the said imprisonment or punishment."[65]

This meant that the defendant should be released in the interim but on this motion the two justices agreed that Perez was to remain

---

[63] *Id.* p. 28.
[64] *Id.*
[65] An Act to amend the Judicial System of the United States, c. 7, s. 1, ch. 31, § 6.

remanded. The Supreme Court, six months later, in an opinion by Justice Joseph Story, ruled that,

> "We are of opinion, that the facts constitute no legal bar to a future trial. The prisoner has not been convicted or acquitted, and may again be put upon his defence."[66]

So, there was no double jeopardy in dismissing a hung jury and the case could be retried while the prisoner remained remanded in custody.

*5. Felix Barbeito and Crew – Piracy and Murder*

| Legal issues to watch for |
|---|
| ❖ Requesting a jury of moiety |
| ❖ Delaying a trial for character witnesses |
| ❖ Planning a piracy with fraudulent currency and forged papers |

The trial of Felix Barbeito, Jose Casares, and Jose Morando, for piracy on the brig *Crawford*, took place in Richmond, in July 1827, before Supreme Court chief justice John Marshall, riding circuit. There were five indictments, four for the murders of Capt. Henry Brightman, and crew members Asa Bicknell, Oliver Potter, and Joseph Dolliver, and one for piracy, which had two counts, one for piracy under the statute of 1820 and a second for piracy under the law of nations. The defendants first requested a jury be summoned *de medietate linguse,* meaning a jury of moiety, comprised of half American citizens and half aliens. The court, after noting that this was discretionary, granted the motion.

When the court reconvened the following Monday, defense counsel Schmidt read an affidavit from the defendants, in which they said that due to the significant coverage in the press, they did not believe they could get a fair trial in Richmond. Further, their evidence and character witnesses were in Cuba and would take some time to arrive, so they wanted a continuance for four months. The defendants also claimed that they were amply funded for the voyage they had taken and had no reason to turn to piracy. Further, their good character was well known in Cuba and the proof of the commercial nature of their voyage could be proven with evidence

---

[66] U.S. v. Josef Perez, 22 U.S. 579 (Mar. 1824).

from there. For these reasons they submitted a motion for continuance until the next sitting of the court, in November.

Prosecutor Robert Stanard vigorously opposed this motion, believing "that delay was to be employed as a means to evade the law."[67] His two principal witnesses were a seaman from Massachusetts, who had to go about his trade and a Cuban resident, who had come here to testify but would be unlikely to make the trip a second time. He also said that press coverage was typical of all trials and the court should be able to find an impartial jury in such a large pool as eastern Virginia. Further, the unavailability of character witnesses was no reason to delay a trial and the material evidence of what occurred happened on the high seas, not on land in Cuba, as his witnesses would testify to.

The court rejected the defense motion, saying the principal events would be those attested to by witnesses on the high seas, so it strongly believed a fair trial was possible. Marshall described the role of the court,

> "It was the duty of the Court, impartially to administer the laws; and in the discharge of this duty, it was as much bound to prevent the guilty from escaping punishment, as it was to protect the accused in their right to an impartial trial. It felt desirous to do both... The Court further declared, that it was certain that it felt no prepossessions unfavorable to the prisoners, and that as it possessed the power to protect them, *it would* certainly exercise that power, and grant a new trial, should it have the least reason to believe, that prejudice had influenced the verdict of the jury."[68]

The first prosecution witness was Edmund Dobson, a mate on the *Crawford*. He described how the ship had sailed from Rhode Island to Cuba, with a crew of seven (Dobson plus commander Henry Brightman, seamen Joseph Dolliver, Oliver Potter, Asa Bicknell, and Nathaniel P. Deane, and cook Stephen Gibbs, with a cargo of American produce. After

---

[67] U.S. v. Jose Caracas, at al. (5th Cir. July 1827), from *A Brief Sketch of the Occurrences on board the Brig* Crawford, *on her Voyage from Matanzas to New York; Together with an Account of the Trial of the Three Spaniards, Jose Hilario Casares, Felix Barbeito, and Jose Morando* (1827), p. 10.
[68] *Id.* p. 17.

unloading that, they took on a cargo of molasses, coffee, and sugar, to be delivered to New York. They also took on the following passengers: Frenchman and piratical leader Alexander Tardy; the three defendants, Felix Barbeito, Jose Hilario Casares, and Jose Morando; Frenchman Ferdinand Ginoulhiac; an Irish passenger [later identified as Eldridge Holloway]; an unnamed American carpenter; and Norman Robinson, part owner of the cargo (the 'supercargo').

Before sailing, the Spaniards had brought aboard a heavy box, which they claimed contained $17,000 in currency (it was later discovered to contain only lead and iron) and had it stored securely. He said the Spaniards and Tardy seemed to know each other. Tardy claimed to be a doctor (he had acquired rudimentary dental skills) and had prescribed something for Brightman for his asthma but this had made him ill. Then Dobson was served some chocolate by Tardy and also became ill, as had many of the crew. He fallen asleep but was awoken by shrieks and found the three Spaniards and Tardy had attacked the crew with knives and guns, assaulted and thrown members of the crew and passengers overboard to their deaths, killed Capt. Brightman, and wounded Dobson. Tardy claimed it was because the Spaniards had thought Brightman had seized their box of currency.

Dobson then relayed the long story of how the few remaining passengers and crew survived a long voyage, supposedly headed to Europe, but which only made it as far as Norfolk, Virginia. Dobson managed to escape, alert local authorities, and fearing all was lost, Tardy killed himself on the ship. Ginoulhiac testified to the same facts. Also testifying were the pilot in Norfolk who came aboard the ship allowing Dobson to escape, the army officers who took possession of the ship after Dobson's alert, and the posse dispatched to catch the three escaping Spanish pirates. A customs officer testified to Spanish papers found on the ship (the originals had been thrown overboard), which were all fraudulent, including a customs document claiming Tandy as the commander and listing a cargo for the voyage from Cuba to Germany, a privateering commission, and a logbook written in Spanish.

The case was submitted to the jury without comment from the defense, as co-counsel Benjamin Watkins Leigh later admitted he could not come up with a theory consistent with the facts to use to defend his clients. The jury voted each of the defendants, in three separate trials with the same evidence, guilty of piracy. One variant was that Morando claimed that he was a servant and so had to follow the commands of the others and he had served honourably in the Spanish army. Given the description of his actions in several murders, the jury did not accept this explanation. The defendants were then sentenced to be executed. The prosecutor did not bother proceeding with the trials under the indictments for murder. Before their executions, the defendants admitted their guilt to the charged acts.

### B.  Jackson to Lincoln

#### 1.  Charles Gibbs and Thomas Wansley – Piracy and Murder

| Legal issues to watch for |
| --- |
| ❖  Excluding juror who would not consider capital punishment |
| ❖  Differential treatment for Black pirates |
| ❖  Time allowed between sentencing and execution |

Charles Gibbs (birthname James Jeffers) and Thomas J. Wansley were brought to trial in New York, in February 1831, for piracy and murder, before district court judge Samuel Rossiter Betts. The prosecutor was James A. Hamilton (son of Alexander), and the defense counsel were Henry E. Davies and N. Bowditch Blunt. The two defendants were accused of murdering captain William Thornber, and mate William Roberts, of the American brig *Vineyard*, and of mutiny, stealing valuable cargo of Mexican silver coins, and scuttling the ship. The ship was on a voyage from New Orleans to Philadelphia, in November 1830. The silver currency belonged to wealthy philanthropist Stephen Girard (who himself would not long survive the defendants).

During the empaneling of the jury, a potential juror named Joseph W. Lockwood stated his opposition to the trial, for which "They found him not indifferent, and he was set aside."[69] William Smith was not empaneled for the same reason. The trial of Wansley opened with defense counsel Davies objecting that the charge of maiming did not include "knowingly and wittingly," as specified by section 13 of the statute of 1790, and that section 10 mentioned only piracy and robbery but not murder, which the Supreme Court had ruled to be separate crimes. The prosecutor said that these objections would be most appropriately brought after the jury had completed its work, by filing a motion in arrest of judgment.

John Brownrigg, one of the four crew members to survive, out of nine who started the journey, was first to testify. He said Wansley, the steward and cook in the ship, had told him he killed the captain by striking him with a pump-break, when the ship was off Cape Hatteras. Brownrigg was aloft at the time but on coming down, saw Wansley wiping blood off and did not see the captain or the mate. Then the crew stole the money in Mexican coins, stored inside ten kegs, and shared it out. Afterwards, they scuttled and burned the ship, came ashore, and buried $5,000 worth of coin, and then went further inland, where they were turned in and arrested.

On cross-examination, he further testified that, when they were trying to come ashore with all their plundered coin, in the long and small boats, they were hit with violent weather and three men (Henry Atwell, Edward Church, James Talbot) in the small boat perished and the four men (Brownrigg, Dawes, Wansley, Gibbs) in the longboat only survived by throwing many of the sacks of coin overboard. He also said he was aloft when the murders happened, but he saw blood when coming down on to the deck, and that Atwell had scuttled the ship. Robert Dawes, 18 years of age, then testified, but his counsel first requested a *nolle proseqi*. The prosecutor said this would come later. Dawes testified that he saw Wansley kill the captain, the plotters to the murder were Gibbs, Wansley, Church, and Atwell, and he confirmed the sharing out of the silver money.

Two justices of the peace had examined Wansley on the complaint of Samuel Leonard, but the jailer had told him to speak the truth, so the court would not admit that examination. Leonard testified that he has seized the

---

[69] U.S. v. Gibbs (S.D.N.Y. Feb. 1831), from *The Trial and Sentence of Thomas J. Wansley and Charles Gibbs, for Murder and Piracy, On board the Brig* Vineyard (1831), p. 4.

men after Brownrigg exclaimed that he would not accompany murderers, and that there were hundreds of dollars found on Wansley when he was captured. Before Brownrigg's disclosure, Leonard had been offered $3 to take the men to Brooklyn but after the disclosure, Gibbs offered him $300. The former owner of the ship testified that the ship was built in Maine and that he had sold it to George Calendar of Boston the previous year, which was confirmed by a clerk in the customs horse. The marshal and another man testified to clothes found on the defendant with Capt. Thornber's name marked on them.

Police officer B.W. Merritt, who had taken Wansley, Gibbs, and Dawes to the jail, testified, over the objections of defense counsel, that Wansley and Gibbs had told him voluntarily the whole story and that Brownrigg was innocent, with another man testifying to the accuracy of Merritt's account. The prosecution rested and the defense only reiterated that they reserved the right to move in arrest of judgment. The court instructed the jury that for the court to have jurisdiction, it had to be proved that the vessel or the defendants were American, but this was up to the jury to determine. Also, that no one could be convicted merely on their own confession, unless other evidence proved that a crime had been committed, for which the jury was to look to the testimony of Brownrigg and Dawes. The jury quickly found Wansley guilty.

Then the trial of Charles Gibbs started the next day, with the same prosecutor but different defense counsel, Seth Perkins Staples and Joseph Patten. The defense objected to a juror, Forbes Clapp, who was on the jury from Wansley trial and the court set him aside, as again was Joseph Lockwood. Dawes testified that Gibbs was the first to strike the mate and helped Atwell and Church throw him overboard. He also described the many conversations on the plot to kill the captain and first mate and how he was offered $1000 for his 1/7 share in the coins, which were worth $54,000, which he agreed to, but Gibbs talked him out of it. Gibbs was also the one who set fire to the ship and was the one at the helm after the murders. Despite various objections raised by defense counsel, the jury found him guilty after deliberating for two hours.

Before sentencing, Wansley was asked if he had anything to say, and he replied,

"he had always known that a difference of colour produced a difference of treatment, where white men were judges. They had taken the blacks from their own country, and scattered them over their own entitlements, and treated them differently from those of their own country. There was an antipathy, as he knew entertained by the whites against the coloured person. He had found it so himself both as regarded the witnesses and jurors in this case and at the hands of the District Attorney. Much false testimony had been given, as he of course had the means of knowing."[70]

The court replied to this by saying,

"that whatever prejudice he might imagine existed, growing out of the distinctions of color, the utmost impartiality had been observed in his case. Admitting the statement that both Brownrigg and Dawes had sworn falsely, the prisoner's own words, just uttered, admitted that they had been guilty of a most horrible crime, that of taking human life, without any provocation whatever. If the Court did entertain a doubt that, in the case of Wansley, the least injustice had been done, or the slightest advantage withheld from him, they would afford him another opportunity of being tried. But there was not a shadow of such a doubt."[71]

Judge Betts sentenced both men to hang. Unlike for most convicted pirates, in this case the court gave the two men six weeks to ponder their deeds before their executions. Gibbs used this time to full effect, by giving interviews and writing a confession[72] which included a warning to youth. In the process, he made himself famous after death, for deeds that may or may not have been true. He claimed, among many assertions, that in a long piratical career, he has captured 40 ships and had always killed all the captives. As the punishment for piracy and murder were the same, there would be no witnesses alive, implying he had killed upwards of 400 victims.

---

[70] *Id.* p. 21.
[71] *Id.* p. 22.
[72] *Mutiny and Murder, Confession of Charles Gibbs, A Native of Rhode Island* (1831).

## 2. Pedro Gibert and Crew – Piracy

| Legal issues to watch for |
|---|
| ❖ British disclaiming jurisdiction over pirates |
| ❖ Using expert testimony to determine when attack occurred |
| ❖ Where all members of a pirate ship considered pirates |

Pedro Gibert and eleven of his crew on the *Panda* went to trial in Boston, in November 1834. They were charged with piracy of the American brig *Mexican*, in September 1832. The British warship *Curlew* had captured them while on slaver patrol and taken them back to England. The prisoners were then shipped over to Massachusetts by the Royal Navy, with the British waving their right to try them in favor of the Americans. They were tried before justice Joseph Story of the Supreme Court, riding circuit, and district judge John Davis. The prosecutor was Andrew Dunlap and the defense counsel David Lee Child and George Stillman Hillard. The trial would last fourteen days, in part due to lengthy cross-examinations of prosecution witnesses by Child.

The indictment stated the crew piratically and feloniously assaulted the master of the *Mexican*, John Groves Butman and his crew members, putting them in fear of bodily harm and death and "piratically, feloniously, violently and against the will"[73] of the master and his crew, robbed cargo worth $20,000. Child asked for a delay to retrieve the logbook of the *Panda* from England, but the court ruled it had no power to order evidence retrieved from there. A motion for separate trials was also overruled. Dunlap described how, on a voyage from Salem to Rio de Janeiro, the *Mexican* was attacked by the pirates, who stole the valuable cargo and confined the crew below, broke their compasses, destroyed the rigging, and set the ship's mainsail afire. The captain was able to get free, dose the fire, and the ship slowly made its way back to Salem.

The owner of the *Mexican* testified that he had sent $20,000 in ten boxes aboard the ship. Capt. Butman testified to the assaults on him and the crew and the theft of the money. The mate, Benjamin Brown Read,

---

[73] U.S. v. Pedro Gibert (1st Cir. Nov. 1834), from *A Report of the Trial of Pedro Gibert* (1834), p. 6.

testified to the same and identified two of the defendants (Ruiz and Boyga) as being aboard his ship that night. Child asked that the defendants be able to switch seats before each prosecution witness was introduced, so the witnesses could not give any details with each other, but this was overruled, as the witnesses were kept in a separate room and brought in singly. Different crewman of the *Mexican* identified the same two defendants and testified to their violent acts. Black American cook Thomas Charles Henry Ridgly identified Boyga, and the *Panda*'s cook, Antonio Ferrer, and Black American steward John Lewis recognized Ruiz.

Josef Perez, a member of the *Panda* crew, then testified against his old shipmates. He identified Ruiz as one of the four men who boarded the *Mexican*, with the other three having died or run away. He testified to the armed acts of piracy of money and some supplies from the *Mexican*, what happened afterwards as they proceeded to Africa, the sharing out of the stolen money, and their capture by the British. Those receiving shares who were on trial included the captain, the mate de Solo, Castillo, Garcia, Montenegro, and Delgado. George H. Quentin of the Royal Navy, who was on the *Curlew* when it captured the defendants and their ship, testified to the lack of any logbooks and the unsuccessful search for the stolen money. After testimony from interpreters used in Africa, several experienced captains provided estimates of where these ships would have met, based on their starting dates and destinations, which was close to where they actually encountered each other.

The prosecution closed its case, and Child introduced his own navigation expert, who turned out to be a slaver, and the next day brought on a several more navigation witnesses. He also introduced a character witness for De Soto, put on several witnesses to impugn Ridgly's character, and another who said that a pirate schooner had been seen in the area of the attack on the *Mexican*. Hillard closed for the defense by noting prejudice against sailors from Cuba or Spain, the presumption that a defendant sent by the British must be guilty, and that identifications are often wrong. He also pled cases of the servant Ferrer and the 15-year-old Costa. Child continued the following morning, trying to disparage the testimony of Perez. Then he said the British navy captain may have taken the stolen money.

Dunlap, clearly exhausted, said,

"on the fourteenth day since the commencement of this trial, to address to you the closing argument for the prosecution. The labors of this case have been unexampled. We can find no parallel to them in the history of the judicial proceedings of this country."[74]

He then said the defendants had had more than a fair trial,

"Had this case, which has already occupied the attention of this court twelve days, at an average of six or seven hours per day, been tried at the Old Bailey, it would have been decided between the rising and the setting of the sun."[75]

Justice Story, in giving instructions to the jury, felt that there was one key point and that was that,

"Only those of the crew, he said, could be convicted, who were proved to have participated in the crime. The mere fact of their being on board the Panda was not sufficient to condemn them."[76]

The jury found guilty of piracy all those against whom evidence had been produced, Gibert, De Soto, Ruiz, Boyga, Castillo, Garcia, and Montenegro. The five other defendants from the pirate ship, such as the cabin boy Costa and the servant Ferrer, were found not guilty.

*3. Crew of the Echo – Piracy*

| Legal issues to watch for |
|---|
| ❖ Ability of Congress to expand definition of piracy |
| ❖ Proving the ownership of a pirate ship |
| ❖ Juries determining constitutionality of piracy statutes |

The crew of the *Echo* was tried in Charleston, in April 1859, for piracy. The captain, Edward Townsend, was not among them, still imprisoned in Florida awaiting trial. There were two trials of the crew, the first for ten of the crew and then a second trial of six others on board the ship when

---

[74] *Id.* p. 65.
[75] *Id.* p. 66.
[76] *Id.* p. 74.

captured. They were charged with piracy under the indictment, with nine counts including that they took onboard hundreds of Black Africans while in that continent, intending to make them slaves, detained them while on the high seas, and variously aided and abetted these crimes, all in violation of the piracy statute of 1820. A previous grand jury, located in Columbia, South Carolina, in December 1858, had declined to bring in true bills against them.

The circuit court judges were Supreme Court justice James M. Wayne and district judge Andrew Magrath. The federal prosecutor was James Conner, and the defense counsel were Leonidas W. Spratt, Robert de Treville, Maxcy Gregg, and Edmund Bellinger. The prosecution first called Lt. C. C. Carpenter of the U.S. brig *Dolphin*, which had captured the defendants off Cuba, over defense counsel objections that the captors stood to gain from the prize money in condemning the *Echo*. Carpenter testified that to the awful conditions for the enslaved persons on the *Echo*, and how it had started with 450 African captives but was down to 320 people by the time it was taken, as three enslaved persons per day had died.

Others testified that: the words "*Putnam*, New Orleans" had been painted over; that the bill of sale to Townsend of the *Putnam* in New Orleans was authentic (he paid for it with funds provided by established slave trader Antonio Almeida, who as supercargo was quietly one of the defendants): that Townsend was a native of Rhode Island and was recognized while in jail: the crew list, shipping articles, and registry of the *Putnam* were all proved; that the charts of the *Echo* showed a continuous line from Africa to her point of capture; and confirmed the miserable state of the victims' health aboard the *Echo*. The prosecution rested and defense decided not to put on any witnesses. For the second trial, six of the jurors who were on the first jury served on the second, claiming they had not already formed an opinion about the next trial and had no bias.

For both trials, with the juries being made up of all white men in soon-to-be seceded, pro-slavery Charleston, the result was pre-ordained. Both times, the results were verdicts of not guilty. More interesting were the arguments made by the defense counsel and prosecutor to close the trials.

First to present his argument was Gregg, who broke the eight counts in the indictments into twelve allegations, five of which had to be true for any count to be true. These included that the defendants had to be members of the crew (claiming one was a passenger); that the *Echo* was owned by Townsend (claiming the citizen of Rhode Island was not the one who purchased the ship in New Orleans) or another American citizen; that those captured were currently free (claiming they were considered slaves under South Carolina law); and that the crew of the *Echo* intended to enslave their victims (claiming there was no proof that the victims were free before).

He then asked the jury to consider whether the statute of 1820 was constitutional, claiming that Congress could not extend the meaning of piracy to include slave trading activities. Bellinger spoke next, making similar arguments about the evidence, the constitutionality of the statute of 1820, and the jury's right to interpret that constitutionality. Spratt then spoke, adding to Greg's five points of proof a sixth, that the acts were done piratically and feloniously. To the first point, he said the shipping documents with the crew's names were not sufficiently validated. When trying to show that this was not piratical, he claimed that no slave owner would stand for losing his property in transit,

> "The same persons who so exclaim against the "horrors of the middle passage," as vociferously exclaim against the horrors of plantation life; but do you believe in it? Do you not know that no human beings upon earth are so considered and so cared for as are our slaves?... negro slave would be the most favored voyager that ever crossed the ocean?"[77]

Connor spoke after de Treville argued further about the jury's ability to pronounce on constitutionality and that Congress had no power to declare the slave trade piracy. Connor, who would shortly become an officer in the Confederate army, tried to show that indeed the statute of 1820 was constitutional and how some of the leading South Carolina political leaders had supported it. He said that he had proved ownership of the ship by the best evidence, the original bill of sale, describing and giving

---

[77] U.S. v. R.T. Bates (4th Cir. Apr. 1859), per *Report of the trials in the Echo cases*, p. 71.

the dimensions of the ship and proved by the subscribing witnesses, in addition to the registry of that vessel with customs. He also proved the identity of the prisoner Townsend, by a witness who has known him and his family since childhood, proving his American citizenship and therefore the ship's ownership by an American.

Regarding the defendants being members of the crew, he said the law said they had to either be members of the crew or ship's company, so it encompassed all onboard. The crew list was filed with customs, which also had Townsend's affidavit. That the enslaved people were taken in Africa was clear from the testimony of the *Dolphin's* crew, their spoken languages, which required an interpreter, and the markings on the charts for the course followed by the *Echo*. He said the statute of 1820 did not require proving that the victims were previously free, only that they were not considered slaves under U.S. law. The issue was seizure and detention with intent to enslave.

He harshly criticized the arguments about how well enslaved people were treated on board the *Echo*, noting again that more than one-third of the 450 victims captured by the *Echo* had died either before it was captured and later in the care of doctors, wondering how such a crime would be punished if it had happened on land in South Carolina. As to whether the jury could consider political opinions, he said,

> "You are told that this question involves great political events. They have no place, no weight, in the decision of a question before a legal tribunal. Public opinion and political expediency have nothing to do with the administration of justice. You are sworn by the law, and nothing goes to you but what is vouched for by the law. You are asked to put aside the law and take the law of public opinion. You cannot do it. Public opinion is to be respected in its proper sphere, but its voice must be silent in a court house, and fearful, terrible indeed, will be the day whenever the hall of justice shall be converted into a political arena, and the verdict of a jury no longer the voice of the law, but the mere echo of public opinion."[78]

---

[78] *Id.* p. 104.

Justice Wayne then gave his charge to the jury, saying contrary to the defense's arguments,

> "it has been said that you are the judges of the law and the fact; that you are constitutional judges; that you have a right to do apart from any instruction you may receive from the judge. It is the duty of this Court to tell you what the law is... you are judges of the fact, whether the law as given to you by the Court is made out by the evidence of which you are to be the exclusive judges... Do you find in the oath which gives you your office, a power to determine upon the constitutionality of the law? If you do, another jury may find a different conclusion, so that no law is established at all. In regard to the constitutionality of the law, by the Constitution of the United States, and by the Constitution of South Carolina, such a decision is confided to the judiciary."[79]

In 1861, another piracy trial, *U.S. v. Nathaniel Gordon*, ruled the later sale of the American-built ship from an American owner to an owner of unknown nationality did not remove it from being an American ship for purposes of the statute of 1820, unless the new owner's nationality was established. And the captain of ship fitted for the slave trade would know of its intended use. Gordon unsuccessfully appealed his conviction and death sentence to the Supreme Court.[80]

*4. Albert W. Hicks – Piracy and Murder*

| Legal issues to watch for |
|---|
| ❖ Use of forensic evidence to prove piracy |
| ❖ Using string of circumstantial evidence to prove piracy |
| ❖ Jurisdiction of court over acts committed in harbors |

Albert W. Hicks, aka William Johnson, was brought to trial in New York in March 1860 for piracy on board the sloop *Edwin A. Johnson*. He was charged with a violent assault upon Capt. George H. Burr on the high seas, or alternatively, in a bay, and piratically and feloniously carrying away

---

[79] *Id.* p. 106-108.
[80] Ex parte Gordon, No. 66 U.S. 503 (1861).

Burr's goods, effects, and personal property, including his watch, money, and apparel. He was also charged with the murder of Burr and two other seamen, the brothers Oliver and Smith Watts, but was tried initially only for the piracy (there were no bodies or witnesses, so the murders were harder to prove). The court was presided over by district court judge David A. Smalley, the prosecutor was led by James I. Roosevelt, assisted by Charles H. Hunt and James F. Dwight, and the defense counsel were Ezra Graves and John Sayles. The trial began in May.

In opening, Dwight noted that piracy was robbery on the high seas, basin, or bay, but unlike robbery on the land, the punishment was death. This was because, when,

> "occurring upon vessels upon the high seas, where the protection for person and property is not so great as it can be on land, where individuals are so much surrounded by the police regulations to protect them and their property."[81]

He then described how the *EA Johnson* was found by another ship, floating, with its sails and furniture is disarray, with blood all over the decks and holes drilled into the deck, in an attempt to drain the blood away. The ship, engaged in the oyster trade, had left Long Island, heading to Virginia, with the captain, the Watts brothers, and one other, William Johnson, and a large sum of cash with which to purchase the oysters. Hicks, aka Johnson, was captured, having on his possession several items belonging to his shipmates, such as the captain's pipe and watch, and was thereafter charged and brought to trial.

A long series of witnesses were introduced by the prosecution. Selah Cowell, the American builder and half-owner of the *EA Johnson,* testified that the defendant was the mate aboard the ship, he had seen him on it the night before its departure from Long Island, and he recognized several of the items from the recovered ship and the handwriting of Burr, who he said was an American. The customs officer testified that the ship was registered as American. The man who chartered the ship testified, over the

---

[81] U.S. v. Albert Hicks (1860), from *The Life, Trial, Confession and Execution of Albert W. Hicks, the Pirate and Murderer* (1860), p. 16-17.

defense's objections, to paying money to Burr to purchase the oysters. He testified that the bag he gave Burr $200 in was the same as that found on the defendant and that he had seen the defendant on the ship.

Many other witnesses testified to various acts of the defendants. This included seeing Hicks on the ship or departing from it, proving that he had pawned the captain's watch; that he had a daguerreotype that had been recently given from a young girlfriend to one the brothers; that the lock of the hair she cut from the younger Watts matched the one found in the pools of blood on the ship; that Hicks had landed with the *EA Johnson's* boat; that he had tried to pay for breakfast with a large denomination coin; that he asked a fellow ferry passenger to count out the money in the bag; that he had come home with a large sum of money he claimed was prize money; that a watchmaker had previously cleaned the captain's watch found on Hicks; and that he had exchanged $150 of the coins for bills at a bank.

Others testified to the following: that the damage to another ship, the *J.R. Mather*, in an accident that night between ingoing and outgoing ships matched that found later the *EA Johnson*. That a single dark figure was seen on that ship. That the collision seemed avoidable, but the *EA Johnson* seemed to swerve into the other ship. That Hicks had told someone on shore that a collision with another ship he was on had killed the captain and thrown the other seamen overboard, while he was only able to escape with the money. The captain of the *J.R. Mather* was out to sea and unable to give trial testimony, so the prosecution asked if his testimony before the magistrate could be introduced instead but the defense objected. When he did not arrive by the next morning, the prosecution noted his testimony would have completed the chain of events in their case but was not essential, so they rested.

Sayles objected to the court's jurisdiction, as this act was not committed on the high seas but in a bay and referenced another trial where it was determined that an act of piracy in Boston harbor should be tried in state courts. The court said this was not a question for the jury, even though Sayles claimed that "the jury were the judges of the law and the facts."[82]   The court ruled it was otherwise, as this was a matter of jurisdiction which only the court determines. Sayles also claimed that,

> "'on the high seas' meant either in the harbor of some foreign country, or beyond any portion of a coast where the sea ebbs and flows... [court] this was the opinion of English lawyers, but did not apply to American laws... [Sayles] We have adopted the English common law... [court] Only to a limited extent."[83]

Graves closed with,

> "The evidence against Hicks was entirely circumstantial, and of such a character as to render it very uncertain; but the most astonishing thing about the prosecution was the charge that this one man should kill these three men, powerful as they were, and not receive a single scratch. There must have been a terrible struggle; blood was spattered over the ceiling, blood everywhere, but no blood on him, no mark or violence on his person."[84]

Dwight concluded for the prosecution, saying,

> "nothing which had been asserted by the witnesses for the prosecution had been contradicted. No attempt had been made to break any one link in the chain of the evidence. The defence would endeavor to induce the jury to believe that Capt. Burr parted with his watch, which he had carried for nine years, to a pawnbroker; that Smith Watts had parted with the clothes which his aged mother had put up for him; that Oliver Watts had parted with the daguerreotype of the girl he loved. The time had not yet come when Yankee sailor boys gave up the pictures of 'the girls they left behind them' without a struggle."[85]

The jury quickly found Hicks guilty, and he was sentenced to executed. Before his execution, he confessed to the murders of the three men and to his extensive life of crime, including untold murders, closing with "I ask no

---

[82] *Id.* p. 36.
[83] *Id.*
[84] *Id.* p. 37.
[85] *Id.*

sympathy, and expect none. I shall go to the gallows cursed by all who know the causes which will bring me there."[86]

*5. William Smith – Piracy*

| Legal issues to watch for |
|---|
| ❖ Being under compulsion by statute to commit piracy |
| ❖ Letters of marque issued by government in rebellion |
| ❖ Jurisdiction of court where pirate is apprehended |

The trial of William Smith, an American citizen, for piracy began in Philadelphia, in October 1861, six months after the Civil War had started, before Supreme Court justice Robert Cooper Grier, riding circuit, and district court judge John Cadwalader. The prosecution team included J. Hubley Ashton, George Hussey Earle, and William Darrah Kelley, while the defense team was comprised of John P. O'Neill, N. Harrison, and George M. Wharton. Smith was accused of attacking the U.S. owned *Enchantress* in July 1860, piratically and feloniously attacking the crew, putting the crew in fear, and stealing the cargo and the ship. The ship was American built and registered and the cargo was owned by American merchants, consigned to Cuba.

On their voyage, they were stopped by a brig flying a French flag, which was later hauled down and replaced by the Confederate flag. This was the ship *Jefferson Davis*, which intended to take the *Enchantress* as a prize. The crew of the *Enchantress* was removed, with only the cook, Jacob Garrick, and several members of the *Jefferson Davis* crew including Smith, remaining on board the prize, intending to sail her into some Confederate controlled port. Unfortunately for them, the U.S. gunboat *Albatross* intercepted them. Foiling their plot to impersonate the crew of the *Enchantress*, Garrick leapt into the sea and yelled out its identity, thereby prompting its capture.

Ashton, in his opening, differentiated the law of piracy as being that of the law of nations and of federal statutes and said that this prosecution was based on the latter. Specifically, this initially was the statute of 1790,

---

[86] *Id.* p. 66.

which made it piracy to engage in hostile acts on the high seas against United States, under the pretense of authority from any person. And later, the statute of 1820 made it piracy to commit robbery on American ships on the high seas, regardless of the citizenship of those who were doing it. The prosecution intended to show that the pirate ship of 100 armed men had put the fear into the men of the small merchant vessel and did use actual violence to do so. The seven witnesses for the prosecution were then called.

The owner of the vessel testified to it being American built, registered and owned. The charterer of the ship testified to some of the cargo and that he and other shipper were Americans. The first officer of the *Enchantress*, Charles Page, testified to the captain and six crewmen, including the captain's son and the cargo that was loaded aboard. He described the events of the day of capture, including Smith being a part of the boarding party, and the theft of some of the cargo. He also said there were two other mariners held prisoner from a previous prize, that the ship was heavily armed, and had been loading ammunition and pointing guns at his ship while they were being told to heave to.

He also described how Garrick was sent back to the *Enchantress*, as the captain of the *Jefferson Davis* did not want him aboard. Garrick testified to the same events until the ships parted, and how he was on the prize ship for sixteen days, until it was recaptured, due to his heroic act and how it was flying an American flag when captured. Then the other seamen who were captured previously by the *Jefferson Davis* testified to seeing Smith on that ship, the weapons on the ship, the use of the term 'marines' for certain of her crew, and the capture of the *Enchantress*.

O'Neill began the defense arguments, saying that the defendant did not have the felonious intent necessary for piracy. Smith was forced to serve in the navy, because he did not have a choice, so he could not have the necessary intent. Harrison then asked to introduce the Confederate constitution, proclamations, and laws, to demonstrate a de facto government with the power to regulate persons within its jurisdiction. The prosecution objected to this, on the grounds that it would have no bearing on the charges and the source, which was not the Confederate government, but an unofficial book which included poetry. There was much debate about this topic, with the focus falling finally on the essential information, which was the ability to the Confederate government to issue letters of marque and reprisal.

The defense put on as its main witness, Edward Rochford, one of the prize crew also charged with piracy. Counsel first had him testify that he knew Smith and his family, for the purposes of understanding why Smith would not wish to be subject to the confiscation laws of his state. Rochford was then asked if he understood that the law of Smith's home state of Georgia required performing military service or leaving the "country." The prosecution objected, and after much discussion, the court ruled he was not a competent witness on the law.

The defense then tried to make an issue of where the defendant was first brought in, to whether this court had jurisdiction, without success. Ashton asked Rochford questions to show that Smith was not forced to go on or stay on his ship, such as in voluntarily taking a train from Savannah to Charleston, after he became a member of the ship's company. When the effort by the defense to introduce all the legal documents of the Confederacy was rebuffed, the defense rested after the court ruled,

"These papers are not received as evidence of any fact except the fact of their own existence."[87]

In closing, Harrison outlined his case as proving that a de facto Confederate government existed sufficient to issue letters of marque and able to demand allegiance from those in territories it had domain over, that the federal courts and military were not available in Georgia to protect the defendant against confiscation laws if he did not serve in the Confederate military, and that this court had no jurisdiction, as the defendant was originally brought into a different judicial district. Wharton again made the point that piracy is only piracy as defined by the law of nations and that Smith was just a poor seaman trying to provide for his family who was compelled into military service by the Confederacy.

---

[87] U.S. v. William Smith (3rd Cir. Oct. 1861), from *Full Report of the Trial of William Smith for Piracy* (1861), p. 52.

Kelley closed for the prosecution, noting that Smith had not attempted to flee his supposed confinement before, during, or after he left the *Jefferson Davis*, the latter period when he oversaw the prize ship. Objecting to the de facto existence of the Confederacy, he said,

> "The United States government extends over the territory of the thirty-four States. If it does not, it has ceased to exist. If it does exist, their proposition is at an end, and no adequate defence to the indictment has been presented. The government that issues letters of marque must have had a peaceable existence."[88]

In his charge to the jury, Justice Grier said that the U.S. government and so the courts had to view those in rebellion against their own country as traitors, and not a de facto government. He also said there was no right of secession in the Constitution and said he saw no evidence for duress in the defendant. Justice Cadwalader said that it was not where a pirate is captured that determines the court of jurisdiction but where the defendant is apprehended for trial. Also, a government that is not legitimate cannot issue valid letters of marque. As to compulsion, a law is not sufficient,

> "Unless actual force was exercised against him personally, or threats and intimidation placed him personally under a reasonable fear of death or serious bodily harm, the allegation of compulsion cannot be sustained."[89]

The jury found Smith guilty and in a following trial, found his fellow prize crew members, Thomas Quigley, Edward Rochford, and Daniel Mullinzs, also guilty. The fifth member of the crew, Eben Lane, was found not guilty, as the government did not put on any evidence and,

> "It was alleged that Lane who had charge of steering the *Enchantress*, as one of the prize crew, steered south in daytime and north by night, when he was not observed, thereby keeping her longer on the ocean., and conducing to her capture."[90]

---

[88] *Id.* p. 93.
[89] *Id.* p. 99.
[90] *Id.* p. 100.

These men were not executed, given the significant political, military, and diplomatic implications of treating the enemy's privateers as pirates. Instead, President Lincoln had them sent back across the Union's military lines to the Confederacy.

# *Chapter 3*

# REGULATION ON SHIPS
# AND IN COURT

In 1670, a surgeon who had fallen in with pirates, Alexander Esquemeling, described how buccaneers in Tortuga regulated the activities on their ships,

> "they deliberate whither they shall go to seek their desperate fortunes, and likewise agree upon certain articles, which are put in writing, which every one is bound to observe; and all of them, or the chiefest part, do set their hands to it. Here they set down distinctly what sums of money each particular person ought to have for that voyage, the fund of all the payments being what is gotten by the whole expedition... First... how much the captain is to have for his ship; next, the salary of the carpenter, or shipwright... Afterwards, for provisions and victualling... also a salary for the surgeon, and his chest of medicaments... Lastly, they agree what rate each one ought to have that is either wounded or maimed in his body... All which sums are taken out of the common stock of what is gotten by their piracy, and a very exact and equal dividend is made of the remainder... They observe among themselves very good orders; for in the prizes which they take, it is severely prohibited... to take anything to themselves... they take a solemn oath to each other, not to conceal the least thing

they find among the prizes; and if any one is found false to the said oath, he is immediately turned out of the society."[1]

This agreement among buccaneers, the earliest pirates in the Americas, illustrates some of the elements which would populate later agreements among those involved in illegal piracy and legal privateering. They both aimed to maximize the prizes captured and to fairly share out the proceeds. When privateers stopped potential prizes, they looked at the ship's papers and queried the crew, determining whether the ship and cargo were legitimate prizes. Taking the prize into port, the privateer captain would file a libel complaint in court. The court used examinations of the ship's papers and the captured crew, and perhaps further evidence, when necessary, to make its determination. The choices were whether the ship and cargo should be condemned and sold, with proceeds going to the captor, or acquitted, with ship and cargo returned to its crew and owners.

The first section of this chapter covers the types of crew agreements, both on pirate ships, looking back to the trials covered in Chapters 1 and 2, and on privateers, looking forward to the trials covered in Chapters 4 and 5. The agreements had certain principles in common, with the ubiquitous provision on the sharing out of captured ships and goods. There were often unique provisions, based on the characteristics of the crew or cruise. When the more formal privateering crew agreements had ambiguities, the parties could end up arguing their perspectives in court.

The second section of this chapter deals with the various types of documents involved in evaluating and determining the status of ships taken as prize, looking forward to Chapters 4 and 5. These include the registration of ships, describing their ownership and nationality, and the bills of lading describing the cargo, shipper, and consignee. When the ship and cargo were litigated against, the libelant would claim them, but this allowed other claimants to respond with their own assertions as to why they should retain or obtain ownership. The prosecution of libels primarily used the written depositions, based on standing interrogatories.

---

[1]Alexander Esquemeling, The Pirates of Panama or the Buccaneers of America, A True Account of the Famous Adventures and Daring Deeds of Sir Henry Morgan and Other Notorious Freebooters of the Spanish Main (1684).

## 3.1 CREW AGREEMENTS

On both pirate and privateer ships, there had to be rules by which the crew worked. For the crew of William Kidd, discussed in Chapter 1, after they turned from privateering to pirating, the ship's articles were revised to include common features of pirate articles, like the shares everyone would receive, payments for injuries, rewards for certain acts like spotting ships, and discipline for other behavior, like drunkenness, cowardice, and mutiny. On a pirate ship, sailing in violation of the law, the agreement was often simplified, using common principles that bound the crew and commander to a course of action and describing how crew would act in certain situations, like battle.

For privateers operating in accordance with the law, the rules were more elaborate. Beyond the legal authority for privateering through legislative acts, instructions from the king or Congress, and privateering commissions, were the ship's articles of agreement. These agreements between ship owners, commanders, and crew dictated the objectives and durations of the cruise, expected crew behaviors in certain situations, and most importantly, how the proceeds from prize ships and cargo would be distributed among these three groups. The articles for the American privateer *Yankee*, during the War of 1812, had all these provisions, and some provisions less frequently used, such as designating a successor in case of the captain's death, the captain and officers appointing an agent for the crew, and prohibiting the rude treatment of female prisoners. The agreements could lead to litigation when the articles were vague or unexpected situations arose, as discussed in the cases below.

### A. Pirates

*1. Agreement to Commit Piracy*

An early example of an agreement between the commander and crew of a pirate ship was the *Camelion*, a slave ship, where the crew had taken over the ship and made the following agreement, in 1683. These acts would soon see them put on trial for piracy.

> "June the 30th day, 1683. Articles of Agreement between us abord of the Camillion," Nich. Clough Comander, that wee are to dispose of all

the goods thatt are abord amongst us, every man are to have his full due and right share only the Commander is to have two shares and a half a share for the Ship and home * the Captain please to take for the Master under him is to have a share and a half. Now Gentlemen these are to satisfy you, as for the Doctor a Share and half, and these are our Articles that wee do all stand to as well as on * and all. These are to satisfy you thatt our intent is to trade with the Spaniards, medling nor make no resistances with no nation that wee do fall with all upon the Sea. Now Gentlemen these are to give you notice that if any one do make any Resistances against us one any factery hereafter shall bee severely punish according to the fact that hee hath comitted and as you are all here at present you have taken your corporall oath upon the holy Evangelists to stand one by the other as long as life shall last.

[signed] John Hallamore, Henery Michelson, Thomas Dickson, Albert Lasen, Symon. Webson, Robert Cockram, Jo. Darvell, William Strother, Arthur Davis, Edwa. Dove, Jno. Morrine, John Watkins, John Renals, Edward Starkey, Robert Dousin, George Paddisson, John Copping, Nicho. Clough, Henry Lewin, Samll. Haynsworth, Daniell Kelly, William Heath, John Griffin."[2]

2.    *Bartholomew Roberts*

Bartholomew Roberts, a crew member of a slave ship, was taken from his ship off Africa in 1719 by the pirate Howell Davis. When Davis was killed, Roberts was chosen to take over as captain, until his own death in action in 1722. While the source of the following, and the related pirate articles are not completely verifiable, they can still be viewed as representative.

"I. Every Man has a Vote in Affairs of Moment; has equal Title to the fresh Provisions, or strong Liquors, at any Time seized, and use them at pleasure, unless a Scarcity (no uncommon Thing among them) make it necessary, for the good of all, to vote a Retrenchment.

II. Every Man to be called fairly in turn, by List, on Board of Prizes, because, (over and above their proper Share,) they were on these Occasions allowed a Shift of Cloaths: But if they defrauded the

---

[2] J.F. Jameson, *Privateering and Piracy in the Colonial World* (1923), p. 141-42.

Company to the Value of a Dollar, in Plate, Jewels, or Money, MAROONING was their Punishment. This was a Barbarous Custom of putting the Offender on Shore, on some desolate or uninhabited Cape or Island, with a Gun, a few Shot, a Bottle of Water, and a Bottle of Powder, to subsist with, or starve. If the Robbery was only between one another, they contented themselves with slitting the Ears and Nose of him that was Guilty, and set him on Shore, not in an uninhabited Place, but somewhere, where he was sure to encounter Hardships.

III. No Person to Game at Cards or Dice for Money.

IV. The Lights and Candles to be put out at eight o'Clock at Night: If any of the Crew, after that Hour, still remained inclined for Drinking, they were to do it on the open Deck; which Roberts believed would give a Check to their Debauches, for he was a sober Man himself, but found at length, that all his Endeavours to put an End to this Debauch, proved ineffectual.

V. To keep their Piece, Pistols, and Cutlash clean, and fit for Service: In this they were extravagantly nice, endeavouring to outdo one another, in the Beauty and Richness of their Arms, giving sometimes at an Auction (at the Mast,) 30 or 40 l. a Pair, for Pistols. These were slung in Time of Service, with different coloured Ribbands, over their Shoulders, in a Way peculiar to these Fellows, in which they took great Delight.

VI. No Boy or Woman to be allowed amongst them. If any Man were sound seducing anny of the latter Sex, and carried her to Sea, disguised, he was to suffer Death; so that when any fell into their Hands, as it chanced in the Onslow, they put a Centinel immediately over her to prevent ill Consequences from so dangerous an Instrument of Division and Quarrel; but then here lies the Roguery; they contend who shall be Centinel, which happens generally to one of the greatest Bullies, who, to secure the Lady's Virtue, will let none lye with her but himself.

VII. To Desert the Ship, or their Quarters in Battle, was punished with Death, or Marooning.

VIII. No striking one another on Board, but every Man's Quarrels to be ended on Shore, at Sword and Pistol, Thus; The Quarter-Master of the Ship, when the Parties will not come to any Reconciliation, accompanies them on Shore with what Assistance he thinks proper, and turns the Disputants Back to Back, at so many Paces Distance: At the Word of Command, they turn and fire immediately, (or else the Piece is knocked out of their Hands:) If both miss, they come to their Cutlashes, and then he is declared Victor who draws the first Blood.

IX. No Man to talk of breaking up their Way of Living, till each had shared a 1000 l. If in order to this, any Man should lose a Limb, or become a Cripple in their Service, he was to have 800 Dollars, out of the publick Stock, and for lesser Hurts, proportionably.

X. The Captain and Quarter-Master to receive two Shares of a Prize; the Master, Boatswain, and Gunner, one Share and a half, and other Officers, one and a Quarter.

XI. The Musicians to have Rest on the Sabbath Day, but the other six Days and Nights, none without special Favour."[3]

3.   *Thomas Anstis*

The articles of Thomas Anstis were provided by a captured crew member of the ship *Good Fortune*, William Whelks, in 1723. Anstis had turned pirate under Howell Davis and remained there under Bartholomew Roberts.

"1st: That the captain shall have one full share as the rest of the company; the master, gunner, carpenter, and boatswain the same.

2nd: If any man should disobey any lawful command of the commanding officers, shall suffer punishment the company and captain shall think fit.

---

[3] Charles Johnson, *A General History of the Pyrates* (1724), p. 230-32.

3rd: If any person or persons should go on board of any prize and should break open any chest without the knowledge of the quartermaster shall suffer what punishment the company and captain shall think fit.

4th: If any person or persons shall be found guilty of thievery from another to the value of one piece of eight, shall be marooned on an island with one bottle of powder, one bottle of water, and shot equivalent.

5th: If any person or personal should be found neglecting in keeping their arms clean unfitting for an engagement shall lose his share or shares.

6th: If any person or persons should be found to snap their arms or cleaning in the hold shall suffer Moses Law, that is 40 lacking one.

7th: If any person or persons shall be found backwards in the time of an engagement, shall be marooned.

8th: If any person or persons shall be found to game on board this privateer of the value of one rial plate, shall suffer Moses Law.

9th: If any person or persons shall go on board of a prize and meet with any gentlewoman or lady of honor and should force them against their will to lye with them, shall suffer death.

10th: If any person or persons should lose a leg or a limb or a joint shall for a limb have 800 pieces of eight and for one joint 200.

11th: If any time we shall come in company with any other marooner and that shall offer to sign their articles without the consent of the company, shall be marooned or run away shall receive the same.

12th: But if at any time we shall hear from England and have an account of an act of grace, they that are of a mind to receive it shall go with their money and goods and the rest have the privateer."[4]

---

[4] Information of William Whelks, before justice of the peace William Blake (Apr. 22, 1723).

## 4.  *John Phillips*

John Phillips was a ship's carpenter, captured by Thomas Antis, who would in turn run his own small pirate ship, until his death in 1724.

> "1. Every Man shall obey civil Command; the Captain shall have one full Share and a half in all Prizes; the Master, Carpenter, Boatswain and Gunner shall have one Share and quarter.
>
> 2. If any Man shall offer to run away, or keep any Secret from the Company, he shall be marroon'd, with one Bottle of Powder, one Bottle of Water, one small Arm, and Shot.
>
> 3. If any Man shall steal any Thing in the Company, or game, to the Value of a Piece of Eight, he shall be marroon'd or shot.
>
> 4. If at any Time we should meet another Marrooner [that is, Pyrate,] that Man that shall sign his Articles without the Consent of our company, shall suffer such Punishment as the Captain and Company shall think fit.
>
> 5. That Man that shall strike another whilst these Articles are in force, shall receive Moses's Law (that is, 40 Stripes lacking one) on the bare Back.
>
> 6. That Man that shall snap his Arms, or smoak Tobacco in the Hold, without a Cap to his Pipe, or carry a Candle lighted without a Lanthorn, shall suffer the same Punishment as in the former Article.
>
> 7. That Man that shall not keep his Arms clean, fit for an Engagement, or neglect his Business, shall be cut off from his Share, and suffer such other Punishment as the Captain and the Company shall think fit.
>
> 8. If any Man shall lose a Joint in time of an Engagement, shall have 400 Pieces of Eight; if a Limb, 800.
>
> 9 If at any time you meet with a prudent Woman, that Man that offers to meddle with her, without her Consent, shall suffer present Death."[5]

---

[5] *A General History of the Pyrates* (1724), p. 397-98.

## 5. George Lowther

George Lowther was another pirate captain who started as a mariner aboard a slaver, pirating until his death in 1723.

"1. THE Captain is to have two full Shares; the Master is to have one Share and a half; the Doctor, Mate, Gunner, and Boatswain, one Share and a quarter.

2. He that shall be found Guilty of taking up any unlawful Weapon on Board the Privateer, or any Prize, by us taken, so as to strike or abuse one another, in any regard, shall suffer what Punishment the Captain and Majority of the Company shall think fit.

3. He that shall be found Guilty of Cowardize, in the Time of Engagement, shall suffer what Punishment the Captain and Majority shall think fit.

4. If any Gold, Jewels, Silver, &c. be found on Board of any Prize or Prizes, to the Value of a Piece of Eight, and the Finder do not deliver it to the Quarter-Master, in the Space of 24 Hours, shall suffer what Punishment the Captain and Majority shall think fit.

5. He that is found Guilty of Gaming, or Defrauding another to the Value of a Shilling, shall suffer what Punishment the Captain and Majority of the Company shall think fit.

6. He that shall have the Misfortune to lose a Limb, in Time of Engagement, shall have the Sum of one hundred and fifty Pounds Sterling, and remain with the Company as long as he shall think fit.

7. Good Quarters to be given when call'd for.

8. He that sees a Sail first, shall have the best Pistol, or Small-Arm, on Board her."[6]

---

[6] *A General History of the Pyrates* (1724), p. 352.

*6.  Edward Low*

Edward Low had turned pirate and worked together with George Lowther, leading to the similarity of their articles. At the trial of a member of his crew, Charles Harris, described in Chapter 1, one of the trial exhibits were Low's ship articles.

> "I THE Captain shall have Two full Shares, the Master a Share and a half, the Doctor, Mate, Gunner, Carpenter, and Boatswain a Share and quarter.
>
> II. He that shall be found Guilty of Striking or taking up any unlawful Weapon either aboard of a Prize, or aboard the Privateer, shall suffer what Punishment the Captain and majority of ⟨◊⟩ Company shall think fit.
>
> III. He that shall be found Guilty of Cowardice in the Time of Engagement, shall ⟨◊⟩ what Punishment the Captain and the majority of the Company shall think fit.
>
> IV. If any Jewels, Gold or Silver is found on board of a Prize to the Value of a ⟨◊⟩ of Eight, and the finder do not deliver it to the Quarter-Master ⟨...⟩ Time, shall suffer what Punishment the Captain and majority of the Company shall think fit.
>
> V. He that shall be found Guilty of Gaming, or playing at Cards, or Defrauding or Cheating one another to the Value of a Royal of Plate, shall suffer what Punishment ⟨◊⟩ Captain and majority of the Company shall think ⟨◊.
>
> VI. He that shall be Guilty of Drunkenness in the Time of an Engagement, shall suffer what Punishment the Captain and majority of the Company shall think fit.
>
> VII. He that hath the Misfortune to loose any of his Limbs in the Time of an Engagement in the Companies Service, shall have the Sum of Six Hundred Pieces of Eight, and kept in the Company as long as he pleases.
>
> VIII. Good Quarters to be given when Craved.

IX. He that sees a Sail first shall have the best Pistol, or Small Arm aboard of her.

X. And lastly, No Snapping of Arms [weapons] in the Hold."[7]

## 7. John Gow

Along with an account of the 1725 English trial and conviction of mutineer turned pirate John Gow, was a listing of his ship's articles.

"I. THAT every Man shall obey his Commander in all Records, as if the Ship was his own, and we under Monthly Pay,

II. THAT no Man shall give or dispose of the Ship's Provisions whereby may be given Reason of Suspicion that every one hath not an equal Share.

III. THAT no Man shall open or declare to any Person or Persons what we are, or what Design we are upon; the Offender shall be punish'd with Death upon the spot.

IV. THAT no Man shall go on Shore till the Ship is off the Ground, and in readiness to put to Sea.

V. THAT every Man shall keep his Watch Night and Day, and precisely at the Hour of Eight leave of Gaming and Drinking, and every one repair to their respective Stations.

VI. WHOEVER Offends shall he punish'd with Death, or otherwise."[8]

## 8. Summary of the Pirate Articles

Among these presented pirate articles, there are provisions that occurred more commonly, such as the division of spoils and compensating for injuries to the crew, and others that stand out as being unique. There were sometimes general procedural articles, such as pledges to stand together and to obey the articles, to vote democratically (although this was not commonly included as a provision), and even a duration of time or an objective the crew had to reach before breaking up. The following divides

---

[7] Tryals of Thirty-Six Persons for Piracy at Rhode Island (1723).
[8] Daniel Defoe, An Account of the Conduct and Proceedings of the late John Gow alias Smith (1725), p. 52-53.

the preceding articles into two groups, those listed once and those listed more than once. It is important to note that some of the articles were from pirates who had served on ships of other pirates and likely copied their articles.

Provisions listed more than once in the preceding pirate articles:

- Allocation of spoils among the captain and crew
- Mandate to follow orders of the captain
- A right to equal provisions including alcohol
- Punishment for defrauding their piratical company
- Punishment for robbery/theft among the crew
- Prohibition on gambling
- Mandate to keep weapons serviceable
- Prohibition on women onboard and assaulting women encountered
- Prohibition on desertion or signing articles for another pirate ship
- Prohibition on giving quarter or being drunk during battle
- Prohibition on fighting amongst crew
- Compensation for injuries received in service
- Requirement to coordinate spoils with the quartermaster

Provisions listed at once in the preceding pirate articles:

- Putting out the lights by certain time
- Work schedule for musicians
- Allocation of living quarters onboard
- Prohibition of (non-working) boys onboard
- Prohibition on keeping secrets from the crew
- Prohibition on smoking or carrying candles in the hold
- Prohibition on snapping weapons (firing without powder)
- Manner of settling disputes onshore

- Monthly pay for the crew
- Prohibition on declaring ship's piratical intentions
- Assignment of all to prize crews, and the extra reward for taking this role
- Prohibition on going ashore until ship is ready to put to sea
- Mandate to keep the watch, night and day, and be on stations at night
- Allowance to seek pardons that are offered
- Reward for spotting potential victims.

## B. Privateers

### 1. Colonial Era

The following are articles of agreement of the privateer *Mars*, from June 1762, during America's time as a colony of Great Britain.

"Imprimis, That the said Dennis McGillycuddy, for himself, and in Behalf of the Owners of the Privateer, shall put on board the said Brigantine a sufficient Number of Great Guns, Small Arms, Powder, Shot, and all other necessary warlike Stores and Ammunition; as also, suitable Provisions sufficient for the said Brigantine, during the whole Cruize; which Cruize is to be understood to be from the time of the said Brigantine's sailing from the Port of New York, until the Time of her returning thither again, for which there shall be no Deduction made out of the said Company's Shares: And in Consideration thereof, the Owner of the said Brigantine or his substitutes, shall have and receive One Half of all Prizes, Goods, Wares, Merchandizes, Monies, Effects, etc. that shall be taken during this Cruize; the other Half shall be divided, and paid to the said Brigantine's Company, by the Captain aforesaid, according to the Rules hereafter stated.

II. That the Captain shall have and receive, for himself, Six Full Shares, and shall be granted all Privileges and Freedoms which have been granted any Captains of Privateers: That the Lieutenants and Master, shall each of them have Three Full Shares, That the Captain's Clerk, Mates, Steward, Prize-Master, Gunner, Boatswain, Carpenter, and

Cooper, shall each of them have and receive, Two Full Shares. That the Gunner's Mate, Boatswain's Mate, Doctor's Mate, Carpenter's Mate, and Cooper's Mate, shall each of them have and receive One Share and a Half.

III. That the doctor of the said Privateer, or whoever is at the Expence of the Chest of Medicines, shall have and receive the Sum of Pounds, if well furnished. Also the doctor shall have and receive for himself Three Full Shares, as also all Medicines and Instruments belonging to any Doctor that shall be taken.

IV. That if any Person spies a Sail, and she proves to be a Prize worth One Hundred Pieces of Eight a Share, he shall receive Forty Pieces of Eight at Six Shillings. And the first Man who enters on boarding a Prize in an engagement, and strikes her Colours, shall receive Half a Share for his Bravery.

V. That all the rest of the said Brigantine's Company, such as shall be deemed able and sufficient Seamen, shall each of them have and receive One Full Share, out of the Effects, Plunder and Prizes, that shall or may be taken by the said Brigantine during the Cruize, Provided, They are not found guilty of the Faults or Crimes hereafter named.

VI. That as to the Proceedings of the Vessel, and under taking any Enterprize at Sea, or on Shore, and into what Port any Prize shall be Carried that shall be taken during the Cruize, shall be left entirely to the Captain's Election.

VII. That whoever of the Company shall breed a Mutiny or Disturbance, or strike his Fellow, or shall Game with Cards or Dice for Money, or any Thing of Value, or shall sell any strong Liquors on board, during the Voyage, he or they shall be fined as the Captain and Officers shall direct. And if any of the Company be found pilfering or stealing any Money or Goods of what kind soever, belonging to the said Privateer or Company, he or they shall forfeit his or their Share or Shares of the Prize-Money or Effects then and afterwards taken by the said Brigantine, during the whole Cruize, to the Owner and Company.

VIII. That if any of the Company in an Engagement with the Enemy, or in the true Service of the Cruize, shall lose a Leg or an Arm, or be so disabled as to be deprived of the Use of either; every such Person shall be allowed out of the effects or Prize first taken, (before any Division be made) the Sum of Six Hundred Pieces of Eight, at Six Shillings; or the Value thereof in Goods, at the Price according to public Sale: But if there be not so much taken at that Time, the vessel and Company shall keep out till they have enough for that Purpose; Provided no extraordinary Accident happens.

IX. That all the small Plunder, shall be brought to publick Sale, and be delivered to the highest Bidder, for which their Shares shall be accountable, excepting the Captain's Perquisites, which are such as did belong to the Captains of Prizes, and such Clothing as the Captain shall think proper to allow the Prisoners. -

X. That if any Person belonging to the said Brigantine, be killed in an Engagement, or die on board, his Share or Shares, of all Prizes taken in his Life-Time, shall be paid to his Executors, if so appointed by Will; but if no Will be made, then his Part of what was got as aforesaid shall go to his Widow, or Heirs at Law, if claim'd in Twelve Months, from the Time of the said Brigantine's Arrival into her commission'd Port; and on Failure thereof, said Share or Shares shall be and belong to the general Interest of the Whole.

XI. That if any of the Company do disannul any of the Officers Commands for the Good of the Cruize, or the general Interest, he or they shall be fined and punished as the Captain and Officers shall direct. And if any of the Company do Assault, Strike or Insult any Male Prisoner, or behave rudely or indecently to any Female Prisoner, he or they shall be punished as the Captain and Officers shall direct. And if any of the Company begin an Attack, either by firing a Gun, or using any Instrument of War, before Orders be given, by the proper Officers, he or they shall be punished; but if any of the said Company do refuse to make an Attack on the Enemy, either at Sea or Land, at the Command and in the Manner ordered by the Captain and proper Officers, or do behave with Cowardice in any Engagement, he or them shall forfeit his or their Share or Shares for such Refusal or Cowardice; and if any of the Company get drunk, or use blasphemous and prophane Words, they shall be punished as the Captain and Officers shall direct: And likewise if any of the Company do desert the said Schooner before her Return to New-York, he or they shall forfeit their whole Shares to the Owner and Company, first paying such Brigantine's Debts as are contracted by the Captain's Knowledge.

XII. That at the Division of any Money or Effects taken this Cruize, Dead Shares shall be deducted out of the Whole, which shall be divided by the amongst the most Deserving and them that does most for the benefit of the Cruize.

XIII. That any Prize or Prizes that shall be taken during the Cruize, shall be with all Speed sent into the Port of New-York, in order that the same may be libelled against in the Court of Admiralty for Condemnation, and to no other Place whatsoever, except said Prize shall be so disabled that she could not proceed to said Port: And any Person or Persons which shall be aiding or assisting, or shall give his or their Consent for sending any Prize or Prizes, into any other Port but the Harbour of New-York aforesaid, shall forfeit his or their Share to the Owner and Company; and that no Division shall be made till they return to the Port of New-York.

XIV. That in Case any neutral Property, or any Property whatever, be taken and sent into Port, and after Condemnation be had, an Appeal should be entered by the Claimants, then, and in such Case, it shall be Lawful with the full Consent of the Captain and Company of the said Privateer, for the Owner, or his Attorney, to compromise, compound, and settle, by giving up any Sum or Part of the Prize, as shall seem most advisable to him for the general Interest, that the Captain and Company may receive each and every one of them their just and lawful Right and Prize Money, and not be kept out of their Money until the Appeal may be determined in England; and in Case no such Compromisation can be made, then a certain Sum, shall be lodged out of the Prizes before taken, to prosecute the said Appeal: And it shall likewise be lawful for the Owner or Agent of the said Privateer to discharge any Capture that may be made during his said Cruize, without the formality of a Prosecution, in order that all unnecessary Charges may as much as possible be avoided.

XV. That it shall not be lawful for the said Officers and Company, or either of them, to demand or sue for the Prize Money so to become due to them, or any Part thereof, until fourteen Days after the Sale of such Prize or Prizes, the Settlement of the Accounts relating to the said Cruize, and the actual Receipt of the Money by the Agent appointed to manage the Affairs of the said Cruize.

XVI. That if it should happen, that the said Briganteen, by Means of any Fight, Attack, or Engagement, be lost, sunk or disabled, so as she may be thereby rendered unfit for any further Service as a private Vessel of War to cruize; that then, and in such Case, the owner of said Brigantine, shall be entitled to take to himself, and for his own sole Use and Property, any Ship or Vessel taken during the Cruize, with her Guns, Tackle, Furniture, Ammunition and Apparel, not exceeding the Value of the Brigantine at the Time of her Sailing; which Ship or Vessel so taken shall be to the Owner in Lieu of the said Brigantine.

XVII. That in Case of the Death of the Commander, the next in Place shall strictly observe and comply with the Rules, Orders, Restrictions and Agreements, between the owner of the said Brigantine and the said Commander.

God Save the King, and Success to the *Mars*, and all her brave Crew."[9]

## 2. Revolutionary War

On the privateer *Revenge*, during the American Revolutionary War, the captain and crew drew up the following agreement.

"Articles of Agreement, made and concluded in New London, between the Owners, Captain, Officers, and Mariners of the armed Sloop called the *Revenge*, bound on a six Weeks Cruize against the Enemies of the United States of America.

---

[9] *Privateering and Piracy in the Colonial World* (1923), p. 581-85.

We, Owners of the said-Sloop do covenant to fit for Sea the said Vessel, in a warlike Manner; and provider her with Cannon, Swivels, Small-Arms, Cutlasses, sufficient Ammunition, and Provisions, with a Box of Medicines, and every other Necessary at our own Expence, for a six weeks Cruize against the Enemies of the Thirteen United States of America; and that said Owners shall be entitled to receive the one Half of all Prize, Effects and Things that shall be taken during the said Cruize; the other Half to be divided amongst the Sloops Company, in the following Proportions – Captain, eight Shares; First and Second Lieutenants, Master and Doctor, four Shares each; two Masters Mates, Boatswain, Gunner and Quarter-Masters, Officer Marines and Carpenter, two Shares each; Prize-Masters, three shares each; all lesser Officers, not more than one and half Shares; Privates, one Share; and Boys, Half a Share.

All Enterprises at Sea or on Shore, shall be solely directed by the Captain. There shall be five dead Shares given to the most deserving Men, to be adjudged by the Committee.

If any one shall loose a Leg or an Arm, in Time of Action, he shall receive Three Hundred Dollars, out of the whole Effects taken. If any Person shall mutiny, or raise any Distrubance on Board, game, steal, or embezzle on, or of, any Prize, whether at Sea of in Port; disobey his Officer, prove a Coward, desert his Quarters, absent himself without the Leave of his superior Office for the Term of twelve Hours, exercise any Cruelty or Inhumanity in cold Blood, he shall forfeit his whole Share or Shares to the Company, and be liable to such corporal Punishment as the Committee shall think fit to inflict. The Committee shall consist of the chief Commanding Officer, first and second Lieutenant and Master.

The Captain shall have full Power to displace any Officers as he shall think proper.

Lastly, the said Commander, Officers, and Men, hereby enter ourselves on the Cruize for a Term of six Weeks, if the Cruize shall last so long, or unless sooner discharged."[10]

## 3. War of 1812

A 1790 U.S. statute[11] required a written agreement specifying the voyage, its term, and the date and time for the seaman to report to the ship, for any voyage to a foreign port or any ship over 50 tons burden sailing to a port in a non-adjacent state. If there was no agreement, the seaman was to be paid the highest wages being given at their port and the commander fined $20 per man without a contract.

On the privateer *Prince de Neufchatel* during the War of 1812, the owners, captain, and crew had the following agreement.

"Articles of Agreement between the owners of the private armed vessel the brig Prince of Neufchatel, Nicholas Millin Commander and the Captain, Officers and Crew of the said Vessel entered into at Boston the 30th November 1814.

Art. 1. The expenses of armoring & provisioning of the said Vessel shall be paid by the Owners for the fitting her out of her Port of departure Only – afterwards everything which may be taken from Captured Vessels such as war-like stores and provisions, sails, rigging, cordage, cannon and generally every thing which may be useful for the service of the Privateer shall be considered as belonging to the Privateer without compensation for the Value thereof in Account.

Art. 2. The cruize shall be for four months at sea, and entirely governed by the will of the Captain. He however shall be subject in every respect to the order of the Owners, or their agents.

Art. 3. None of the crew shall be allowed before the period fixed by the preceding article to demand a discharge until the grounds upon

---

[10] Articles of Agreement for the sloop Revenge (June 27, 1778).
[11] An Act for the government and regulation of Seamen in the merchants service, c. 1, s. 2, ch. 29.

which his application shall be founded, shall be approved by the Captain.

Art. 4. The said Captain shall have the right of putting from on board the Vessel, and of depriving in whole or in part of his right to prize money any person who shall by his bad conduct have merited that punishment by sentence given against him by a tribunal composed of four Officers and the said Captain making five, without right of appeal by the delinquent even the said delinquent be absent.

Art. 5. If any person shall purloin any Captured articles and it should be proved against him, he shall loose [lose] all his shares.

Art. 6. In case of putting into a foreign Country, the Crew obligates themselves to do all necessary repairs to the Privateer without making any claims for payment.

Art. 7. In case of putting into a port or place, the Officers and petty Officers as well as Seamen and Crew obligate themselves to remain on board, each one his turn. Or all hands if the said Captain so directs.

Art. 8. Any man who during the continuance of the cruize shall abandon the Privateer without permission from the Captain may be declared a deserter and shall loose [lose] all his shares of prize to which he otherwise might claim.

Art. 9. Any man embarked on board for a station, he shall be incapable of fulfilling, either from ignorance or bad conduct, shall be triest by tribunal similar to that mentioned in the 4th article and displaced by the said Captain, who may put him in that station which shall be assigned him by such tribunal.

Art. 10. In whatever part of the United States or where so ever else the Privateer or her prize shall put in, the Owners shall not be held to pay for or furnish to any person whatsoever passage to the place from which the vessel shall have been fitted out.

Art. 11. Who ever shall first discover a Vessel which proves to be a good prize shall have in such regard half a share extra.

Art. 12. The prize master shall have no claims to the effects or merchandize which may be found in the cabin of a prize but there should be allowed him one share extra from the proceeds of the prize he shall succeed in getting into port.

Art. 13. In case of boarding an enemy Vessel of war, the first person on board the enemy Vessel shall receive in that respect six shares extra, the second six shares, the third & fourth five shares, the fifth & sixth four shares, the seventh & eighth three shares, the ninth & tenth each two shares, the eleventh & twelfth each one share, the thirteenth & fourteenth a half share, and the fifteenth up to the twentieth, one quarter of a share.

Art. 14. In case of boarding a merchant Vessel, the first on board of the enemy shall receive two shares extra, the second two shares, the third & fourth one share, the fifth & sixth one half a share, the seventh & eighth up to the tenth, one quarter a share.

Art. 15. When a prize shall arrive in Port, the prize crew shall be obligated to serve on board the Vessel and to remain on board until the prize shall be unloaded; whoever fails in his duty may be replaced by a man out of his portion of prize.

Art. 16. After unloading a prize Vessel, there shall be allowed to the Captain and prize crew who bring the Vessel in – A board suited to their respective stations, until the owners or agent of the Privateer shall discharge them.

Art. 17. If the Privateer shall be in Port where there are any of her prizes, the Crew may be required to work, where the general interest requires; those who fail in their duty may be replaced by day laborers paid out of their share of prizes.

Art. 18. The Captain shall have the right of putting on board of prizes the Officers and Crew he may see fit without liberty to any to complain.

Art. 19. The advances if any are paid by the owners to the crew shall be repaid out of the first prizes that arrive with the addition of fifty percent thereon and if no prizes arrive, it will be the owners' loss.

Art. 20. The Captain shall have the right if he sees fit to double the prize money of those who in an engagement with the enemy loose [lose] a leg or an arm.

Art. 21. Any officer who gets drunk at sea will be put before the mast and be entitled only to the same number of shares as the prize master mates, and the Captain shall have the right of replacing the delinquent and giving the new officer the same number of shares as to the old.

Art. 22. A commission of two percent on the net proceeds of all prizes will be allowed to the Captain to be taken out of the whole net proceeds.

Art. 23. Neither the Captain of the Privateer nor the prize master shall have the right to select an agent on their arrival. Shall be their duty to give notice thereof to the owners or agents of the Privateer and if they delay doing so, they will be answerable for the consequences of such neglect.

Art. 24. ____, ____, & _____ are hereby irrevocably made the agents of the Captain, Officers, and Crew to receive their Prize Money and do everything that relates to the present cruize, with powers of substitution, and they shall be allowed five percent commission on the gross proceeds of all prizes and prize goods.

Art. 25. No transfer of shares or parts of shares by the commander, officers, or crew shall be unless first requested by the agent _____, _____,& _____, in the district where the prize may be in a register expressly for the purpose, and such transfer shall take place only from the time of being so registered.

Art. 26. On shipping each man, a ticket is issued payable to him as bearer for one quarter of a share, provided he conforms to the articles of agreement. That quarter of the shares will be paid to the bearer and the rest to the crew.

Art. 27. One half of the net proceeds of all prizes is to be allowed to the Owners and the other half to the Captain, Officers and Crew.

Art. 28. The half of the Captain, Officers and Crew shall be divided among them as follows, subject however to the alternations that may result from the foregoing articles.

Commander 12 shares; 1st lieutenant 10; 2nd lieutenant 8; 3rd lieutenant 7; 4th lieutenant and doctor 6; lieutenant marines and prize masters 4; gunner and boatswain 3; carpenter 2 and 1/2; cook, sail master, quarter master, steward, armorer, gunners mate, and first boatswain 2; second boatswain and carpenters 1 and 3/4; segreant marines and able seaman 1 and 1/2; ordinary seaman, corporal, and musicians 1; marines 3/4; and boys 1/2."[12]

## 4. Summary of the Privateer Articles of Agreement

The articles of agreement, sometimes called the shipping articles, presented above clearly evolved to become more sophisticated over time, as the use of privateering became more prominent. The following elements were common to these articles:

- List of munitions, armaments, stores, supplies, and provisions that were to be put onboard at the owner's expense
- Scope of the cruise, including departure and return ports and the duration of the cruise
- Division of the prize proceeds between owners, usually half, and the captain and crew, usually the other half
- Share allocation amongst the captain and different ranks of the crew for their one half of the proceeds
- Extra shares for those crew spotting or entering prizes first
- Dead shares, which were set aside and awarded to chosen members of the crew, based on their meritorious acts
- Prohibitions of various acts (e.g. mutiny, theft, gambling, assault, desertion)
- Penalties for prohibited acts, including loss of shares and being sent off the ship

---

[12] Articles of Agreement for the brig Prince de Neufchatel (Nov. 30, 1814).

- Discretions and powers given to the commander during the cruise
- Payments for disabilities of crew members incurred during service
- Prohibitions on selling more than half a crew member's share before the ship sails or prizes are taken

Other articles that were often included:

- The owners are responsible for the initial fitting out, after which needed items had to be claimed from other ships
- Advances to the owners were to be paid back first
- Loss or significant damage to privateer ship allowing the owner to claim a prize ship
- Prohibitions on maltreating prisoners or abusing women encountered on ships
- Line of succession if captain was killed during the cruise
- How to pay shares for crew members killed during the cruise
- No claims in prize merchandize found by the prize master
- Obligation to remain onboard a prize until the cargo is unloaded
- Detailed responsibilities of prize masters and crew
- Punishments for those who pilfered any part of a prize
- Appointing an agent for the crew during the cruise
- Obligation of crew to repair a ship having to enter a foreign port
- The role and commission rates of prize agents and who had the ability to select these agents

5. *The Dash*

The privateer *Dash* had captured a prize, the *Five Sisters*, in August 1814, the ship was libeled and condemned in the district our in Massachusetts, sold, and the proceeds were paid to the marshal of the admiralty court. Claims were made upon these proceeds by three members of the crew, Ross, Slater, and Marshall, which were disputed by the owners. Ross claimed five shares, Slater four shares (they were both officers), and seaman Marshall one share. The owners filed a petition that the shares of these men should instead come to them, as the men had only shipped (worked) for wages, not prize shares. The men then produced the articles of agreement, which stated that,

> "The net amount of all prizes and prize goods taken during the voyage to be divided in the following manner, viz. one moiety to the owners of the vessel, and the other to be shared among the officers and crew in the proportion set against their names respectively."[13]

The list in the agreement showed the crew's names and two columns for wages and shares, with shares written in for only some of the crew. There was a later document, dated two months after the capture of the prize ship, signed by the owners, showing 59.5 total shares, as opposed to only 18 in the articles of agreement. The district court ruled against the owner-petitioners and the case was appealed to the circuit court. Supreme Courtice Justice Joseph Story, riding circuit, wrote the opinion of the court. He first noted that the prize act of June 1812 required distribution according to an agreement among the owners and crew and if there was not an agreement, then the proceeds would be split half and half, with the crew's shares being split in a manner like that described by statute for the navy.[14]

He said that both by statute, and by the letters of marque issued to the ship, that the crew had a vested interest in all condemned prizes. The amount allocated to each crew man could either be determined by the written agreement or by statutory specification. These interests were legal interests, which could be assigned but only by a written agreement. Noting that less than half of the officers and crew had shares against their names in the articles of agreement, this construction would be contrary to the intent to the prize act, and so was inadmissible. The owners' argument was that these three men had accepted higher wages in exchange for being excluded from shares. The court termed this an implied assignment to the owners and ruled that the presumption of payment of higher wages could not defeat the men's vested interests in the prize proceeds, decreeing payment to the three men, and assigning costs to the owners.

---

[13] The Dash, 7. F. Cas. 2 (Cir. Ct. D. Mass. 1815).
[14] An Act for the better government of the Navy of the United States, c. 6, s. 1, ch. 33.

*6.    The America*

The privateer *America* took on a quartermaster, Charles Still, in August 1812, before cruising in September. The privateer took several prizes, including the *James and Charlotte*, before Still led a mutiny. This resulted in him being clasped into irons for the remainder of the voyage, subsequently convicted before a court martial, and sentenced to receive 100 lashes. After he was held in chains, the privateer captured more prizes. Upon the proceeds of some of the condemned prizes being paid to the prize agent, Still made a claim for his share, based upon the articles of agreement. The prize agent refused to pay and Still initiated a suit. The articles of agreement stated, in the fourth article, that,

> "'if any person shall be found causing disturbance or mutiny, or shall be guilty of any misdemeanour, in which peril may arise to the cruise, the offender shall be punished (even to the forfeiture of his share or shares) at the discretion of the captain and officers.' And by the twelfth article it was agreed, that 'all and every one of said company agree to serve on board the private armed ship America, for the term of four months from the said vessel's departure from the port of Salem.'"[15]

The court, in an opinion by chief justice of the Massachusetts Supreme Judicial Court, Isaac Parker, ruled that the provision in the articles of agreement did not apply, because the captain and crew had not passed sentence on Still's act (a court martial had). Further, it could lead to forfeiture of all his shares, as it allowed for either total or partial forfeiture, based on the seriousness of the offense. The court also said that the corporal punishment meted out by the court martial was all the punishment available, and it did not affect Still's rights to prize proceeds. The court then considered how much of his one and a half shares he was due. Noting that seamen are apportioned wages based on the amount of time they spend on a vessel before dying or departing, the same principle should apply to prizes. Because he voluntarily acted criminally, his contract ended at that point. The prize proceeds of which he had taken part in securing would be allocated to him, but none after the act of mutiny.

---

[15] Luscomb v. Prince, 12 Mass. 576 (1815).

## 7. The Brutus

The privateer *Brutus* left Boston, at the beginning of November 1814, and captured several prizes, which were sent in to port with prize crews. Due to battle and weather damage, the *Brutus* was forced to land in France for repairs, in January 1815. Repairs were not completed until early February 1815, meaning the three-month period specified in the shipping articles had expired. The crew insisted that they were no longer bound by the first set of articles, so the captain was forced to make a second set, which almost all the crew signed, including some additional crew members. The ship's owners had entered into articles of agreement with the captain and crew in October 1814, which in part specified,

> "1. The schooner shall cruise, where the owners or a majority of them, may direct. 2. Three fifths of the net proceeds, of all the prizes and prize goods, taken during the cruise, are to belong to the owners; the other two fifths to belong to the captain, officers and crew, and to be divided among them according to the number of shares set against their names. 3. No one of the company shall, before the end of the cruise, sell more than half his shares. 4. The captain, officers and crew, agree to repair on board immediately, when ordered, and to remain for three months from time of sailing, unless the cruise is sooner completed in the opinion of the owners."[16]

The crew left France, and on their cruise back to Boston, captured several valuable prizes. After these were condemned and sold, a supplementary libel under the first set of articles was initiated by a prize master from the original crew, who had taken his prize back to the United States and so could not join the second set of articles, and by a set of assignees from the original set of shares. They both contended that the owners did not end the cruise in France and start a new cruise, and the commander, William Austin, himself a signer of the articles of agreement, could not terminate them, and had no authority to bind the owners in a new agreement. They also asserted that the time in France repairing should not count against the three months allocated for cruising.

---

[16] The Brutus, 4 F. Cas. 490 (Cir. Ct. D. Mass. 1815).

Justice Story, again writing the opinion of the circuit court, after decrying the poor draftsmanship of the shipping articles, ruled that the articles must be viewed as being for a cruise of three months, not for a contract of being onboard for a period of three calendar months. He also defined a cruise as a voyage for a specific purpose, to "make captures jure belli,"[17] with a definite point of commencement and termination. This meant, under the prize act of 1812, that a cruise was not extinguished by arrival at a port not its intended port of termination, unless there was some express act doing so.

Upon the expiration of the term in the articles, ships were required to take the most direct route home, where the cruise would terminate. Cruising would not be allowed (going out of one's way to make a capture) on this direct route back home, but if prizes were captured, they would belong to those who had signed the first articles. The first cruise had not legally terminated until it reached its home port. So, the prize master and the assignees were to share fully in the proceeds for prizes captured on the privateer's journey home from France.

### 8. The Macedonian

In November 1814, the privateer *Macedonian* took on as prize master, Amos Blanchard. The crew all signed articles of agreement, including,

> "Art. 5. That the cruise shall be where the owners may direct. If they see cause to leave it to the captain, he shall have full power to alter or prolong the cruise; and it shall not be considered as ended until the arrival of said vessel at Portsmouth. Art. 12. It is agreed that this cruise shall be considered not more than one hundred, nor less than ninety days. The captain is to end the cruise, whenever all his men that can be spared are put on board prizes." "Art. 15. And finally we do by these presents bind ourselves each to the other, for the faithful performance of all, and singular the provisions and covenants above specified, in consideration of our becoming the crew of said schooner *Macedonian*, and it shall be binding upon us to all intents and purposes, as if we had received monthly wages for the time fixed for

---

[17] *Id.*

said cruise. Art. 8. Should any man desert, or not render himself on board, after verbal notice by the agents, or by publishing the same in one public newspaper, he shall forfeit all his share or shares."[18]

The ship captured a prize, which Blanchard was put in the charge of, but the *Macedonian* soon after was damaged and had to return to port for repairs. When the ship was ready for sea again, despite a public notice recalling all the crew, only 14 men of the crew of 80 showed up. The owners then voted to end the cruise and begin a second cruise, which was made up of mostly new men, with the same articles of agreement. Before sailing again in January 1815, Blanchard came to the ship but begged off returning, claiming he was on parole from naval activity. His prize had been recaptured and he was only let ashore by the British on the condition that he would not continue in the fighting. This was attested to by others. The *Macedonian* sailed without him in early January, about two months after originally departing, and captured several prizes.

The questions before the court were whether Blanchard was entitled to shares in prizes captured from the January re-sailing of the privateer, and if so, was this limited to those within the 90 days stated in the articles of agreement. The plaintiff cited the *Brutus* case as asserting that this cruise was unlawfully terminated, but the circuit court said this case was different, as it was the owners, not the commander, who terminated the first cruise and that they did so in good faith, given that so many of the original crew had not returned. The court ruled the first cruise lawfully abandoned, and as the plaintiff had not signed the new articles or taken any part in the second cruise, he had no legal right to proceeds from any prizes captured since the privateer departed again in January.

---

[18] Blanchard v. Haven, 3 F. Cas. 625 (Cir. Ct. D. N.H. 1818).

## 3.2 SHIP'S PAPERS AND COURT DOCUMENTS

There were many different types of documents onboard sailing ships that were inspected by privateer boarding crews and used later in libels before the admiralty court. The most important documents were those that showed the ownership of the ship and cargo. The former included the ships' registration, which listed the port where it was built, fitted out, or sailed from, and its owner. The cargo was described in bills of lading (from Old English *hladan*, to load), which detailed the goods on the ship, who owned them, and who would be receiving them.

There were many other types of documents that could be found on ships, including the ship's journal, leases or charters of the ship, various types of passports to travel freely in areas controlled by the issuer, and disparate letters from the ship's owners to the master, and from the consignor of goods to the consignee or the shipper. There may also be contracts or documents for the sale or assignment of the ship or its goods, with conditional clauses based upon various events, such as the consignee rejecting the goods, not being able to reach a certain port due to weather, or there being, or not being, a market available to sell the ship or goods.

When the ship was captured and brought to court for libel, a preparatory examination was undertaken. This involved investigating the captured ship's papers and its crew members who were taken away by the privateer. The crew members were typically asked to answer a list of predefined questions, called standing interrogatories, which were recorded as depositions. These two sources allowed the court to make a preliminary decision on whether to condemn a ship. A libel, essentially a complaint, would be entered, most commonly by the privateer commander, demanding the ship and cargo. This would be opposed by the current owners of the ship and cargo, or their agents, especially in cases where they believed they were fully justified in sailing where and when they did, with that specific cargo. Depositions of parties interested in contesting the libel would be taken, and if the case were not yet clear, further evidence might be requested. The court would then decide to condemn or acquit the ship and cargo, with some form of appeal process typically available.

## A. Ship's Papers

### 1. *Ship Registration – Britain*

A British act of 1786 specified the form that each British ship's registration should be in and the details required, as shown below. An oath was also required to be taken by the shipowners as to its title and an examination was carried out by government officials to ensure the ship's measurements were as listed. Registering fraudulent measurements would lead to a fine, and any ship leaving port without a clearance certificate would be forfeit. The certificates had to be produced at each port that the ship called upon, to the appropriate government official.

"In pursuance of an act, passed in the twenty-sixth year of the reign of King George the Third, intituled, An act [here insert the title of the act, the names, occupation, and residence, of the subscribing owners], having taken and subscribed the oath required by this act, and having sworn that he, [or, they] together with [names, occupation, and residence of non-subscribing owners,] is [or, are] sole owner [or, owners] of the ship or vessel called the [ship's name] of [place to which the vessel belongs), whereof [master's name] is at present master, and that the said ship or vessel was [when and where built, or captured, and date of condemnation]; and [name and employment of the surveying officer] having certified to us that[:]

the said ship or vessel is [whether British, Foreign, or British plantation built], has [number of decks] decks, and [number of masts] masts, that her length, from the fore part of the main stem to the after part of the stern post aloft, is [number of feet and inches], her breadth at the broadest part, whether above or below the main wales, [number of feet and inches), her heighth between decks (number of feet and inches, if more than one deck, and if not, then] the depth of the hold [number of feet and inches], and admeasures [burthens] tons that she is a [kind of vessel, and how built], has [whether any or no gallery] gallery, and [kind of head, if any] head; and the said subscribing owners having consented and agreed to the above description and admeasurement, and having caused sufficient security to be given, as is required by the said act, the said [kind and name of the vessel] has been duly registered at the port of [name of the port].

Given under our hands and seals of office, at the custom-house in the said port of [name of the port], this [date] day of [name of the month], in the year [words at length]."[19]

## 2. Ship Registration – United States

From the very beginning of the republic, the United States required registration of U.S.-built, or previously acquired, ships. Under a statute from 1789, Congress described the form of the registration certificate, following on from the British act a few years previous. Fraudulent use of the certificate of registry would lead to forfeiture of the ship.

"In pursuance of an act of the Congress of the United States of America, intituled An act for registering and clearing vessels, regulating the coasting trade, and for other purposes, [here insert the name, occupation and residence of the subscribing owner] having taken and subscribed the oath or affirmation required by the said act, and having sworn or affirmed, that he, together with [names, occupation and residence of non-subscribing owners] is (or are) sole owner (or owners) of the ship (or vessel) called the [ship's name] of [place to which the ship or vessel belongs] whereof [master's name] is at present master, and is a citizen of the United States,

and that the said ship (or vessel) was [when and where built] and [name of surveying officer] having certified to us, that the said ship, or vessel, has [number of decks] and masts, that her length is _____, her breadth _____, her depth _____, and that she measures _____ tons, that she is [here describe the vessel and how built], has _____ gallery and head; and the said subscribing owners having consented and agreed to the above description and measurement, and having caused sufficient security to be given as is required by the said act, the said [kind of vessel and name] has been duly registered at the port of Given

---

[19] An Act for the further increase and encouragement of shipping and navigation, 41 Geo. III c. 60.

under our hands and seals of office, at [port] this ____ day of ____, in the year [words at full length.]"[20]

Like Britain, the United States also required an oath from the owner of the ship regarding its ownership,

"I, _____, of [place of residence and occupation] do swear or affirm, that the ship or vessel _____ of _____ [take the description from the certificate of the surveyor or other person authorized by this act] was built at in the year _____ or was the entire property of _____ on the sixteenth day of May, one thousand seven hundred and eighty-nine, and hath continued to be the property of a citizen or citizens of the United States, that, ____ the present master, is a citizen of the United States, and that I, ____ and [the other owners' names, occupation, and where they respectively reside, viz: town, place, county and state, or if resident in a foreign country, being an agent for, and partner in, any house or co-partnership] am or are sole owner or owners of the said ship or vessel, and that no other person whatever hath any property therein, and that I, the said _____, [and the said owners, if any] am or are truly a citizen or citizens of the United States, and that no foreigner, directly or indirectly, hath any part or interest in the said ship or vessel."[21]

### 3. Bills of Lading – Overview and Cases

The other key document onboard a prize ship was the bill of lading for the cargo, which came in many different forms and styles, and evolved over time to have more purposes. Arising initially as an entry in a book of lading, or register, kept by a public official, bills of lading were needed in case the book of lading was lost at sea, and to provide copies to the shipper, the carrier, the consignee, and their various agents. Bills of lading were not needed when vessels were wholly leased, under charter parties. As it became more common for shippers to lease only parts of their ship for the cargo of different shippers, bills of lading became more prominent. The bill of lading was originally used as a receipt for the shipper, provided by the

---

[20] An Act for Registering and Clearing Vessels, Regulating the Coasting Trade, and for other purposes, c. 1, s. 1, ch. 11, § 2.
[21] *Id.,* § 6.

master of the ship, who would typically sign the bill of lading only when he had received all a shipper's goods on board.

Quickly there arose questions regarding whether the quantity and quality of the goods in the bills of lading was accurate. Over time, bills of lading began to list the specific quantities and qualities of the named and marked goods put on board by a shipper. Questions also arose on the responsibility for goods in containers not visible to the master, and for the condition of goods. From that foundation, bills of lading took on other functions, such as memorializing a contract for carriage previously agreed between the shipper and the owner or master of the vessel. It also became a document of title, as the bill of lading was used as a negotiable instrument that could be endorsed by the shipper, consignor, or other seller, over to a new owner, possibly the consignee, or another buyer. The legal characteristics of bills of lading were recognized through legal cases of this period, arising from the customary practices of merchants, before being formalized as legal obligation in statutes, from the mid-19th century onwards.

In *Lickbarrow*, a British bills of lading case, was decided for the plaintiffs at trial, reversed on appeal with a ruling that a bill of lading only evidenced a contract of carriage, and the House of Lords then ordered a new trial, which came in 1794.[22] This matter began as an order, in 1786, from British merchant James Freeman, residing in the Netherlands, to a merchant house there, for a cargo of corn and a ship to carry it to Liverpool. The invoice stated the cargo was to be shipped on the account and risk of Freeman. The bills of lading showed the merchant house, Turing & Son, as the shipper, were signed by the ship's master, and had a blank space for whom the goods were to be delivered to, based on the order of the shipper or his assigns. Four copies were distributed, two to Freeman endorsed by Turing, one to the merchant house, and one to the ship's master. Freeman sent his endorsed bills of lading to the plaintiffs, W.N. Lickbarrow and R. Wright, with instructions they should receive and sell the cargo upon arrival in Liverpool.

---

[22] Lickbarrow v Mason, 1 B. & P. 565 (1794).

Lickbarrow and Wright filled in the deliver-to blanks on the bills of lading from Freeman, with their own names. Freeman then drew bills of exchange on them, as Turing had on him. Before the ship arrived at Liverpool, Freeman became bankrupt and absconded. Turing had to honor the bills of exchange they drew on Freeman, as did Lickbarrow and Wright, for bills of exchange Freeman drew on them. Turing endorsed their copy of the bill of lading to Mr. Mason, to take delivery in Turing's name. Mason, the defendant, took delivery of the cargo when it arrived in Liverpool and sold it. The jury ruled that bills of lading were negotiable while the ship is at sea, and transferred ownership in the named cargo, as the customary practice of merchants. It was also customary for shippers to transfer such ownership by endorsing and delivering the bill of lading to the new owner, and for the recipients to enter their names into the blank spaces in the bill of lading. However, as the bill of lading had already been non-fraudulently endorsed by the consignee (Freeman) to a third-party (Lickbarrow), the later transfer to Mason was not valid, so the court gave judgment for the plaintiffs.

In *Barrett*, the master of a ship was sued, because three cases of velvets that he took on board in Liverpool for a voyage to Boston were not delivered to the consignees. Instead, they were retained by the master, as they were damaged. In the signed bill of lading, he had committed to delivering these to the consignee in good order and well-conditioned, with the only exceptions the dangers of the sea and navigation. The water-damaged goods were finally delivered to the consignees. At trial, both sides put on evidence that the goods were either properly or improperly stowed away. There was no evidence that they were damaged by the dangers of the sea. Despite the bill of lading stating, based on the shipper's assertion, that the goods were in good condition, the trial judge, as a matter of law, ruled that it "was not conclusive evidence that the goods were in good order within the cases, when received on board the vessel."[23] The appeals court re-worded this to be that the bill of lading should be viewed as prima facie evidence but not conclusive in all cases.

---

[23] Barrett v. Rogers, 7 Mass. 297 (1811).

In *Walter*, the master signed bills of lading for ten bales of skins aboard the ship *Laura*. The bills of lading were sold to Lynde Walter but when the ship arrived in Boston from Montevideo, half of the bales were missing. Three had been sold before the ship left Montevideo and two more had been sold to the owner, who was sailing with the ship, as the official cargo all belonged to him. He was not aware of the storage of these extra bales aboard the ship, which had been placed aboard by the master. The question was whether the owner was responsible for the masters' acts of creating bills of lading for ten bales but only shipping five. The lower court held for the plaintiff, finding that the owner must have had knowledge of the bales being shipped, having bought some himself. The court of appeals ruled that the instruction to the jury was incorrect, in that the owner could only be liable for acts of the master regarding goods legitimately taken onboard as cargo for the voyage, not for goods fraudulently listed on bills of lading and not taken onboard as legitimate cargo.[24]

*4. Bills of Lading – Later Statutes and Cases*

The legal status of bills of lading are further explained by several later statutes and cases, which surveyed the law during this earlier period. In 1855, by statute in Britain, the following problems with bills of lading were recognized,

> "Whereas by the Custom of Merchants a Bill of Lading of Goods being transferable by Endorsement the Property in the Goods may thereby pass to the Endorsee, but nevertheless all Rights in respect of the Contract contained in the Bill of Lading continue in the original Shipper or Owner, and it is expedient that such Rights should pass with the Property; And where is frequently happens that the Goods in respect of which Bills of Lading purport to be signed have not been laden on board, and it is proper that such Bills of Lading in the Hands of a bona fide Holder for Value should not be questioned by the Master or other

---

[24] Walter v. Brewer, 11 Mass. 99 (1814).

Person signing the same on the Ground of the Goods not having been laden as aforesaid."[25]

This act transferred all rights and liabilities in the carriage contract to the consignee or endorsee and mandated that the signed bill of lading was conclusive evidence against the master that the goods have been shipped, unless the consignee had notice when receiving the bill of lading that the goods had not been loaded or if the master could prove fraud on the part of the shipper or consignee.

A U.S. Supreme Court case, in 1871, provided a summary of the U.S. law on bills of lading, up to that time,

"Different definitions of the commercial instrument, called the bill of lading, have been given by different courts and jurists, but the correct one appears to be that it is a written acknowledgment, signed by the master, that he has received the goods therein described from the shipper, to be transported on the terms therein expressed, to the described place of destination, and there to be delivered to the consignee or parties therein designated. Regularly the goods ought to be on board before the bill of lading is signed, but if the bill of lading, through inadvertence or otherwise, is signed before the goods are actually shipped, as if they are received on the wharf or sent to the warehouse of the carrier, or are delivered into the custody of the master or other agent of the owner or charterer of the vessel and are afterwards placed on board, as and for the goods embraced in the bill of lading, it is clear that the bill of lading will operate on those goods as between the shipper and the carrier by way of relation and estoppel, and that the rights and obligations of all concerned are the same as if the goods had been actually shipped before the bill of lading had been signed.

Such an instrument is twofold in its character -- that is, it is a receipt as to the quantity and description of the goods shipped, and a contract to transport and deliver the goods to the consignee or other person therein designated, and upon the terms specified in the same

---

[25] An Act to Amend the Law relating to Bills of Lading, 18&19 Vict. c. 111.

instrument. Beyond all doubt, a bill of lading, in the usual form, is a receipt for the quantity of goods shipped and a promise to transport and deliver the same as therein stipulated. Receipts may be either a mere acknowledgment of payment or delivery or they may also contain a contract to do something in relation to the thing delivered. In the former case and so far as the receipt goes only to acknowledge payment or delivery, it, the receipt, is merely *prima facie* evidence of the fact, and not conclusive, and therefore the fact which it recites may be contradicted by oral testimony, but insofar as it is evidence of a contract between the parties, it stands on the footing of all other contracts in writing, and cannot be contradicted or varied by parol evidence."[26]

Addressing only two of the three properties usually ascribed to bills of lading, in contrast to the British *Lickbarrow* case of 1855, the Court made clear, in 1881, its view on the negotiability of bills of lading in the United States, which was not resolved until the 20th century,

"A bill of lading is an instrument well known in commercial transactions, and its character and effect have been defined by judicial decisions. In the hands of the holder, it is evidence of ownership, special or general, of the property mentioned in it, and of the right to receive said property at the place of delivery. Notwithstanding it is designed to pass from hand to hand, with or without endorsement, and it is efficacious for its ordinary purposes in the hands of the holder, it is not a negotiable instrument or obligation in the sense that a bill of exchange or a promissory note is."[27]

In 1893, a U.S. statute required, for bills of lading for international shipments from the United States, that,

"it shall be the duty of the owner, or owners, masters, or agent of any vessel transporting merchandise or property from or between ports of the United States and foreign ports to issue to shippers of any lawful merchandise a bill of lading, or shipping document, stating, among

---

[26] The Delaware, 81 U.S. 579 (1871).
[27] Pollard v. Vinton, 105 U.S. 7 (1881).

other things, the marks necessary for identification, number of packages, or quantity, stating whether it be carrier's or shipper's weight, and apparent order or condition of such merchandise or property delivered to and received by the owner, master, or agent of the vessel for transportation, and such document shall be prima facie evidence of the receipt of the merchandise therein described."[28]

*5. Bills of Lading – Example*

The following are examples of three translated bills of lading, from 1740, for cargo onboard the *Princess of Orange*. The characters beginning each description were unique marks identifying the goods.

"(1)

I, Juan Milidoni, Master under God of my Ship named the *Princess of Orange*, now Laying ready at the Island of Theneriffe, to sail with the first good and fair Wind God shall Send, to Sail for the Island of Curacao, where my rightfull discharge is to be.

I acknowledge to have recd. under the Deck from you, Mr. Peter Doscher, junr.

M.R. Fifty pipes of wine

V.P. Thirty pipes of wine, all Dry and well conditioned and marked as in the Margent, all which I promise to deliver if God Grants me a Safe Voyage with my Ship at Curacao aforesaid, to Mr. Mestre, and In absence to Messrs. Rodier and Lecier, or to his Factor or Deputy, paying me for the freight thereof according to agreemt., with avaridge according to the Custom of the Sea, and to fulfill what is aforsaid, I bind my Selfe, all my goods, and my said Ship, with all her apparell. In testimony whereof I have Sign'd 4 Bills of Lading with my name, or my Clerk in my behalf, all of one tenour, one whereof being fullfil'd the other to Stand void. written in Sta. Crux upon the Island Theneriffe the 16th Xber 1740.

Insides and Contents unknown.

---

[28] An Act relating to the navigation of vessels, bills of lading, and to certain obligations, duties, and rights in connection with the carriage of property, c. 52, s. 2, ch. 105.

Juan Milidoni

(2)

DCN. 18 pipes Vidonio wines of the outward marks.

C M.    5 pipes Malvasia wines in whole pipes 2 half pipes

C M.    and 4 quarter Casks

the residue Z.  1 Bag of venice Thread buttons

2 quarter cask Vidonio of the first mark

1 Bar'l. of Raisons and figs

8 Distil Stones

60 Stone Mortars

1 Bag of Venice thread buttons cont'g 504 gross

All Shipped By Capn. Juan Milidoni on bourd the Dutch Snow Call'd the *Princess of Orange*, whereof he is M[aste]r. and are for his proper Acct. and Risk, Consigned to himself, in his Absence to Mr. Mastre and in the absence of both to Messrs. Rodier and Le Cire In Curacao.

(3)

DCN. 15    pipes Vidonio wines of the without mark.[19]

DCN. 7-1/2 idem Malvasia wines in 5 whole pipes and 5 half pipes of the without mark.

All Shipped by Capn. Juan Milidoni on board the Dutch Snow Called the *Princess of Orange* whereof he is Mas'r. and for Acct. of the new Company in Venice Consign'd to himselfe, in his absence to Mester, and in the absence of both to Messrs. Rodier and LeCire in Curacao."[29]

---

[29] *Privateering and Piracy in the Colonial World* (1923), p. 483-85.

## B.  Court Documents

*1.  The Libel – War of Austrian Succession*

The libel was the initial complaint put before the court of admiralty, to start the process of condemning (or acquitting) a captured prize or cargo. In the libel of the ship *Amsterdam Post* in 1740 in Massachusetts (see Chapter 4), the following was the libel entered.

"New Engl'd Prov. of the Massa's Bay, Boston, July 23, 1740.

To the Hono'ble Robt. Auchmuty, Esqr., Jud. of Vice Adm'ty.

The Libel of Philip Dumaresq, Commander of the Private Man of War Sloop *Young Eagle* of Boston, Sheweth,

Whereas on the 23d of Octob'r last his Majesty Caused Publick Proclamation to be made of an Open War with the King of Spain, requiring all his officers and Soldiers to do all Acts of Hostility in prosecution of this War against the King of Spain, his Vassals and subjects, and afterwards on the 15th of January last the said Philip, Commander of the sloop aforesaid, and her men, being duly Commissioned with Letters of Marque and Reprisals against the King of Spain, his Vassals and Subjects, to attack, Seize, Take and make Prize of their Ships, Vessells and Goods,

met with the Sloop the *Amsterdam Post* about three or four Leagues off of the Grand Canary Island, standing in for Santa Crux in Teneriffe in the King of Spains Dominions, Commanded by Aeneas Mackay, a British Subject but made free of Amsterdam, man'd with British Subjects and furnished with various Papers and Evidences to make her seem to be either an English or Dutch Sloop, as might best suit the occasion, and upon Examination finding that she was the Property of certain Subjects of the King of Spain or Inhabitants of the Canaries within his Dominions, and by them during this present War sent from Teneriffe aforesd to Cork in Ireland

and there Laden with thirty nine Barrells of Beef, Forty Barr'ls of Pilchards, eighty nine BBlls of Butter, fifty four boxes of Candles, a hundred eighty nine Hides of Leather, five Bar'ls of Hatts, two Boxes of

Soap and five Bar'ls of Wax for acco't of the same owners and was then returning directly to Teneriffe for their Supply, He the said Philip therefore Seized and Took the sd Sloop *Amsterdam Post* and her Cargo as a Lawfull Prize, as he Lawfully might do, Wherefore the said Philip Dumaresq prays the consideration of this Hono'ble Court upon the premises properly and only in their Cognizance, that a Short Day [early date] may be assigned to Hear and pass upon this Libel and Matters therein contained and that the said Sloop and Cargo may be Decreed and declared a Lawfull Prize, etc."[30]

## 2. The Libel – Seven Years' War

In the case of the ship *La Virgin del Rosario*, in 1756, in New York (see Chapter 4), the following libel was submitted.

"Province of New York, Court of Vice Admiralty. To the Honourable Lewis Morris Esqr, Commissary and Judge of the Court of Vice Admiralty for the province of New York. The Lybell of Richard Haddon of the City of New York, Marriner Commander of the private vessell of Warr called the *Peggy* in behalf of himself and the Owners and Company of the said Schooner *Peggy* in all Humble Manner Sheweth unto your honor that his most Gracious Majesty George the Second, by the Grace of God of Great Brittain france and Ireland King, Defender of the Faith, Vfd. by his Commission under the seal of the Court of Vice Admiralty of New York Bearing date the Twenty Ninth Day of September in the year of our Lord one thou sand Seven hundred and fifty Six writeing as is therein Re cited

did thereby Grant Commission to and Lycence and Authorize Jasper Farmer and Nathaniell Marston of the City of New York Merchants to Sett forth in warr Like manner the said Schooner called the peggy under the Command of the said Richard Haddon, therewith by force of Arms to Attack, Surprize, Seize and take by and with the said Schooner and the crew thereof any place or fortress upon the Land or any Ship or Vessell, Goods, Amunition, Arms, Stores of Warr or Merchandize belonging to or possessed by any of his said Majesties Enemies in any

---

[30] *Privateering and Piracy in the Colonial World* (1923), p. 357-58.

Sea, Creek, Haven or River and Such other Ships, Vessells and Goods which are or shall be Lyable to Confiscation pursuant to the treaties between his Said Majesty and Other princes, States and potentates and to bring the same to such port as should be most convenient in Order to have them Legally Adjudged in his said Majesties high Court of Admiralty of England or before the Judges of such other Admiralty Court as Shall be Lawfully Authorized within his Majesties Dominions, which being Condemned it Should and might be Lawfull for the said Richard Haddon to sell and Dis pose of Such Ships, Vessells, and Goods, Amunition, Arms, Stores of Warr or Merchandise so Adjudged and Condemned in Such sort and Manner as by the Course of the Admiralty hath been Accustomed as by the said Commission may more fully Appear,

and the said Richard Haddon Doth further Show unto your Honour that in pursuance of his Said Commission on or About the Seventh Day of December Last past being on the High Seas within the Jurisdiction of this Court in the said Schooner Peggy with his Company and Crew on Board the Same in or About the Latitude of twenty-one Degrees and Eighteen Minutes North Longitude Eighty Seven " Degrees fifty Seven Minutes West from London he did meet with, sett upon and take a Certain Schooner Belonging to the Subjects of the french King Enemies of our Said Lord King George the Second,

having on Board ten Doubleloons," five thousand seven hundred and Sixty four Dollars, one hundred and five pistereens," and Some Small Silver as also one Bracelett, twenty Gold rings, Some Silver Buckells, six Swivell Guns, Some Shott, one Cask of Powder, Some Cutlasses and one Kegg of Indigo being the Money, Chattles, Goods and Effects of the Subjects of the french King, Enemies of our Said Lord King George the Second, which money, Bracelett, Rings, Buckells, Swivell Guns, Shott, powder, Cutlasses and Indigo Belonging to the Subjects of the french King and Enemies of our Said Lord King George the Second the said Richard Haddon hath brought into this his Majesties port of New York in the said Schooner Peggy in Order to have the Same Legally Condemned by the Sentence and Decree of this Honourable Court (But the said Schooner being unfitt to Come upon a Winters Coast and he the said Richard Haddon having a Great Number of prisoners Delivered her to a Number of them to Carry them to some french port After takeing out of her the Money, Goods and Chattles aforesaid)

Wherefore the said Richard Haddon Humbly prays your Honour that the said Money, Bracelett, Rings, Buckells, Swivell Guns, Shott, Powder, Cutlasses and Indigo Aforesaid belonging to the Subjects of the french King and Enemies of our Said Lord the King may by the Sentence and Adjudication of this Honourable Court be Condemned as Lawfull prize to the Use of the said Richard Haddon and the Owners and Company of the said Schooner Peggy According to the Common Right of Nations and the Law of Arms in Such Case used."[31]

*3. Standing Interrogatories – War of Austrian Succession*

The following were a set of interrogatories used in the libel of the *Amsterdam Post* (see Chapter 4).

"Interro. The First. Was the Sloop called the Amsterdam Post, Aeneas Mackay Master, taken as a Prize, by whom, when and where?

Interro. 2d. What was the Lading of the Sloop Amsterdam Post?

Interro. 3. Are the Papers now produced before you and now Lodged in this Court, the Papers that were taken on Board the said Sloop as you know, or have heard, how, and in what manner?

Interro. 4. Did you hear the sd Master of the Sloop aforesd Declare where he took in his aforesaid Loading?

Interro. 5. What was done with the Cargo after the Vessell and Cargo was thus taken?

Interro. 6. Is the Sloop now under Seizure the same Sloop that was thus taken?

Interro. 7. What became of the hands belonging to said Sloop?

Interro. 8. Do you know or have you heard what Nation those hands were of?

---

[31] *Privateering and Piracy in the Colonial World* (1923), p. 529-33.

Lastly, Do you know anything further relating to sd Vessell and Cargo or any other former Voyages the said Vessell had made and where to?"[32]

### 4. Standing Interrogatories – Seven Years' War

This set of interrogatories was used in 1756 in Antigua, for the libel of the ship *Princess of Orange,* alias *Flying Fish*, captured by the privateer *Mary*.

"1. Where was you born, and where do you now live, and how long have you lived there, and where have you lived for seven years last past? are you subject to the Crown of Great Britain, or of what Prince or State are you a subject?

2. When, where, and by whom was the schooner and lading, goods and merchandises, concerning which you are now examined, taken and seised, and into what place or port were the same carried? whether was there any resistance made, or any guns fired against the said schooner, or persons who seised and took the same, and what and how many, and by whom?

3. Whether was you present at the time of the taking or seizing the schooner and her lading, goods and merchandises, concerning which you are now examined, or how and when was you first made acquainted thereof? whether was the said schooner and goods taken by a man of war, or a private man of war, and to whom did such man of war, or private man of war belong? had they any commissions to act as such, and from and by whom, and by what particular vessel, or by whom was or were the said schooner seized and taken? to what kingdom, country, or nation did the said schooner so seized and taken belong, and under the colours of what kingdom, country, or nation did she sail at the time she was so seized and taken? was the said schooner, which was taken, a man of war, privateer, or merchantman?

4. Upon what pretence was the said schooner seized and taken? to what port or place was she afterwards carried? whether was she condemned, and upon what account, and for what reason was she

---

[32] *Privateering and Piracy in the Colonial World* (1923), p. 359-61.

condemned, and by whom, and by what authority was she so condemned?

5. Who by name was the master of the vessel concerning which you are now examined, at the time she was taken and seized? how long have you known the said master? who first appointed him to be master of the said schooner, and when did he take possession thereof, and who by name delivered the same to him? where is the said master's fixed place of habitation with his wife and family, and how long has he lived there? what countryman [i.e., of what country] is he by birth, and to what Prince or State subject?

6. What number of mariners belonged to the said schooner at the time she was taken and seized? what countrymen are they, and where did they all come on board? whether had you, or any of the officers or company, or mariners, belonging to the said schooner or vessel, any part, share, or interest in the said schooner concerning which you are now examined, and what in particular, and the value thereof, at the time the said schooner was so taken, or the said goods seised?

7. Whether did you belong to the schooner or vessel concerning which you are now examined, at the time she was taken and seized? how long had you known her? when and where did you first see her? of what burthen was she? how many guns did she carry? and how many or what number of men did belong to, or were on board the said schooner at the time she was taken, or at the beginning of the engagement before she was taken? and of what country building was she? what was her name, and how long had she been so called? whether do you know of any other name she was called by? and what were such names, as you know or have heard?

8. To what ports and places was the said schooner or vessel concerning which you are now examined bound, the voyage wherein she was taken and seized? to and from what ports or places did she sail the said voyage before she was taken and seized? where did the voyage begin, and where was the voyage to have ended? what sort of lading did she carry at the time of her first setting out on the said voyage, and what particular sort of lading and goods had she on board

at the time she was taken and seized, proceeding upon a lawful trade? had she at that time any, and what prohibited goods on board her?

9. Who were the owners of the said schooner and vessel and goods concerning which you are now examined, at the time she was taken and seized? how do you know they were the owners of the said schooner and goods at that time? of what nation are they by birth, and where do they live with their wives and families? and to what Prince or State are they subjects?

10. Was there any bill of sale made to the owners of the said schooner? in what month or year, and where and before what witnesses was the same made, and when did you last see it, and what is become thereof?

11. In what port or place was the lading, which was on board the schooner at the time she was taken and seized, first put on board the said schooner? in what month and year was the lading so put on board? what were the several qualities and quantities, and particulars thereof? whether were the same laden and put on board the said schooner in one port, or at one time, or in several ports and places, and how many by name, and at how many several times, and what particulars and what quantity at each port? who by name were the several laders or owners thereof, and what countrymen are they? Where were the said goods to be delivered, and for whose account, and to whom by name did they then really belong?

12. How many bills of lading were signed for the goods seized on board the said schooner? whether were the same colourable, and whether were any bills of lading signed, which were of a different tenor with those which were on board the said schooner at the time she was seized and taken? and what were the contents of such other bills of lading, and what are become thereof?

13. What bills of lading, invoices, letters, or any instruments in writing, or papers, have you to prove your own property, or the property of any other person, and of whom in the schooner and goods, concerning which you are now examined? produce the same, and set forth the

particular times when, and how, and in what manner, and upon what account, and for what consideration you became possessed thereof?

14. In what particular port or place, and in what degree of latitude were or was the schooner, concerning which you are now examined, taken and seized? at what time, and upon what day of the month, and in what year, was or were the said schooner so taken and seized?

15. Whether was there any charter party signed for the voyage, wherein the schooner, concerning which you are now examined, was taken and seized? what is become thereof? when, where, and between whom was the same made? what were the contents thereof?

16. What papers, bills of lading, letters, or other writings, any way concerning or relating to the schooner concerning which you are now examined, were on board the said schooner at the time of the seizure of the said schooner? were any of the papers thrown overboard by any person, and whom, and when, and by whose orders?

17. What loss or damage have you sustained, by reason of the seizing and taking of the said schooner concerning which you are now examined? to what value does such loss or damages amount? and how and after what manner do you compute such loss and damage? have you received any and what satisfaction for such the loss and damage which you have sustained, and when and from whom did you receive the same?"[33]

### 5. Standing Interrogatories – War of 1812

A standard set of interrogatories was used in British colonial courts of admiralty during the War of 1812, such as the following set employed in the Halifax court.

"Standing Interrogatories

To be administered on behalf of Our Sovereign Lord George the Third, by Grace of God, of the United Kingdom of Great Britain and Ireland, King, Defender of the Faith. To all Commanders, Masters, Officers,

---

[33] *Privateering and Piracy in the Colonial World* (1923), p. 525-29.

mariners, and other Persons found on board any Ships and Vessels, which may have been, or shall be seized or taken as Prize by any of His Majesty's Ships or Vessels, which have or shall have Commissions or Letters of Marque and Reprisals, concerning such captured Ships, Vessels, or any Goods, Wares, and Merchandizes on board the same; examined as Witnesses in preparatory during the present hostilities with the United States of America. Let each witness be interrogated to every of the following Questions; and their answers to each Interrogatory written down.

1. Where were you born, and where have you lived for these seven years past? Where do you live? and how long have you lived in that place? To what Prince or State, or to whom are you, or have you been a subject, and of what Cities or Towns have you been admitted a Burgher or Freeman, and at what time and in what manner were you so admitted? How long have you resided there since you were admitted a Burgher or Freeman, or where have you resided since? What did you pay for your admission? Are you a married man, and if married, where do your wife and family reside?

2. Were you present at the time of the taking and seizing the ship or her lading, or any of the goods or merchandizes concerning which you are now examined, and Commission? What and from whom?

3. In what place, Latitude, or port, and in what year, month, day, was the ship and goods, concerning which you are now examined, taken and seized? Upon what pretence and for what reasons were they seized? Into what place or port were they carried, and under what colours did the said ship sail? What other colours had you on board, and for what reason had you such other colours? Was any resistance made at the time when the said ship was taken; and if yea how many guns were fired, and by whom, and by what ship or ships were you taken? Was such vessel a ship of war, or a vessel acting without any Commission as you believe? Were any other, and what ships, in sight at the time of capture?

4. What is the name of the Master or commander of the Ship or Vessel taken? How long have you know the said Master, and who appointed

him to Command of the said ship? Where did such Master take possession of her, and at what time, and what was the name of the person who delivered the possession to the said Master? Where doth he live? Where is the said Master's fixed place of abode? If he has no fixed place of abode, then let him be asked, Where was his last place of abode, and where does he generally reside? How long has he lived there? Where was he born, and of whom is he now a subject? Is he married, if yea, where does his wife and family reside?

5. Of what tonnage or burthen is the Ship which has been taken? What was the number of Mariners, and of what country were the said Seamen or mariners? Did they all come on board at the same port, or at different ports, and who shipped or hired them, and when and where.

6. Had you, or nay of the Officers or Mariners belonging to the said Ship or Vessel. concerning which you are now examined, any and what part, share or interest in the said Ship or her Lading? If yea, set forth who and what goods or interest you or they have? Did you belong to the said Ship or vessel at the time she was seized and taken? In what capacity did you belong to her? How long have you known her? When and where did you first see her, and where was she built?

7. What is the name of the Ship? How long has she been so called? Do you know of any other name or Names by which she has been called; If yea what were they; Has she any Passport or Sea brief on board, and from whom? To what Ports or Places did she sail during her said Voyage before she was taken? Where did her last Voyage begin, and where was the said Voyage to have ended? Set forth the quality of every cargo the ship has carried to the time of her capture from the time you have known her, and what ports such cargoes have been delivered at? From what Ports and at what time, particularly from the last clearing Port, did the said Ship sail, previously to the capture? Under whose direction and management has she usually been, with respect to her employment in Trade? With whom do you correspond on concerns of the Vessel and her cargoes? I what country was she built, as far as you know, or have reason to believe?

8. What Lading did the said Ship carry out at the time of her first setting sail on her last voyage, and what particular sort of Lading and goods had she on board at the time when she was taken? In what year and in what month was the same put on boar d? set forth the different species of Lading, and the Quantities of each sort.

9. Who were the Owners of the Ship or Vessel, concerning which you are now examined, at the time when she was seized? How do you know that they were the Owners of the said Ship at that time? Of what Nation or Country are such Owners by birth? Where do they reside, and where do their Wives and Families reside? How long have they resided there? where did they reside before, to the best of your knowledge? To whom are they Subjects?

10. Was any Bill of sale made, and by whom, to the aforesaid Owners of the said Ship; and if any such was made, in what month and year? Where, and in the presence of what Witnesses, was such Bill of Sale made? Was any and what engagement entered into concerning the Purchase further than what appears upon the Bill of sale? If yea, was it verbal or in writing? Where did you last see it? and what has become of it?

11. Was the said Lading put on board in one Port and at one time, or at several Ports and at several times, and at what Ports, by name? Set forth what quantities of each sort of Goods were shipped at each Port.

12. What are the names of the respective Laders or Owners, or Consignees, of the said Goods? What Countrymen are they? Where do they now live and carry on their business or trade? How long have they resided there? And where were the said Goods to be delivered, and for whose real account, risk or benefit? have any of the said Consignees or laders any, and what Interest, in the said goods? If yea, whereon do you found your belief that they have such Interest? Can you take upon yourself to swear that you believe, that at the time of the lading the Cargo, and at the present time, and also if the said Goods shall be restored and unladen at the destined Ports, the Goods did, do and will belong to the same Persons, and to none others? What is the ground of your knowledge or belief?

13. How many Bills of Lading were signed for the Goods seized on board the said Ship? Were any of those Bills of Lading false or colourable, or were any bills of Lading signed which were different in any respect from those which were on Board the Ship, at the time she was taken? What were the contents of such other Bills of Lading, and what became of them?

14. Are there, in Great Britain, any Bills of Lading, Invoices, Letters or Instruments, relative to the Ship and Goods, concerning which you are now examined? if yea, set forth where they are, and in whose possession, and what is the purport thereof, and when they were brought or sent into this Kingdom?

15. Was there any Charter-Party signed for the Voyage in which the Ship, concerning which you are now examined, was seized and taken? What became thereof? When, where and between whom, was such Charty-Party made? What were the contents of it?

16. What Papers, Bills of lading, Letters, or other Writings, were on board the Ship at the time she took her departure from the last clearing Port, before her being taken as Prize? Were any of them burnt, torn, thrown over board, destroyed or cancelled, concealed or attempted to be concealed, and when, and by whom, and who was then present?

17. Has the ship, concerning which you are know examined, been at any time, and when seized as prize, and condemned as such? If yea, set forth into what port she was carried, and by whom and by what authority, or on what account was she condemned?

18. Have you sustained any loss by the seizing and tasking the ship, concerning which you are know examined? If yea, in what manner do you compute such, your loss? have you already received any indemnity, satisfaction, or promise of satisfaction, for any part of the damage which you have sustained, or may sustain by this capture and detention, and when, and from whom?

19. Is the said Ship or Goods, or any, and what part, insured? If yea, for what Voyage is such Insurance made, and at what premium, and when and by what Persons, and in what Country was such Insurance made?

20. In case you had arrived at your destined Port, would your Cargo, or any Part thereof, on being unladen, have immediately become the property of the consignees or nay other Person, and whom? Or was the Lader to take the chance of the Market for the Sale of his Goods?

21. Let each Witness be interrogated of the Growth, Produce, and manufacture of what Country and place was the lading of the Ship or Vessel, concerning which you are know examined, or any part thereof?

22. Whether all the said Cargo, or any part thereof, was taken from Shore or Quay, or removed or trans shipped from one Boat, Barque, Vessel or Ship, to another? From what and to what Shore, Quay, Boat, Barque, Vessel, or Ship, and when and where, was the same so done?

23. Are there in any Country, besides Great Britain, and where, or on board any and what Ship or Ships, Vessel or Vessels, other than the Ship and Vessel, concerning which you are now examined, any Bills of Lading, Invoices, Letters, Instruments, Papers, or Documents, relative to the said Ship or Vessel and cargo, and of what Nature are such Bills of lading, Invoices, Letters, Instruments, Papers, or Documents, and what are the Contents?

24. Were any Papers delivered out of the said Ship or Vessel, and carried away in any manner whatsoever? And when and by whom, and to whom, and in whose custody, possession, or power, do you believe the same now are?

25. Was Bulk broken, during the Voyage in which you were taken, or since capture of the said Ship? And when and where, by whom, and by whose orders? And for what purpose, and in what manner?

26. Were any Passengers on board the aforesaid Ship? Were any of them secreted at the time of Capture? Who were the Passengers by name? Of what Nation, rank, profession, or occupation? Had they any Commission? For what purpose, and from whom? From what place were they taken on board, and when? To what place were they finally

destined, and upon what business? Had any, and which, of the Passengers any and what property or concern, or authority, directly or indirectly, regarding the Ship and Cargo? Were there any Officers, Soldiers or Mariners, secreted on board, and for what reason were they secreted? Were any of His Britannic Majesty's Subjects on board, or secreted or confined at the time of capture? How long and why?

27. Were, and are, all the Passports, Sea Briefs, Charter-Parties, Bills of Sale, Invoices and Papers, which were found on board entirely true and fair? Or are any of them false or colourable? Do you know of any matter or circumstance to affect their credit? Were they obtained for this ship only? And upon what oath, or affirmation of the persons therein described, or were they delivered to, or on behalf of the person or persons who appear to have been sworn or to have affirmed thereto, without their having ever, in fact, made any such oath or affirmation? How long a time were they to last? Was any duty or fee payable and paid for the same? And is there any duty or fee to be paid on the renewal thereof? Have such Passports been renewed, and how often? And has the duty or fee been payable for such renewal? was the Ship in a Port in the Country where the Passports and Sea Briefs were granted? And if not, where was the Ship at that time? had any person on board any Let-Pass or Letters of Safe-conduct? If yea, from whom and for what business?

28. If it should appear that there are in Ireland, or the British American Colonies, or in any other Place or Country, besides Great Britain, any Bills of Lading, Invoices, Instruments, or Papers relative to the Ship and Goods, concerning which the Witness is now examined:- Then Interrogate, hoe were they brought into such a Place or Country? In whose possession are they, and do they differ from any of the Papers on board, or in great Britain, or Ireland, or elsewhere, and in what particulars do they differ? Have you written or signed any Letters or Papers, concerning the Ship and her Cargo? If yea, what was their Purport? To whom were they written and sent, and what is become of them?

29. Towards what Port or Place was the Ship steering her course at the Time of her being first pursued and taken? Was her Course altered upon the appearance of the Vessel by which she was taken? Was her Course at all times, when Weather would permit, directed to the Place or Port for which she appears to have been destined by the Ship Papers? Was the Ship before, or at the time of her capture, sailing beyond, or wide of the said Place or Port to which she was so destined by the said Ship Papers? At what distance was she therefrom? Was her course altered at any and, at what time, and to what other Port or Place, and for what reason?

30. By whom, and to whom hath the said Ship been sold or transferred, and how often? At what time and at what place, and for what sum or consideration, hath such sum or consideration been paid or satisfied? Was the sum paid, or to be paid, a fair and true equivalent? Or what security, or securities, have been given for the payment of the same, and by whom, and where do they live now? Do you know or believe in your conscience, such sale or transfer has been truly made? And for the purpose of covering or concealing the real property? Do you verily believe that if the Ship should be restored, she will belong to the persons now asserted to be the Owners, and to none others? Are there any private Agreements for the return of the Ship to her former Owners at the conclusion of the war, or at any other period?

31. What Guns are mounted on board the Ship, and what arms and Ammunition were belonging to her? Why was she so armed? Were there on board any other Guns, Mortars, Balls, Shells, Handgranades, Muskets, Carbines, Fuzees, Halberts, Spontoons, Swords, Bayonets , Locks for Muskets, Flints, Ram-rods, Belts Cartridges, Cartridge-Boxes, Pouches. Gun-Powder, Salt Petre, Nitre, Camp Equipage, Military Tools, Uniforms, Soldiers Clothing or Accoutrements, or any sort of Warlike or Naval Stores? Were any such Warlike or Naval Stores, or things, thrown overboard, to prevent suspicion at the time of the Capture? And were, and are any such Warlike Stores, before described, concealed on board under the Name of Merchandize, or any other colourable appellation, in the Ships Papers? If yea, what are

the marks on the Casks, Bales, and Packages, in which they were concealed? Are any of the before-named articles, and which, for the sole use of any Fortress or Garrison in the Port or Place to which such a Ship was destined? Do you know or have you heard of any Ordinance, Placart, or law existing, in such Kingdom or State, forbidding the Exportation of the same by private persons without a Licence? Were such Warlike or Naval Stores put on board by any Public Authority? When, and where, were they put on board?

32. What is the whole which you know or believe, according to the best of your knowledge and belief, regarding the real and true property and destination of the Ship and Cargo concerning which you are now examined, at the time of Capture?

*Additional*

33. Did the said Ship, on the Voyage in which she was captured, or on, or during any, and what former Voyage or Voyages, sail under the Convoy of any Ship or Ships of War, or other armed Vessel or Vessels? If yea, Interrogate for what reason, or purpose, did she sail under such Convoy? Of what force was or were such convoying Ship or Ships? And to what State or Country did such Ship or Ships belong? What Instructions or Directions had you, or did you receive on each and every such Voyages, when under Convoy, respecting your sailing or keeping in company with such armed or convoying Ship or Ships, and from whom did you receive such Instructions or Directions? had you any and what Instructions or directions, and from whom, for resisting or endeavouring to avoid or escape from capture, or for destroying, concealing, or refusing to deliver up your Ship's Documents and Papers? Or any and what other papers, that might be, or were put on board your said Ship? If yea, Interrogate particularly as to the Tenor of such Instructions, and all particulars relating thereto? let the Witness be asked if he is in possession of such Instructions, or Copies thereof, and, if yea, let him be directed to leave the same with the Examiner, to be annexed to his deposition.

34. Did the said Ship, during the voyage in which we was captured, or on or during any and what former voyage or Voyages, sail or attempt

to enter any Port under Blockade by the arms or Forces of any, and which of the Belligerent Powers? If yea, when did you first learn or hear of such Port being so blockaded, and were you at any and at what time, and by whom warned not to proceed to, or to attempt to enter such blockaded Port? What Conversation or other Communication passed thereon? And what course did you pursue upon, and after, being so warned off?"[34]

### 6. Summary of the Standing Interrogatories

The standing interrogatories attempted, through increasingly detailed questions developed over time, to discover a core set of information, in the following areas:

- The details of the capture, who was it done by, when and where, whether there had been resistance, and what ship, cargo, merchandize, crew, and passengers were seized

- The specifics of the cargo, its quantity, quality and descriptions and its origin, which nation's product or produce was it, where was it loaded on the ship, what was its destination, and whether the bills of lading matched all cargo on the ship or were falsified

- The ship's papers, their nature and descriptions, whether they were true or fraudulent, whether other papers existed elsewhere that may arise during condemnation, and whether any papers had been lost or destroyed before, during, or after the capture

- Nationalities of the crew, the owners, the consignees, and any passengers

- Ownership in the ship and cargo and whether there were any sales or leases of the ship

- What had happened since the capture to the ship, cargo, and crew, whether bulk had been broken, and whether the ship being examined was that which was captured

- Whether there had been any damage that had occurred during the seizure of the prize or since its capture

---

[34] 165 Eng. Rep. [i] (1752-1865).

The other types of questions that might be asked included:

- Armaments aboard the ships
- Any commissions issued to the ships
- The status of any insurance coverage
- Color hoisted by the captured ship during its voyage
- Whether it had sailed in a convoy during its voyage
- Prior names of the captured ship
- Prior condemnations of the captured ship
- Personal experiences with the master and the loading of the ship
- The actual versus stated course of the ship during its voyage

*7. Sentence of the Court*

The admiralty court, after reading the depositions answering the standing interrogatories and reviewing the ship's documents, plus considering any additional evidence, would then sentence the ship and cargo. By no means were the decisions for the ship and cargo the same in prize proceedings, especially in the cases of neutral ship owners transporting cargo that might be intended for enemies. And the cargo itself was certainly subject to differing judgments, based upon the many factors explored in the standing interrogatories, so different parts of the cargo could be condemned while other parts acquitted. These judgements would also cover the tackle, apparel, and furniture of captured ships and the merchandise and personal property aboard the prize ship.

One example of a court sentence, during the Seven Years' War, was an admiralty court decision by admiralty judge Thomas Salusbury, on a captured French ship,

> "Therefore we Sir Thomas Salusbury... do hereby pronounce, decree, and declare that the said ship *La Mignone* and her tackle, apparel, and furniture, and the goods therein were rightly and duly taken and seized by His Majesty's said ships of war the *Aeolus*, whereof John Elliott, esquire, was commander, and the Isis, whereof Edward Wheeler, esquire, was commander, and the officers, mariners, and others then being in the service of the said ships ; And that the said

ship *La Mignone*, her tackle, apparel, and furniture, and the goods taken therein, did at the time of the capture and seizure thereof, as far as appears to us, belong to the French king and his vassals or subjects, enemies of the crown of Great Britain, and as such ought to be accounted and reputed lyable and subject to confiscation, and to be adjudged and condemned as and for good and lawfull prize;

And we do also pronounce, decree, and declare that the *said La Mignone* was and is a French ship of war, and had a commission on board from the French King to act as such; and that she was taken in fight by His Majesty's said ships of war the *Aeolus*, whereof the said John Elliott was commander, and the *Isis*, whereof Edward Wheeler, Esquire, was commander; And that the said French ship of war *La Mignone* had alive and on board her, at the beginning of the engagement between them, one hundred and thirty eight men; And we so adjudge and condemn the said ship, her tackle, apparel, and furniture, and the goods therein taken, as and for good and lawful prize, as being a French ship of war, and goods of the enemies of the crown of Great Britain, or otherwise liable to confiscation, by this our definitive sentence, or final decree, which we read and promulgate by these presents."[35]

---

[35] Sentence, condemning La Mignone as prize, Adm. Ct. Prize Sentences, 40, No. 115, from *Documents Relating to Law and Custom of the Sea*, ed. R.G. Marsden.

# *Chapter 4*

# PRIVATEERING – BRITAIN, EDWARD III TO GEORGE III

The history of privateering may have begun in the ancient world, with the Greeks and Romans, who kept military prizes for the good of the state, before allowing individual distributions. As it later evolved in the maritime nations of Europe, from the thirteenth century onwards, specific methods were developed to resolve complaints on the piratical taking of goods transported by the sea. To settle claims of theft of a merchant's water-born cargo, rulers could issue letters of reprisal against the specific offender, if the courts had no remedy. When the offender was a citizen of another country, diplomacy could be attempted. If diplomacy did not work, an arrest could be made of the offender's goods within the victim's country. If that was not possible, then general letters of reprisal could be granted to the victim against any of the other country's merchants.

Letters of marque were also issued when the reprisals required crossing national borders (*marche*). These two instruments would over time become joined as letters of mark and/or reprisal. The term later came to signify privateering activities by merchantmen carrying cargo. Privateering commissions, on the other hand, were granted to privately-owned armed warships which carried no cargo. These two types of authorizations to private armed ships were meant to harass an enemy during war, supplementing weak national navies. Over time, "letters of marque and reprisal" and "privateering commission" would often be used interchangeably for designating a national effort to prod privately-owned ships to attack its enemies' merchant shipping during times of war.

The first section of this chapter reviews privateering laws enacted in England/Great Britain. These statutes permitted the Admiralty or colonial governors to issue letters of marque and reprisal to private ship owners, who would be required to post security to guarantee the behavior of the commanders of their ships. Nations did not wish privateer captains to descend into outright piracy, so it was important that they followed specific instructions. Privateers would be directed to capture only enemy ships, not those of friendly or neutral nations, unless they were assisting an enemy. Captured ships and cargo were to be brought into a port, not raided at sea, so courts of admiralty would determine whether the ship and cargo were lawful prizes able to be condemned for use of the captors. This section covers statutes for private armed ships, not public ships of war (i.e. navies), which operated under related but different rules.

The second section addresses the trials of these ships and cargos before the courts of admiralty and vice admiralty. Initially, all ships were sent to England for trial but with the growth of the British colonial possessions, courts of vice admiralty handled libels (suing in admiralty by initiating a complaint) in more remote locations, including in America. The trials examined here happened in the 18th century, during the various wars of Britain when privateering laws were in effect. The courts handled a wide variety of issues in acquitting or condemning ships and cargo.

These legal issues included what was considered contraband, use of neutral shipping to avoid confiscation, setting salvage rate based upon merit, use of American passports to avoid American privateers, Admiralty droits, general carriers making general claims to prize cargo, condemnation based on enemy laders, consigners, or exporters, claims for recapture of a ship by its former owner, allocating a prize between captor and re-captor, when cargo was not on a condemned ship, use of false passes and neutral colors, entitlement to additions made to a recaptured ship, priority of the crown over other claimants, suborning perjured testimony, common law courts overruling an admiralty court arrest, sureties paying for privateering violations, and inconsistencies between documentation and testimony.

## 4.1 STATUTES

Events involving the main features of privateering were recorded in Britain as early as the 13th century. In 1205, the sixth year of the reign of John I, there was a grant of half of the cargo of a prize ship to the crew who captured it.[1] In 1216, the captors of a prize, after giving the king his half, were to return the other half of amounts taken back to the owner of the captured ship, as apparently it was not legitimately taken.[2] In 1293, a court was appointed to hear a case from merchants of Spain and Portugal against those of Bayonne in France (then under English rule), both claiming the other had taken their goods.[3] In the same year, the king stayed certain letters of marque and reprisal issued against Castille.[4] In 1295, a letter of reprisal was granted to a merchant whose goods were taken in Lisbon,

> "liberty to make reprisals upon people of the realm of Portugal, and particularly upon those of the city of Lisbon aforesaid, and upon their goods, wheresoever he may find them... [and] to retain and keep them for himself, until he... shall be fully satisfied for [the loss of] his goods so spoiled as aforesaid, or their value as declared above, together with expenses reasonably incurred by him."[5]

### A.   14th to 17th Century

*1.   Municipal Statutes*

The system that would develop over time began with the power residing in the king to receive all maritime prizes captured and brought to England. The king, through proclamation or Parliamentary statute, would grant this power to privately owned ships to take prizes and receive all or most of the proceeds of a lawful prize. The courts of admiralty would be given a

---

[1] Patent Rolls, 6 John, m. 3 (1205), from *Documents Relating to Law and Custom of the Sea*, ed. R.G. Marsden.
[2] Patent Rolls, 1 Hen. III, m. 4 (1216), from *Documents Relating to Law and Custom of the Sea*, ed. R.G. Marsden.
[3] Chancery Miscellanea, Bundle 13, File I, No. 16. (1293), from *Documents Relating to Law and Custom of the Sea*, ed. R.G. Marsden.
[4] Patent Rolls, 21 Edw. I, m. 7 (1293), from *Documents Relating to Law and Custom of the Sea*, ed. R.G. Marsden.
[5] Vascoii Rolls, 23 Edw. I, m. 22 (1295), from *Documents Relating to Law and Custom of the Sea*, ed. R.G. Marsden.

commission to adjudicate whether the prize was lawful, the cost allocations, and other matters related to the capture. The first statutory mention of letters of marque was in 1353, in a law passed by Parliament for the protection of foreign merchants selling in England. This new law referenced the already existing system of marque,

> "provided always, That if our liege people, merchants or other, be indamaged by any lords of strange lands or their subjects, and the said lords (duly required) fail of right to our said subjects, we shall have the law of marque, and of taking them again, as has been used in times past."[6]

Letters of marque were mentioned in a statute passed more than sixty years later, in the reign of Henry V, in 1416. This came as a response to continued violations of the statute of 1414[7] by those at the borders with Scotland. The 1414 act appointed conservators in each port to deal with murder, robbery, and other crimes on the high seas and in ports, and required prizes captured from the king's enemies to be brought before the conservator. The 1416 statute allowed those who were aggrieved by such breaches of the truce, who had not yet received restitution, to have a letter of marque issued to them so that they could privately pursue the recovery of their damages.[8]

By the time of Henry VIII, privateering was burdened by the shares in prizes that had to go to the lord admiral, the need for letters of marque, and the concomitant funds for bail/security. To give privateering a boost, a royal proclamation[9] was issued in 1544 that allowed private ship owners to sail on privateering missions against the enemies of the country without an express letter of marque. This reduced the upfront costs and, also cut out

---

[6] A merchant-stranger shall not be impeached for another's debt but upon good cause. Merchants of enemies countries shall sell their goods in convenient time, and depart, 27 Edw. III stat. 2 c. 17.

[7] Breaking the truce and safe conduct shall be high treason; In every port there shall be a conservator of the peace and safe conduct, 2 Hen. V c. 6.

[8] In what cases letters of marque may be granted, 4 Hen. V c. 7.

[9] Proclamation, made 20 Dec. 36 Henry VIII, licensing all subjects to equip vessels to sea against the Scots and Frenchmen; enjoining upon officers of port towns to help that this liberty may have substantial effect; and forbidding the taking of mariners, munition or tackle from such as so equip themselves.

the allocation to the lord admiral, increasing the take for the owners and crew of the privateer. Privateering continued to be encouraged during the reign of Elizabeth, from Francis Drake and other adventurers, in official or unofficial letters of marque during the many conflicts between England and its enemies, such as Spain and France. In 1585, she issued letters patent to the lord admiral, saying

> "Whereas we have been credibly advertised that the King of Spain hath made stay of late of all the ships, goods, debts of our loving subjects within the realms of Spain and Portugal, and hath caused likewise such of our said subjects as were there for the trade of merchandise to be retained in prison; Whereupon divers of this our realm, merchants, owners, and others, interested in the goods and persons so stayed and detained, have made humble suit unto us for letters of reprisal, having no other means by any order of justice to be yielded to them, and that they may be licensed to stay and take the goods of the subjects of the King of Spain wheresoever, upon the seas or in any part without our dominions, to answer the losses and damages by them sustained and the reasonable charges they shall be at for the taking thereof;

> These are therefore to will and require you and by virtue of these presents to authorize you, as our Admiral, to grant your Commissions for the taking of the goods of the subjects of the King of Spain to such our loving subjects so damnified and in such manner and form and according to such articles and orders as shall be agreed upon and advised by the Lords and others of our Privy Council, or by any six of them, and set down by them [&c] in writing under their hands and delivered unto you."[10]

During the reigns of the Stuart kings in the 17th century, who sought peace with the usual enemies of England, there were fewer letters of marque, except during the English Civil War and those issued by James II from France, where he had fled after being pushed out during the Glorious Revolution. By the end of the 17th century, in the reign of William III and

---

[10] Letters Patent to the Lord Admiral, authorizing him to issue letters of reprisal (1585).

Mary, a statute passed in 1692 addressed the current conflict with France, setting down many of the rules of privateering,

> "whereas it would much tend to the annoying and damageing their Majesties Enemies and to the better secureing the Trade and Commerce of this Kingdom if greater numbers of Ships were equipp'd and set out in warlike manner by their Majesties Subjects. To which end it is requisite that all fitting encouragement should be given to all Merchante Owners and Setters out of and all the Officers, Marriners, and Seamen comanding and serving in any private Man of Warr for the seizeing, surprizeing, and takeing of Ships and Vessels belonging to their Majesties Enemies... all Ships and Vessels with their ladings and all Goods and Merchandizes that shall be taken or seized as Prize either by their Majesties Ships of Warr or by any Ships sett forth as Privateers... and brought into some of their Majesties Ports of this Kingdom... until such time as the same shall be adjudged lawfull Prize."[11]

The goods and merchandise on the prizes were to be divided with four-fifths going to the privateer owner and crew and one-fifth to the crown, after deduction for duties. The ship and all its tackle and apparel were to go the privateer captor solely. Those commanders and crew embezzling from the prize ships or acting in collusion with a potential prize ship would forfeit any interest in sharing out the prize ship and cargo. There was an extra reward of ten pounds for each ordnance on a prize ship taken, sunk, or burnt. Recaptures of ships made prize by the enemy would be rewarded as a percent of the value of the ship and cargo, and the time it took to recapture the prize. If recaptured in less than one day, the salvage fee was one-eighth the value; if recaptured in more than one but less than two days, the salvage fee was one-fifth the value; and if recaptured in more than two days but less than four days, the salvage fee was one-half the value.

---

[11] An Act for continuing the acts for prohibiting all trade and commerce with France, and for the encouragement of privateers, 4&5 Will. III & Mary c. 25.

## 2. International Treaties

Besides municipal statutes declaring the rules for privateering, international treaties also contributed significantly to setting the limits on what privateers could do. As Britain was frequently at war, the various peace and alliance treaties it signed often included restrictions placed upon the roles of privateers or on adjudicating their captured prizes. The following provides a partial description of how privateering was addressed in the various treaties, in the 17th century. England had only just started to become an important naval force after the defeat of the Spanish Armada, which led to many wars to expand or protect its commerce and geopolitical ambitions, and therefore to the use of privateering to help facilitate those goals.

The Treaty of London, negotiated with Spain in 1604 between new monarchs, after the hostilities between the countries brought about during the reigns of Elizabeth I and Phillip II of Spain, specified that all past damages done to each other would no longer be claimed and,

> "each party shall hereafter abstain from all booty, depredation, offenses, and spoils, both by sea and land and fresh waters, in any of the kingdoms, dominions, places, or jurisdictions of the other, wherever they may be situated. Neither shall they [i.e., the aforesaid princes] consent that any of the aforesaid be done by their vassals, the inhabitants of their kingdoms, or their subjects and they shall cause restitution to be made of all booty, spoils, depredations, and damages which shall hereafter be committed."[12]

The Treaty of Madrid, again negotiated with Spain, in 1630, after further conflict, gave varying start dates as to when privateering would be terminated, based on location,

> "except for captures made within the strait of the Narrow Seas after the space of fifteen days, and between the Narrow Seas and the Islands after the space of three months, and beyond the Line [equator] after the space of nine months fully ended, to be reckoned from the publication of the peace, or immediately after notice of the peace is

---

[12] Treaty between Spain and Great Britain concluded at London, Aug. 18/28, 1604.

sufficiently given within the said limits and places by declarations or by authentic documents which should be respectively shown, because an accounting must be made concerning these and restitution made. And hereafter each party shall abstain from all depredations, captures, offenses, and spoils, both by land and by sea and fresh waters in all the kingdoms, dominions, places, and jurisdictions of the other, wherever situated; nor shall they consent that any of the aforesaid wrongs shall be committed by their vassals, inhabitants of their kingdoms, or subjects, and they shall cause restitution to be made of all booty, spoils, and captures, or for damages proceeding or resulting therefrom."[13]

The Treaty of Westminster, this time negotiated with France, in 1655, focused partly on privateering losses over the prior decade plus,

"whereas since the year 1640 a great many captures have been made at sea and heavy losses have been inflicted upon each nation, its people and subjects, by the other, it has been agreed that immediately after the ratification of the present treaty, three commissioners shall be named by each side, armed with sufficient authority to consider, examine, estimate, and liquidate such captures and losses, and fix and determine the compensation, payment, and satisfaction for them, according to the claims produced and presented before them by either party, their subjects, and peoples... nor shall the aforesaid letters of marque be restored to their full force, or other new ones be granted."[14]

The Treat of Breda was negotiated with the Netherlands, after the Second Anglo-Dutch War in 1667 (and similarly the 1674 Treaty of Westminster ending the Third Anglo-Dutch War), banned privateering during the term of the agreement, after it was properly notified across the world. Those who violated that prohibition could be brought to justice, by either party,

---

[13] Treaty of peace and commerce between Spain and Great Britain, concluded at Madrid, Nov. 5/15, 1630.
[14] Treaty of peace between France and Great Britain, concluded at Westminster, Nov. 3/13, 1655.

"that all ships, with their equipment, and cargoes, and all movable goods which during this war, or at any time heretofore, have come into the power of either of the aforesaid parties, or of their subjects, shall be and remain to the present possessors, without any compensation or restitution; so that each may become and remain proprietor and possessor in perpetuity of that which has been thus seized, without any controversy or exception of place, time, or things...

to avoid all matter of strife or contention hereafter, which is sometimes wont to arise concerning the restitution or liquidation of such ships, merchandise, and other movables, as both parties, or either of them, may claim to have been taken or seized in places and coasts far distant, after the conclusion of peace, and before it shall have become known in those places, it is agreed, that all such ships, merchandise, and other movables, as may chance to fall into either party's hands after the conclusion and publication of the present instrument, within [certain periods, depending on the distance]... shall be and remain unto the possessors without any exception or further distinction of time or place, or without any consideration of restitution or compensation...

But in case the offenders against this treaty do not appear and submit themselves to judgment, and give satisfaction within the respective times above expressed, according to the distance of the places, they shall be declared enemies of both parties, and their estates and goods and revenues of whatever kind shall be confiscated, and used for full and due satisfaction of the injuries caused by them; and their persons also, when they come within the power of either party, shall be liable to such punishments as each shall deserve for his offences."[15]

A treaty of neutrality, negotiated between Britain and France regarding America, in 1686, specified the security that privateering ship owners had to provide for any injuries their ships would cause the other party,

---

[15] Treaty of peace and alliance between the United Netherlands and Great Britain, concluded at Breda, July 21/31, 1667.

"all their subjects who fit out ships at their own expense... shall be prohibited from all injury and harm toward the other party, but shall give security and be restrained from damage on any account and satisfy the interested party by reparation and restitution, under obligation of person and goods... For this reason all captains of vessels fitted out for warfare at private expense, before receiving their letters of marque or special commissions shall be required hereafter to give, before a competent judge, through suitable men, solvent and having no part or interest in such ship, suitable security in the sum of a thousand pounds sterling or thirteen thousand livres; and when the men exceed the number of one hundred and fifty, in the sum of two thousand pounds sterling or twenty-six thousand livres, to the effect that they will give satisfaction for any injuries whatever which they or their officers or any others serving them may in their cruise commit against the present treaty... under penalty of the revocation and cancelling of their commissions and letters of marque, in which it shall always be mentioned that such security has been given by them (as above said); it is moreover agreed that the ship itself shall be held to satisfy injuries committed by it."[16]

## B.   18th and 19th Century

### 1.   Anne

The wars of Spanish Succession from the early 18th century were the reason for passing a statute arming privateers.[17] This law called for the deployment of 43 ships, under the direction of the Royal Navy, which could be used in a line of battle if so needed. If these ships were lost in battle or to the sea or taken by the enemy, they were to be replaced. The rights to prizes captured by privateers were the same as those for a Royal Navy ship, meaning the commander and crew would have sole rights to the value of the ship and goods of a prize legally captured and condemned, excepting custom duties owed. Embezzling by a commander required him to forfeit treble the value of what was taken. Prize ships not sold but instead taken

---

[16] Treaty of neutrality in America between Great Britain and France, concluded at Whitehall, Nov. 6/16, 1686.
[17] An Act for the better securing the trade of this kingdom by cruisers and convoys, 6 Ann. c. 13.

into the Royal Navy had their own method of appraisal, as they would not be sold. A bounty payment of 5 pounds sterling was to be made for every man captured aboard a prize vessel. Privateering was encouraged in the American colonies in another act that same year[18] that would serve as a model for future privateering statutes.

2. *George II*

In 1739, as conflict with Spain was breaking out, the king issued instructions to privateers, which clarified the difference between letters of marque and privateering commission,

> "it shall be Lawful for the said Commanders of Merchant Ships and Vessells, Authorized by Letters of Marque or Commissions for Private Men of War, to set upon by force of arms and to subdue and take the Men of War, Ships and other Vessells whatsoever, as also the Goods, Moneys and Merchandizes, belonging to the King of Spain, his Vassals and Subjects, and others Inhabiting within any of his Countries, Territories or Dominions... But so as that no Hostility be committed, nor Prize Attacked, Seized or taken within the Harbours of Princes and States in Amity with Us."[19]

Further instructions included directions for the commander to send the master and pilot of the prize, along with its papers, to the court of admiralty for interview and inspection, to not break bulk on the cargo and merchandize before the verdict of the court was given, and that condemned ships and cargo belonged to the privateer's owner and crew, except for items made in India, Persia, or China, which were to be held for re-export. Prisoners were not to be treated inhumanely, ships from countries in amity with Britain were not to be attacked, and those applying for commissions or letters of marque had to provide information on the ship, its crew, and armaments, and pay a bail for security of £3,000 for a ship of 150 men or more and £1,500 for a smaller ship.

---

[18] An Act for the encouragement of the trade to America, 6 Ann. c. 37.

[19] Instructions for the Commanders of such Merchant Ships and Vessells as may have Letters of Marque or Commissions for Private Men of War against the King of Spain, his Vassals and Subjects or others Inhabiting within any of His Countries, Territories or Dominions (Nov. 30, 1739).

In 1740, a privateering statute was passed that spelled out in greater detail the rules for targeting Spanish ships. It gave the crews the sole rights to lawfully captured prizes and allowed any British owner of a ship, upon giving bail and security, and taking an oath that the pledging party could cover that amount, to request a commission or letter of marque,

"of such ship or vessel, for the attacking, surprising, seizing, and taking, by and with such ship or vessel, or the crew thereof, any place or fortress upon the land, or any ship or vessel, goods, ammunition, arms, stores of war, or merchandizes, belong to or possessed by any of his Majesty's enemies, in any sea, creek, haven, or river; and that such ship or ships, vessel or vessels, arms ammunitions, stores of war, goods, and merchandizes whatsoever, with all their furniture, tackle, or apparel so to be taken by or with such private owner or owners, ship or vessel, according to such commission and commissions, being first adjudged lawful prize in any of his Majesty's courts of admiralty."[20]

The court of admiralty was given limited timeframes to determine whether the prize was lawful, including five days for a preliminary exam, time to advertise so claimants to come forward and post security, to examine papers and witnesses, and to proceed to a determination of condemn or acquit for the ship and cargo. Salvage fees for British ships retaken from the enemy were specified. If retaken by a navy ship, the re-captor's commander and crew would receive 1/8 the value of the ship and cargo, but if retaken by a privateer, the privateer would receive 1/8 of the value if retaken in less than 24 hours; 1/5 the value if retaken in less than 48 hours; 1/3 the value if retaken in less than 96 hours; and 1/2 the value if retaken in greater than 96 hours since it was originally captured or if it has been set out as a man of war. Admiralty courts in America could preside over prize cases for privateers, except in cases of captured Spanish treasure ships. Any privateer ship that colluded in the capture of a prize ship would itself be classified as a prize, and subject to condemnation.

---

[20] An Act for the more effectual securing and encouraging the trade of his Majesty's subjects to America, and for the encouragement of seamen to enter his Majesty's service, 13 Geo. II c. 4.

In 1741, the governor of Rhode Island, under this statute, issued a privateering commission to a Capt. Norton, requiring that he keep a journal of all his prizes, gathered information on the enemy, and had his crew follow these instructions. The commission began,

"Know Ye therefore That I do... grant Commission to, and do license and authorize the said Benjamin Norton to set forth in Hostile manner the said Sloop called the *Revenge* under his own Command, And there with by Force of Arms (for the Space of Twelve months from the Date hereof, If the war shall so long continue) to apprehend, seize and take the Ships, Vessels and Goods belonging to Spain, or the Vassals and Subjects of the King of Spain... and to bring the Same to such Port as shall be most convenient, In order to have them legally adjudged in such Court of Admiralty as shall be lawfully authorized within his Majesty's Dominions, which being condemned, It shall and may be lawful for the said Benjamin Norton to sell and dispose of such Ships, Vessels and Goods so adjudged and condemned in such Sort and manner as by the Course of Admiralty hath been accustomed."[21]

In 1744, another privateering statute was passed, this time targeting French ships, but essentially the same as the statute of 1740. One provision gave the government an open-ended ability to commission privateers in future wars.

"That his Majesty be, and he and his heirs and successors are hereby impowered from time to time during the continuance of this present or any future war, to grant or make any charter, commission, or grant, charters, commissions, or grants, for the better or more effectual enabling any society or societies, or particular persons, to join in any expeditions or adventures, by sea or land, and to sail to and in any seas, for the attacking, surprizing, taking, or destroying any ships, goods, moveables, and immoveables, settlements, factories, creeks, harbours, places of strength, lands, forts, castles, and fortifications, now belonging, or hereafter to belong to, or to be possessed by any enemy of his Majesty... [giving] full and undoubted properties, rights,

---

[21] Commission of Capt. Benjamin Norton, by Richard Ward, Governor of Rhode Island (June 2, 1741).

and titles of, in, and to, and the full enjoyment of all and every the ships, ammunition, stores of war, goods, chattels, moveables, and immoveables, settlements, factories, places of strength or security, lands, forts, castles, or fortifications, now belonging to, or possessed by, or hereafter to belong to, or to be possessed by any enemy of his Majesty, his heirs or successors, which such society or persons shall take, or cause to be taken from any such enemy; together with all the proceed, profits, and advantages, which may accrue of or by the same, or any of them.[22]

In 1756, in the middle of the Seven Years' War, this statute was again enacted[23] for the duration of this new war with France. Instructions for privateers were issued in 18 articles. The first two articles allowed for the seizure of ship, cargo, money, and merchandise belonging to French subjects or of ships carrying contraband (arms or armaments) for the French. Articles 3-12 included what port to bring the prize into for libel, the use of condemnation proceeds, the requirement to follow the issued letters of marque, and the need to render aid to other allied ships in distress. Articles 13-15 required turning over prisoners to the commissioners in port and not ransoming them, that ships were not ransomed, commanders ignoring instructions would lose their shares and could be subject legal proceedings, and commanders were required to turn in their journals. The final articles discussed punishments and the requirement for surety bonds.

The 1756 statute was amended a few years later, as privateering had become so popular that many smaller vessels including those barely armed had taken to boarding vessels of both enemies and neutral shipping,

"That no such Commission as aforesaid shall be issued for or granted to any Person or Persons by virtue of this Act, unless the Ship or Vessel for which the same shall be granted in Europe, shall be of the Burthen

---

[22] An Act for the better encouragement of seamen in his Majesty's service, and privateers, to annoy the enemy, 17 Geo. II c. 34.

[23] An Act for the encouragement of seamen, and the more speedy and effectual manning his Majesty's navy, 29 Geo. II c. 34.

of one hundred Tons, and carry ten Carriage Guns, being three Pounders, and forty Men at the least."[24]

Neutral ships made prize had to be brought into port and not ransomed off. Neutrals that had only contraband cargo could have just that cargo removed as a prize, and not the remainder of the cargo or the ship.

### 3. *George III*

With the American Revolutionary War underway, Parliament enacted a statute[25] in 1777 like the acts under George II, but built off the Prohibitory Act of 1776, which had closed trade with the American colonies.[26] While the Prohibitory Act allowed for prizes, these were only for ships captured by the Royal Navy. This new act allowed for the issuing, and revocation, of commissions for privateers to seize the ships and cargo of the Americans and any British ship trading with the American rebels. It gave the privateer owner and crew the sole proceeds from the sale of lawfully captured ships and cargo, unless they were sailing in a convoy, in which case there would be no sharing of prizes with privateers.

To be granted a commission, the applicant had to specify the dimensions of the ship, the burden it could carry, the number of guns and expected crew size, and the ability of those providing bail and security to have the necessary wealth to cover that amount. The ship had to be checked by the customs officer where it was being fitted out, who would issue a certificate upon all the submitted details matching his inspection. The commission would be voided if the commander departed port without a certificate and any customs officer who issued a false certificate who be fired and fined. If any commander of a privateer ransomed a prize back to

---

[24] An Act to explain and amend an Act made in the twenty-ninth Year of his present Majesty's Reign, intituled, *An Act for the Encouragement of Seamen, and the more speedy and effectual Manning his Majesty's Navy*; and for the better Prevention of Piracies and Robberies by Crews of private Ships of War, 32 Geo. II c. 25.

[25] An Act for enabling the commissioners for executing the office of lord high admiral of Great Britain, to grant commissions to the commanders of private ships and vessels, employed in trade, or retained in his Majesty's service, to take and make prize of all such ships and vessels, and their cargoes, as are therein mentioned, for a limited time, 17 Geo. III c. 7.

[26] 16 Geo. III c. 5.

its crew and set it free without bringing in to be condemned, he was to be considered a pirate and would suffer the same fate as a pirate.

Aboard privateers or merchant ships with letters of marque, the rules for the crew were generally the same as those of the crews in the Royal Navy. As any such crimes required a court martial and that meant naval officers were required for the panel, the offender had to be confined until the privateer could arrange to meet these navy ships. Ships in American waters were to obey local laws not allowing servants or enslaved persons to be taken into their crews without the permission of the servant's or slave's master. In 1779,[27] after France had joined the war on the American side, Parliament again enacted a statute with similar provisions as the statutes of 1740 and 1777, with French ships now a legal target, soon to be followed by the ships of Spain[28] and the Netherlands.[29]

In 1793, with the start of the Napoleonic Wars, the privateering statute was re-enacted[30] in that the Admiralty could issue letters of marque and reprisal to registered British ships, with only the captor's owners entitled to the proceeds from the sale of the condemned ship and cargo. Anyone ransoming their ship, cargo, or merchandise was no longer considered a pirate subject to death but instead would be fined 500 pounds. Five pounds were to be paid for each man on each ship captured.

---

[27] An Act for the encouragement of seamen and the more speedy and effectual manning of his Majesty's Navy, 19 Geo. III c. 67.

[28] An Act for extending the provisions of two acts, made in the eighteenth year of his present Majesty's reign and In the last session of parliament, with respect to bringing prize goods into this kingdom, to Spanish prize goods; and for repealing so much of the said last-mentioned act as relates to the certificates for prize tea and East India goods exported from this kingdom to Ireland; for the removal of East India goods condemned as prize at any out-port to London for sale; and' of prize goods for exportation; and for reducing the duty on foreign prize tobacco, 20 Geo. III c. 9.

[29] An Act for extending the provisions of three acts, made in the eighteenth, nineteenth, and twentieth years of his present Majesty's reign, with respect to bringing prize goods into this kingdom, to prizes taken from the states general of the United Provinces; for declaring what goods shall be deemed military or ship stores; for regulating the sale of and ascertaining the duties upon East India goods condemned as prize in the port of London; for permitting the purchasers of prize goods condemned abroad to import such goods into this kingdom, under the like regulations and advantages as are granted by law to captors themselves; and for reducing the duties on foreign prize tobacco, 21 Geo. III c. 5.

[30] An Act for the encouragement of seamen, and for the better and more effectually manning his Majesty's navy, 33 Geo. III c. 66.

Orders in council were then used to further direct privateers towards enemy ports under blockade, instead of going freewheeling on their own,

> "That it shall be lawful for the commanders of His Majesty's ships of war and privateers, that have or may have letters of marque against France, to seize all ships, whatever be their cargoes, that shall be found attempting to enter any blockaded port, and to send the same for condemnation, together with their cargoes."[31]

The same year, exemplifying how shares of prizes were allocated, George III issued a proclamation regarding the distribution of prizes during the conflict with France. Although focusing primarily on distributions to the officers and crews of Royal Navy ships, it started by focusing on privateers.

> "WHEREAS... We have ordered that general reprisals be granted against the ships, goods, and subjects of France, so that as well our fleets and ships, as also all other ships and vessels that shall be commissionated by letters of marque, or general reprizals... shall and may lawfully seize all ships, vessels, and goods belonging to France... and bring the same to judgment in any of our courts of admiralty within our dominions; we, being desirous to give due encouragement to all our faithful subjects who shall lawfully seize the same... do now make known... by this our proclamation... that the neat produce of all prizes taken... be given to the takers... but subject to the payment of all such or the like customs and duties... if the same were or might have been imported as merchandize... that all prizes taken by ships and vessels having commissions of letters of marque and reprizals... may be sold and disposed of by the merchants, owners, fitters, and others, to whom such letters of marque and reprizals are granted, for their own use and benefit, after final adjudication, and not before."[32]

In 1803[33] and 1805,[34] with the Napoleonic Wars ramping up, the privateering statute was revived, and then revised again in 1809.[35] In

---

[31] Order in council, Additional instructions to the commanders of His Majesty's ships of war and privateers that have or may have letters of marque against France (June 8, 1793).

[32] "A Proclamation granting the Distribution of Prizes during the present Hostilities (Apr. 17, 1793).

[33] An Act for the encouragement of seamen, and for the better and more effectually manning his Majesty's navy; for regulating the payment of prize-money, and for making provision for

1813, with the War of 1812 started against the United States, the privateering statute from the Napoleonic Wars was targeted now at American shipping, goods, and citizens.[36] However, after that war, by the start of the next major conflict involving the British, the Crimean War in 1853, the government had re-thought the role of privateering, which the queen proclaiming that.

> "Her Majesty further declares, that being anxious to lessen as much as possible the evils of war, and to restrict its operations to the regularly organized forces of the country, it is not her present intention to issue letters of marque for the commissioning of privateers."[37]

Privateering was banned internationally under the Declaration of Paris, in 1856, for those nations signing or ratifying it. This included the usual European maritime powers of Britain, France, Spain (decades later), the Netherlands, Sweden, Russia, and other European nations and states which relied heavily upon shipping for their economies.[38] It did not include the United States, which still had a small navy and long memories of how important the role privateering had played in its success in earlier wars, as discussed in Chapter 5.

---

the salaries of the judges of the vice- admiralty courts in the island of Malta and in the Bermuda and Bahama islands, during the present War, 43 Geo. III c. 160.

[34] An Act for the encouragement of seamen, and for the better and more effectually manning his Majesty's navy during the present War, 45 Geo. III c. 72.

[35] An Act for to explain and amend an Act made in the Forty-fifth Year of His present Majesty, for the Encouragement of Seamen, and for the better and more effectually manning His Majesty's Navy during the present War; and for the further Encouragement of Seamen, and for the better and more effectually providing for the Interest of the Royal Hospital for Seamen at Greenwich, and the Royal Hospital for Soldiers at Chelsea; and to extend the Provisions of the said Act to Cases arising in consequence of Hostilities commenced since the passing of the said Act, 49 Geo. III c. 123.

[36] An Act to extend Two Acts of the Forty fifth and Fort ninth years of His present Majesty to American Prizes, 53 Geo. III c. 63.

[37] Royal declaration (Mar. 28, 1854).

[38] Declaration Respecting Maritime Law, Paris (Apr. 16, 1856).

## 4.2 TRIALS

The seizure of prizes and condemnations in English prize courts were established from the late 13th century. In 1296, Edward I ordered that goods captured aboard a ship belonging to his Flemish allies be restored but those of his Spanish enemies condemned to the captors. In 1297, a Flemish ship was to be restored to its owners if its seizure occurred before Flanders became an enemy by aligning with France. In 1357, Edward III upheld the admiral's ruling that Portuguese goods recaptured from the French were properly condemned to the English re-captor. In 1443, Henry VI ordered a stay on restoration of a ship and goods to a Breton accused of piratically seizing an English ship and goods. In 1589, the admiralty court condemned the *St. Anthony of Olinda* and its cargo as being Spanish property. In 1697, the admiralty court condemned the French ship *Bonaventure* and its cargo but noted that its captor had absconded with the ship and cargo and was therefore liable to the king for its full value.

Under privateering statutes, suspected enemy ships or neutral ships assisting an enemy could be stopped and boarded by privateers, to inspect their paperwork and crew. With reasonable suspicion established, such vessels became prizes, a prize crew was put on board, the cargo sealed off, and the ship sent to a port where a court of admiralty oversaw the libel of the ship and cargo. The court could separately acquit or condemn the ship, its tackle, apparel, and furniture, and the cargo, in any variety of combinations. The court of admiralty in Britain operated under procedural rules that somewhat differed from vice admiralty courts in America. The following trials, during the reigns of George II and George III, explore different aspects of libels typically initiated by the privateer commander and opposed by claims from the owners of the ship and cargo. Acquittals returned the ship or cargo to the owner, condemnation led to public auctions, whose proceeds went to the privateer ship owners, commanders, and crew. Ships recaptured from an enemy earned a salvage fee for the privateering re-captor but not necessarily if that ship belonged to a neutral country.

## A. Trials before the Court of High Admiralty

*1. Meds Guds Hielpe*

---

Legal issues to watch for

❖ Requirement for a passport to escape privateer
❖ Items considered contraband
❖ Whether treaty terms must be explicit

---

The Swedish ship *Meds Guds Hielpe* (With God's Help) was seized by the British privateer *Eagle* in 1745, in the middle of the War of Austrian Succession. In the trial before the high court of Admiralty in August 1745, the ship was brought in for condemnation, as it did not carry a proper passport as specified in the England-Sweden treaty of 1661.[39] This treaty had been signed after the restoration of Charles II, but the key provisions were similar to their treaty of 1656, which clarified the more general provisions of a 1654 treaty.[40] The passport, asking that the ship not be molested on its journey, was required to specify the sending government official who certified the owner and captain as citizens of that country, the intended destination, the cargo's description and quantities, and with the owner declaring,

> "upon their said oath, that the said goods above specified, and no others, are already put on board, or are to be put on board the abovenamed ship for the said voyage, and that no part of those goods belongs to any one whatsoever, but the persons abovementioned; and that no goods are disguised or concealed therein by any fictitious name whatsoever, but that the merchandize abovementioned is truly and really put on board, for the use of the said owners and no others."[41]

This treaty had also specified a long list of items which were considered contraband not to be supplied to the enemy of either and subject to seizure by the privateer:

---

[39] Treaty of commerce and friendship between Great Britain and Sweden (Apr. 1654).
[40] Treaty of commerce and friendship between Great Britain and Sweden (Oct. 1661).
[41] Treaty of commerce between Great Britain and Sweden (July 1656), art. IV

"bombs with their fuses and other appurtenances, fire-balls, gunpowder, matches, cannonball, spears, swords, lances, pikes, halberts, guns, mortars, petards, granadoes, musket-rests, bandaliers, saltpetre, muskets, musketballs, helmets, headpieces, breastplates, coats of mail, cuirasses and the like kind of arms; soldiers, horses, with all their furniture, pistols, holsters, belts and all other warlike instruments; and also ships of war."[42]

The cargo of the *Meds Guds Hielpe* was only pitch and tar, which was suspected of being for the French, an enemy of the British in this conflict. The court looked at the treaty's contraband list and came to the view that these were merely examples, instead of a complete list. It said that goods belonged to one of three categories:

"1st. For immediate use of war in the manner they are, and those are contraband. 2nd. Of a mixed nature, which may be of use for war and for other purposes, and these sometimes are, and sometimes are not, contraband. 3rd. Things for pleasure, and which are of no use in war, and those are not contraband."[43]

Pitch and tar fell into the second category. The court of admiralty judge Henry Penrice assumed that pitch and tar were specifically prohibited items according to the instructions given to the privateer, so the *Eagle* was justified in seizing the ship, ruling it a lawful prize and condemned the ship and the cargo. This ruling was appealed to the lords of the Admiralty, with the appellant asserting that the statutes of 1654 during the Cromwell protectorate specified the list of contraband items but the treaty of Charles II in 1661 did not.

Appellants' counsel Dr. Paul also argued that the instructions to privateers required them to follow treaties, that pitch and tar were of no use without tallow, that the ship should not have been condemned even if there was contraband aboard, and that if the cargo seized was not enumerated in the treaty, it cannot be contraband. The crown's position, from solicitor general William Murray and attorney general Dudley Ryder,

[42] Treaty of commerce between Great Britain and Sweden (July 1656), art. II.
[43] The Meds Guds Hielpe, Prize Cases Determined in the High Court of Admiralty.

was that contraband is anything that can be used in war. The lords, including John Willes, chief justice of Common Pleas, sided with the lower court, condemning both the cargo and ship.

## 2. Jong Vrouw

| Legal issues to watch for |
| :--- |
| ❖ Using neutral shipping to avoid confiscation |
| ❖ Fraudulent transfer to a neutral ship |
| ❖ Interpretation of foreign laws |

In May 1758, during the Seven Years' War, the Dutch ship *Jong Vrouw* (Young Woman) was captured by the British privateer *Nelly's Resolution*. The ship took on merchandize like coffee, sugar, and wool in Cadiz, Spain, mostly purchased from two French ships anchored there. She was captured just outside the harbor. The claim was that her cargo was enemy (French) owned and destined for France. To refute that, the bills of lading, signed by the master. Seeke Jeekes. and the owners, showed that the goods were shipped for Spanish, and other, neutral nation owners. Also, a notarized affidavit of the 30 owners at Cadiz attested that they were the sole owners of the entire cargo onboard.

In July, the admiralty judge in Gibraltar did not condemn the ship or certain non-contraband cargo like cheese and wine. These were returned to the owners and freight was paid for the shipping. The rest of the cargo was condemned, as produce from the French West Indies colonies, intended for France. The owners, including Nicholas Tardy, started an appeal, which did not reach the law lords until 1761. There were objections to the affidavits interpreting the French and Spanish law. It was asserted that the condemned goods must have been required transboarding and payment of duties in Cadiz for the sales of the goods, which were originally destined for Marseilles. The court,

> "thought it reasonable that some opportunity should be given for further explanation by affidavits as to the laws .and practice of Spain in relation to transboarding goods from French to neutral ships, and as to the laws and practice of France in relation to the importation of the produce of French settlements in America into France on board a

neutral bottom from a port in Europe; and that the claimants should be at liberty to supply the oaths and depositions already made by declaring whether the property was to continue theirs after the arrival and delivery of the goods at Marseilles, and likewise to supply the defect in their oaths by declaring that the price was actually and bona fide paid to the original proprietors, and how and where."[44]

It took three more years, in 1764 after the war had ended, for the case to be resolved. The court ruled that this was a false conveyance, with the intent of using neutral ships to cover an enemy ship and continue the goods on their original voyage to original destination. It viewed the sale as,

"a mode of unfair assistance to complete the original voyage in favour of the original proprietors, the original consignees, and the public revenue of the enemy arising from the duties."[45]

*3. The John and The Renard*

| Legal issues to watch for |
|---|
| ❖ Setting salvage rate based upon merit of the recapture |
| ❖ Setting salvage rate based upon prior laws |
| ❖ Higher rates for capturing prizes fitted out for war |

In a condemnation during the American Revolution, a prize ship taken by the French, the *John*, had been recaptured by a British privateer, never having been taken to port and condemned by the French. But at that time, while war had been declared against France, the new privateering statute against the French had not yet been passed. So, the court had to consider at what rate the privateer should be allowed for the salvage fee. The court noted that both navy men at war and privateers were awarded 1/8 the value of the ship and cargo under the privateering act that targeted American ships. However, this statute had not created the tiered rates for privateer recaptures, based upon when it was recaptured. The captors complained that the tiered rates used in prior wars, such as the statutes of George II, would be appropriate.

---

[44] The Jong Vrouw, Prize Cases Determined in the High Court of Admiralty.
[45] *Id.*

The court, in the transition from admiralty judge George Hay to James Marriott in November 1778, said that it was not bound by rules in prior privateering statutes that had expired with those prior wars. In finding a rule for the salvage fee for privateers,

> "The simplest rule was the best in everything, and that the decision in the French cases of recapture should square with the clause in the American Act; therefore pronounced for an eighth salvage, yet not so as to preclude the discretion of the Court to give a greater, and even a very great salvage, in other cases, where there should be very great merit in retaking. There was no resistance in this case on the part of the enemy; but when the action should be attended with loss of lives and blood, and damage of recaptors, they might expect a proportionable salvage; observing that this country owed much at this time to the activity of private armaments; and while privateers observed strictly the law and the King's instructions, in doing no injury to British or neutral innocent subjects, they would meet with every suitable and just encouragement."[46]

The following month, another recapture, of the *Renard*, came before the court. This British ship was captured by the French, judicially condemned in France, made a privateer, and then retaken by the British privateer *Lark*. The court had to decide whether, having been condemned by the French, there was salvage value in this prize. The lawyers for both sides asserted the writings of great civil law writers Hugo Grotius and Cornelius van Bynkershoek and common law compiler Robert Brooke to argue how long and in what circumstances a prize had to be taken to no longer be considered a prize. The court dismissed such theoretical arguments. Instead, it looked to the prior prize acts and noted that a privateer received half the value for a ship kept over 96 hours and likewise, a privateer or man of war which recaptured a ship now fitted out for war, was rewarded a salvage fee of half the value. So, the court ruled that, in absence of a current statute against the French, it would use these old rules and give the privateer owner and crew half the value of the *Renard*.

---

[46] The John, Decisions in the High Court of Admiralty, 1 H. & M.

*4.    The Sally and The Louisa*

---

### Legal issues to watch for

❖    Condemning ship and cargo for violating Prohibitory Act
❖    Use of American passports to avoid American privateers
❖    Allocation of costs to claimants

---

In October 1777, the *Sally* was brought to court for condemnation. She has been captured by the letter of marque *Sarah Golborough*, and there were various claimants for the cargo and ship. Edward Savage had been a loyalist judge in South Carolina who refused to take an oath of loyalty to the new state and so was expatriating. He claimed that his three casks of indigo were for his subsistence, not trading. Col. Probart Howarth, a loyalist military and his four casks of indigo, were similarly claimed and in both cases, these casks were ordered restored to the men. Similar claims from Mr. Carne for seven casks of indigo and the remaining cargo and the ship by William Savage were rejected, as neither had been required to take the loyalty oath in Carolina, meaning they were not under a threat of death if they returned. Both men also had insured their cargo and the ship, so theirs was a trading concern properly banned by the Prohibitory Act.

In November 1778, the *Louisa* came before the court of admiralty. Captured by a privateer from Jersey commanded by Capt. Winter, the *Louisa's* master, Mr. Macurdy, believing Winter to be an American, produced a passport and certificate signed by the American commissioners in France, one of whom was Benjamin Franklin.[47] The papers said that the ship was owned by Macurdy and Joshua Johnson of Britain. Its intended voyage took it from London to Portugal, to take on cargo of salt and bark for a voyage to New York. Its English papers were used to cover up its American destination. Macurdy, British by birth but living in America, claimed he bought the ship as a prize in Jamaica. He, Johnson, and Mathew Ridley, Johnson's partner in a London merchant, claimed the ship and cargo.

The king's advocate, William Wynne, asserted that such passports were available in blank, to be used to as needed by the American

---

[47] See THOMAS J. SHAW, THE LEGAL HISTORY OF THE REVOLUTIONARY WAR, chapter 2.

commissioners, and they could be purchased for protection. He did allow that the ship was not intended to go to the American side, just to British-controlled New York. Dr. Harris, for the owners, claimed Ridley was unaware of action of his partner and that costs should not be given against them, as condemnation was sufficient punishment, but the prize acts did stipulate double costs as bail for claimants. The court condemned the ship and cargo, with Marriot claiming he was not bound by the prize acts in awarding costs. Shocked that English traders would be supporting the rebel cause, he ruled,

> "he would condemn them in treble costs generally, ex officio, and as much as the proctors could swear to; that it was his duty to do as much justice as he could to the whole kingdom in this instance, in putting a check to every sort of support and encouragement from home of a system involving the ruin of all good men's lives and properties; a system treasonable and traitorous. That here was a clear fact proved from the evidence of the guilty party, of aiding, abetting, and having intercourse with the self-established and declared enemies of the king and nation; and he only wished his court had a longer arm to reach such a sort of treason; that if Mr. Macurdy, Mr. Johnson, and Mr. Ridley, were dissatisfied with the decree, they might appeal if they dared."[48]

5. *Le Grand Terrein*

---

<u>Legal issues to watch for</u>

❖ Using letter of marque granted after prize capture
❖ Use of admiralty droits
❖ Whether to granting part of prize to non-commissioned privateer

---

In November 1778, the case of *Le Grand Terrein*, a French ship captured on August 9th by the British privateer *Tartar*, came before the court of admiralty. The ship had sailed from French controlled islands in the Caribbean, with a cargo of cotton, rice, indigo, and tobacco, but the latter item was written up as coffee and sugar on the bills of lading, for fear of seizure by the British as produce of the new world. The privateer had a

---

[48] The Renard, Decisions in the High Court of Admiralty, 1 H. & M.

commission to seize American ships and had applied for one against French shipping, but this was only granted on August 10th, the day after it had captured the French prize.

The admiralty advocate and proctor asserted that because the ship was not commissioned at the time of the seizure against French shipping, the rights to the ship should become a droit of the admiralty. In 1665, the king had given the Admiralty several droits (rights) regarding ships in various cases, retaining the rights to commissioned ships sailing against the country's enemies. The Admiralty got the permanent rights to ships and cargos made prize by non-commissioned captures, as well as to wrecks, and flotsam and jetsam. The court agreed, saying for privateers to act upon commission not yet granted would set a dangerous precedent, leading to all kinds of pirates and other applying for commissions or letters of marque.

The court also ruled it was not worthwhile to examine the tobacco on board the ship separately from the other cargo. While it may turn out to be American produce, the captors could not claim that having possession of the tobacco after the commission for French ships was in hand gave them any right, "for the property of prizes vests or not at the time of taking."[49] Moving the prize from one port to another, in this case from Torbay to Jersey, did not increase the captors' rights. The captors also claimed that, for purpose of encouraging captures of enemy ships, the court should award them at least part of the ship and cargo. Marriot, in reply, said somewhat sarcastically,

> "In regard to encouragement, that was a matter of petition and reference. The court (under a former judge) had rewarded amply, two clear thirds to uncommissioned captors; but more might and would be given by the court, under circumstances of greater merit, as in cases of fighting, and extraordinary bravery. The court will adhere to no one general precedent, but all the king's true subjects, who shall engage the actual enemy, although without commission, shall be amply rewarded; and it is, therefore, only now a contention, not on the part of the Board of Admiralty, tending (as was said) to discourage the

---

[49] Le Grand Terrein, Decisions in the High Court of Admiralty, 1 H. & M.

public service, but a struggle of the agent of the privateer, attacking the collector of admiralty droits, who shall have the agency. The captors seem to go out of the way to get that which they might have in the common road, at a less expense."[50]

6. *La Prosperite, or Welfaren*

| Legal issues to watch for |
|---|
| ❖ General carriers making general claims to prize cargo |
| ❖ Claimants must take risk of cargo |
| ❖ Destination port and lack of documents indicating smuggling |

The ship *La Prosperite,* or also *Welfaren*, sailing under a French pass, was captured by the British privateer *Tyger*, on the voyage from Nantz to Dunkirk. The master of the ship, Ljbvien Gotthard Matheisen, claimed it at the libel for the city of Lubeck Germany, and claimed the cargo generally. The specific claimants for the cargo included Martinus Tak of Flanders for ten bales of handkerchiefs and Mr. Dutihl of the Netherlands for a quantity of brandy. Both asserted these items of cargo were for their accounts but not their risk. Coffee, linen, and cotton-wool were for the account of Mr. Rocca, from Spain. All the bills of lading were defective in not naming at whose risk the goods were shipped.

There was much discussion at court about whether common carriers like this could put in general claims for the goods, to be followed up by specific claimants to the cargo. There was also concern by the libelants that this allowed the claimants to inspect all the documents and create new claims. The court said it was necessary, in the case of neutral common carriers like in this case, to allow them to make general claims to the cargo. This then allowed those with a specific interest in the various items of cargo to arrive later and make their own claims. The court also did not agree with trying to keep the evidence away from neutral cargo owners, that they should have the ability to view the necessary documents to make their claims.

---

[50] *Id.*

The court also said, though, that those making specific claims were required to show that the goods were not only on their account but also at their risk. They should also show that none of the Britain's current enemies would have an interest in the cargo if the cargo were released by the court and delivered to its port of destination. If the court allowed claims based upon one's account without any risk, then this would be used to cover up trade with France or America. It was also important consider the port of destination. As Dunkirk was a known smuggling location, even if the goods were not being sent to an enemy, they would likely end up being smuggled, and as such could not be returned to the claimants.

The claimants for the varied items of cargo brought their cases in the court's sitting in February 1779. The first was Tak, who produced a certificate from magistrates in the Netherlands that the handkerchiefs were his property, and no French person had an interest in them. However, while the bill of lading mentioned acquittances for the duties to be owed in France, these were not introduced as evidence by Tak. The court interpreted this to mean that he likely intended to smuggle these goods into England from France. Mr. Dutihl offered no further evidence regarding the brandy. Mr. Rocca produced merely a notarial document outlining the intended voyage of his goods from Barcelona, but this was objected to, as his declaration was not made under oath. The court ruled the cargo condemned,

> "The court observed that the whole cargo carried with it the appearance of a smuggling transaction. If parties equivocate, or do not make oath in their own person, or produce those material documents which clearly did exist on board, or must be now in their hands, it is unnecessary to inquire what the nature of those acquittances was; for it must be presumed that they were made out for the enemy and his property; otherwise why conceal or subduct them? No affidavits of property can aver against a positive proof of subduction of titles on board the, ship, and which were in custody of the master, especially such titles being public instruments."[51]

---

[51] La Prosperite, Decisions in the High Court of Admiralty, 1 H. & M.

7. *The Wanderingsman* and *The Veranderen*

| Legal issues to watch for |
|---|
| ❖ Return of ships to neutral masters |
| ❖ Payment for consuming cargo |
| ❖ Condemnation of enemy laders, consigners, or exporters |

The *Wanderingsman* was a Swedish ship, sailing from Brittany to Sweden, which was captured by the privateer *Resolution*. The ship and cargo were then claimed by Swedish merchants as neutral property. There were three bills of lading, which described different scenarios, originating with French citizens. The first was for wine and vinegar, on the account of the merchants but with the risk unclear. The second was for various goods, which did not specify on whose account or risk they sailed. The third was for salt, on the account and risk of the merchants. There was also coffee aboard, on the account and risk of French merchants in Bordeaux. The master also said that he had a stake in some of the cargo.

The court ruled that there was no need for further proof on the first bill of lading, especially as the captors had drank some of it. But for the second bill required more evidence, while the third for the salt was restored to the claimants. The coffee was condemned, as it was the property of a French merchant, but with freight charges deducted. The court ruled that the ship should be returned to the master, that even though he had some interest in the cargo, it was not unusual for masters to have such an interest. The captor was allocated the cost of the hogshead of wine that they had drunk, payable to the master.

The *Veranderen* (Change) was a Dutch and Prussian owned ship, traveling from Bordeaux to Dunkirk, with a Dutch master and Prussian crew that was captured by the privateer *Two Brothers*. On examination of the master, it turned out he had purchased his Dutch citizenship and was Prussian, as was the vessel. So, the ship was returned to the master, a part owner, as belonging to a neutral. The cargo on board that was laden by French merchants Amand and Son, to the risk and account of other French consignees. Claims on the cargo were entered by different individuals, one was an Austrian national who claimed that his goods were privileged by treaty aboard a Dutch ship.

The court noted that the bills of lading did not specify any of these claimants. The pass the ship was traveling under was not in the form required by treaty, as the master had not taken a witnessed oath. The pass had been acquired for the master by the broker who loaded the ship. The ship was not Dutch and had never been in the Netherlands. The cargo was condemned if it was the property of the French laders (the master testified that the cargo was on the account of the laders), of the French consignees, or was for export to French controlled areas in the Americas. Bond for export had given at a French custom house, based on several acquittances.

8.   *The Rebecca*

| Legal issues to watch for |
|---|
| ❖   Claim for recapture of ship by former owner |
| ❖   Evidence needed to prove national ownership |
| ❖   Evidence of loyalist expulsion beyond reject loyalty oaths |

In August 1778, an American ship, the *Rebecca*, traveling from Charleston to Bordeaux, was captured by two British privateers, *The Duchess of Kingston* and *Triumph*. The ship was claimed by its former owner, John Strettel, as a recapture, saying he had purchased the ship in 1776, and in 1777 it was captured by an American privateer. Three men put in claims to the cargo of indigo and tobacco, asserting that they were banished loyalists not subject to the Prohibitory Act. The captors responded that these three men were merely acting as exiled loyalists to avoid the Prohibitory Act provisions, and the ship here was 300 tons burden, while the paperwork for Strettel's purchase showed a ship's burden of only 180 tons.

The court ruled the loyalists, who either refused to take the oath of allegiance in South Carolina or had sufficient letters explaining their situation, were exempted from having their cargo confiscated, as it was their necessary support. The rice in the cargo was condemned as American produce. The ship itself had several claims and counterclaims. The captors noted that there was no affidavit from anyone who had inspected the ship, just Strettel's affidavit and the bill of sale, with an ordinary warranty included. The court said that the warranty did not prove title, as the sellers could have just been acting as attorneys. Evidence was needed that the sellers had title, such as the ship's register, to prove it was British, and not American, property.

The captors tried to introduce an affidavit from Mr. Chase, the master of the *Rebecca*, who claimed that the ship was foreign owned, saying

> "the ship belonged to Quakers at Philadelphia; that Catton, being an eighth part-owner of the ship, and the remainder being the property of the Quakers, on the first news of the prohibitory act, the ship being then at Falmouth, set off for London, and there made a false bill of sale, with a view to prevent the ship being seized by government, and then sailed with false papers for St. Kitt's, where he took in a lading of sugars, when he was met by the American privateer, and the cargo was condemned at Dartmouth, in Massachusetts Bay, as British property, and the ship as having carried on trade with Great Britain, and for having fired upon two American privateers."[52]

The court rejected this evidence, produced on the same day as the preliminary inspection of the crew took place in Guernsey, as highly irregular, castigating the commissioner who took it and insisted only on the use of the standing interrogatories. Instead, the court ruled the ship to be British and so a recapture, because under the privateering act directed at American ships (discussed above), any British ship that was retaken from the Americans was to be restored to its original owner, in this case, Strettel.

*9.   The Lucretia and The Sarah and Bernhardus*

| Legal issues to watch for |
|---|
| ❖   Determining captor when same prize taken twice by British ships |
| ❖   Allocating prize between captor and re-captor |
| ❖   When military cargo is contraband |

During passage from Charleston to Surinam, the *Lucretia*, an American ship, was captured by the commissioned privateer *Thynne*. With a prize

---

[52] The Rebecca, Decisions in the High Court of Admiralty, 1 H. & M.

crew onboard, they sailed the *Lucretia* for ten days before being recaptured by an American privateer, which had the *Lucretia* for thirteen days. Then it was in turn recaptured by Royal Navy ships and sent in for condemnation. The naval captors insisted that this was not a recapture, limited by statute for navy ships to 1/8 the value but was instead an American prize, as the *Thynne* had lost possession of it. And that the property could not vest in the *Thynne*, as the *Lucretia* had never been condemned. The original captors from the *Thynne* argued based on prior admiralty caselaw that in cases like this, all subsequent takings are considered recaptures.

The court found this case to be unique and that if the *Thynne* had not acquired property in the prize because they never brought it into court, the same was true of the American privateer who recaptured it. The court's opinion was that all captures belong to the crown, until such time as they are lawfully condemned. But that the prize act had taken away the crown's right to the prize, such that the *Thynne* should lawfully be considered the captor of the *Lucretia*. The naval ships should be considered the re-captors of the *Lucretia*, but instead of salvage fee limited to the usual 1/8, they should share half the value, with the original captor receiving the other half.

The privateer *Active* had captured a neutral Danish ship, the *Sarah and Bernhardus*, which was carrying a cargo of deal (boards of wood), fourteen carriage guns (cannon), and 8,000 iron shot. The ship traveled from Norway, with a first stop in Le Havre France, with orders to sell the wood there and the cannon and shot if possible but if orders were not sufficient, then to return home. The ship was then to proceed to Portsmouth England, if the winds were against them, and try and sell the cargo there. The cargo was claimed by the Danish widow Ancker and her sons, which was intended to be delivered to merchants in Le Havre. The court found that the Danish ship did not have bad intent, as there was no war with France notified to it at that time of sailing. The ship was ordered restored to the family but as much of the cargo as was needed would be sold for the crown's military use. The cargo was not considered contraband, as specified under the third article of 1660 treaty with Denmark, as war with France was not declared at the time of the capture.

## 10. The Juffrouw Gerarda and Le Theodore and The Postilion

| Legal issues to watch for |
|---|
| ❖  Need to inspect passport of neutral ship |
| ❖  Current residence proves nationality |
| ❖  Privilege afforded to enemy residing in neutral country |

A Dutch ship, the *Juffrouw Gerarda* (Miss Gerarda), was captured by the British privateer *Joseph*, while traveling from Rotterdam to Le Havre. The privateer, to avoid being levied costs and damages for the capture of the ship, asserted that the master of the *Juffrouw Gerarda* had refused to provide his passport. The master, Mr. Stoffels, counterclaimed that he had offered all his papers but that the privateer's commander had only looked through his bills of lading, handing the remaining documents back. He was also not examined by the responsible commissioners for several months after being brought to port in England. The court said that it was the duty of any privateer to ask to see the passport of a neutral ship. Not having done that, the court ruled the ship and cargo restored and allocated full costs and damages against the privateer.

A privateer had stopped *Le Theodore* on a voyage from St. Domingo to Nantz and the court had condemned the ship and general cargo as being French. Two passengers made claims for their money, jewels, and clothes they had with them when their baggage and bodies were searched. They claimed to be citizens of Germany and Tuscany. The court however ruled that they were residents of the French isle of St. Domingo, going to France on a French ship, and therefore were liable to having their goods condemned as belonging to the enemy. It was not place of birth but their having resided there for some time that classified them for these purposes. They had no family back in Europe and were not being barred from returning to the French isles, like some of the American loyalists expatriating from the former British colonies.

The German ship, *Postilion*, with a French owner and master, M. Lienau, was brought before the court for condemnation. He was currently living as a resident of Hamburg. The captor sought the condemnation based up the French nationality of M. Lienau. The court, however, ruled that because he was a resident of Hamburg and therefore a neutral, the ship and cargo should be restored to him, and the privateer allocated costs and damages. The court used the example of a German residing in France, who would be subject to having his goods condemned, as the privateering statute applied to all inhabitants of territories controlled by France. In the opposite situation, with a Frenchman residing in Germany, he should be given the protection afforded those in that neutral state.

## B.    Trials before Courts of Vice Admiralty

*1. Amsterdam Post*

---

<u>Legal issues to watch for</u>

❖   Use of neutral nationality to mask ownership of vessel
❖   Taking prize to a port with an admiralty judge with a commission
❖   Cargo not on vessel condemned

---

In August 1740, during the War of Austrian Succession, a libel for the ship *Amsterdam Post* was brought by Philip Dumaresq, commander of the privateer *Young Eagle* at the Boston court of vice admiralty. The libel noted that with the acquired letters of marque and reprisal against ships from Spain, he had captured the ship *Amsterdam Post* off the Canary Islands. He claimed that the ship belonged to the Spanish and carried two sets of papers, one as a Spanish ship, to deal with Spanish privateers and one as a neutral Dutch ship, to deal with English privateers. Robert Auchmuty was the admiralty judge and Jonathan Read was the attorney general of the colony leading the libel. When asked who had claims, Jacob Wendell claimed the ship for merchant Peter Devernet of Amsterdam and the cargo for Devernet and his son Isaac, who resided in Tenerife.

The ship had a British commander, Aeneas Mackay, who had been naturalized as a Dutch citizen. The ship had traveled from Spain to Ireland, taken on cargo such as beef, fish, butter, hides, candles, hats, and soap, for the return journey to Tenerife. John Rous, the lieutenant of the *Young Eagle*, stated that the master had told him that the ship had worked the Spain to Ireland route, that until recently it was an English ship, that there was plenty of water on board the ship, so they had no need to stop where they were seized to take on more water, and that the ship had only adopted Dutch colors after the war between Britain and Spain began. He also described that an English Mediterranean pass (used by English ships to avoid certain Barbary pirates) and a Spanish clearance for an English ship were found onboard.

Capt. Dumaresq testified that in Gibraltar, he was told by the admiralty judge that he had no current commission to try any prize captures. Going then to Madeira, an official came onboard the prize from the local judge of the poor, who confiscated the cargo as needed locally. There were then many documents introduced to try to demonstrate one version of events or another. This included a letter from magistrates in the Netherlands declared that Mackay had taken an oath that the vessel was owned by a Dutch national and no one else, a let pass and a tonnage certificate from the admiralty in Amsterdam, Mackay's naturalization oath and Amsterdam house lease, a certificate that the goods onboard the ship matched the manifest, the captain's journal and crew statements about their travels between Ireland and Spain, and a certificate from various Tenerife merchants claiming Mackay had always sailed with Dutch colors.

Auchmuty condemned both the ship and the cargo, ruling that the vessel was British, manned by a British crew, as shown by the English Mediterranean pass granted to Mackay by the Admiralty. He said Mackay acquired the Dutch citizenship and the Dutch papers, sailed to Ireland, and bought the cargo and then planned to return to Spain, with two sets of bills of lading, one stating that the cargo was to be delivered to a fictious person in Madeira and the other that the cargo was to be delivered to Devernet in Tenerife, implying that Isaac Devernet and his deceased brother residing in Spain were the likely owners. He also said that despite the cargo being forced off the ship in Madeira by the local officials, it was still proper to condemn it, along with the vessel, for the benefit of the privateer captors.

2.   *Princess of Orange* and *Le Levrier* and *Elizabeth*

| Legal issues to watch for |
| --- |
| ❖   Use of false passes and neutral colors |
| ❖   Seizing a ship under a flag of truce |
| ❖   Intervention in libel by a government official |

In June 1741, during the same war, the *Princess of Orange*, a snow class of ship led by Juan Milidony, was captured by the privateer *George* around Aruba. The prize was in turn captured by Royal Navy ships but returned when the identity of her original captor was determined. She was sailing with a cargo of wine from Tenerife, on Dutch passes but there were no Dutch seamen aboard, just Spanish. Capt. Seth Drummond of the *George* had also captured another prize which was renamed the *Victory*, led by Capt. John Sibbald, which brought the prize into Philadelphia. The libel came before judge Andrew Hamilton of the vice admiralty court. Drummond subsequently dying, Sibbald was named captain of the *George* and the one who initiated the libel.

Milidony produced a bill of sale from him to a Dutch merchant named Peter Doscher. There was a letter from Doscher, with instructions to the consignee Mr. Mastere, for the sale of his part of the cargo and the ship itself in Caracao, sale of the captain's part of the cargo if he should die, and what to do if the ship could not be sold (supply for a return voyage to Europe). Affidavits from the crew asserted that the Dutch passes and colors were false, and that the cargo was owned by Spanish merchants. One of the seamen, Gaspas Fajardo, claimed that the ship was built in Ireland and taken prize by a Spanish privateer, and sold to Milidony. The cargo instead belonged to two natives of Tenerife (see Chapter 3 for the bills of lading). Another testified to the same facts, and that Milidony had told them that their Dutch pass and colors should protect them from the English. The ship and cargo were condemned by the court.

In 1747, Capt. Arthur Helm's privateer *Polly* captured the French ship *Le Levrier* (Greyhound) off St. Christopher, despite the ship having a pass from British general Matthews at Barbados, for the exchange of 40 prisoners from Martinique, and flying a flag of truce. The prize ship was sent into St. Christopher, libeled, and then acquitted. However, the property taken from French passengers was sent to New York, where it mixed with a suit requested by the French consul against Capt. Helm for seizing the *Le Levrier* in violation of a flag of truce. His defense was that the prisoners had been offloaded prior to meeting the privateer, so something seemed suspicious. The court, in September 1747 and January 1748, ruled that while the property taken was a lawful prize, the captain was liable for the loss of use of the ship during the six days from its capture until its release.

The ship *Elizabeth* was captured by the privateer *Knowles*, whose Capt. Seth Place tried to libel it in New York in May 1748. The collector of customs, Mr. Kennedy, asserted that she was not a prize but a violator of the navigation laws, by flying a false flag of truce, and he would initiate his own libel against the ship. The claimant, Bartholomew Fabre, asserted that she was a lawful cartel (large prisoner exchange), flying a flag of truce. The court first had to deal with a petition from the crown for William Smith to represent them but as he was Place's lawyer, it was rejected, and Benjamin Nicoll was appointed. The court ruled that neither Place nor Kennedy had produced sufficient evidence and so acquitted the ship.

The court did not allow the customer collector to intervene directly in the libel. The ship, being in poor condition, was to be sold at Fabre's request, with proceeds to the owners, net of costs. It came out in later proceedings, in May 1751, that Place and Fabre had made an agreement, to allow the taking of the ship and cargo, except for certain parts of the cargo that Fabre owned. The court later ruled that as this was not a legal capture, no part of the cargo that remained with Place could be condemned. This allowed Kennedy to seize it for violating the customs laws, for the 54 hogsheads of sugar condemned by Kennedy's libel.

3.  *Le Heureuse* and *Speedwell and Confirmation*

---

### Legal issues to watch for

❖  Actions necessary for onlookers to share in a prize
❖  Recapture periods and locations under a peace proclamation
❖  Salvage fee due if recapture outside allowed period

---

The privateer *Royal Catherine* captured the ship *Le Heureuse* (The Happy) with Royal Navy ships *Brave Hawk* and *Phoenix* nearby. In the libel in New York by Capt. John Burgess, in July 1748, both the naval ships tried to intervene to claim a share, but the privateer resisted their involvement in the capture. The *Phoenix* was about three leagues to the leeward and in sight of the prize, whose crew claimed that they did not surrender because of the *Phoenix* and would not have surrendered because of her presence, only doing so because of the power of the *Royal Catherine*. The *Brave Hawk* seemed to be too far away and could not be distinguished. Given that neither naval ship had an impact on the capture, the court ruled for the privateer.

As the court stated the rule,

"It is the Common Received opinion that one Privateer being in sight when Another Privateer takes a Prize; she that is in sight is entituled to a Share tho she did not fight, neither was Aiding or assisting. All Cases of the Kind Depend on the particular Circumstances of each Case. If one Privateer attacques the Enemy, and another Vessell is in sight, and her bearing down upon the Enemy is the reason that the Enemy Strikes to the Privateer, that vessell in justice ought to be entituled to a share tho she was a Merchantman, because it was through her means that the Privateer became possessed, but being in Sight only cannot entitle them to a share, except the enemy be Intimidated by them. For it is plain except I am aiding and assisting in taking a Prize, I ought not in Justice to be Intituled to a share."[53]

The *Royal Catherine* later brought two recaptured ships, the *Speedwell*, and the *Confirmation*, to libel, in October 1748. The ships had

---

[53] Le Heuseuse, Cases in the vice admiralty in the province of New York.

been captured by the French and then recaptured after the royal proclamation to cease hostilities, per claimant Joseph Haynes. Even if this was true, the privateer asserted a right to a salvage fee. The proclamation had different time frames, based on where in the world a capture took place, determining whether a prize had to be restored. The further from England, the longer the time allowed for word of the cessation of hostilities to reach them. The claimants asserted that the capture happened north of Cape St. Vincent and six weeks after the proclamation, so the ships were liable to be automatically restored by the French and could not therefore be legally recaptured by the privateer.

The court noted, in February 1749, that the prizes had already been condemned, as agreed by the libelants and the claimants, before word of the cessation of hostilities reached New York. The judge, Lewis Morris, Jr., then reviewed the proclamation and said the period of six weeks was for ships at a distance more than the distance from England to Cape St. Vincent, not for being north of the latitude of Cape St. Vincent. As the ships had been quite a bit further away than that, the time limit of six weeks did not apply, and so the ships were legally recaptured before the end of hostilities. The prior condemnation of the ships would stand unless overturned on appeal.

*4. Ave Marie and Sambo St. Frerar and Experience*

| Legal issues to watch for |
|---|
| ❖  Entitlement to additions made to a recapture |
| ❖  Fraud during a libel re-addressed in later proceedings |
| ❖  Flying false colors during an attack |

The privateer *Hester* captured the Spanish ship *Ave Maria*, which had previously been the British ship *Lark* before capture by the Spanish, so it was a recapture. Under the statute, a recapture was returned to her former owner. However, in this case, the Spanish had added to the *Lark*, so the question during the libel, in July 1748, was whether the additions were the property of the former owner or the re-captor? The court read the privateering statute of 1740, emphasizing that in a recapture what is restored is the ship and goods that existed at the time the ship was taken.

The ruling was that the Spanish owned goods on the ship and the additions made to the *Ave Maria* belonged to the captors, the ship net of the additions was to be returned to the original British owners, and the salvage fee payable for restoration was one-half the value.

The Spanish ship *Sambo St. Frerar* was captured by the British privateer *Morning Star* off Haiti, by Capt. Linus King. and brought to New York for condemnation, in December 1748. As there were no claimants, the condemnation was successful. In April 1749, the petition of Manuel Joseph Dele Mar was read in court, asserting that the ship had been captured illegally, that the only person brought from the ship was a cabin boy not old enough to testify, and the Spanish interpreter used was not the usual one employed by the court. Noting that the time of appeal had already expired, the court nevertheless defended both the use of the selected interpreter (the usual interpreter was occupied) and the cabin boy, at the age of 16, seemed old enough to answer interrogatories. Nonetheless, the court was willing to bring King into court to answer against the accused illegalities.

The privateer *Rainbow*, flying French colors, captured the *Experience*, whose crew had abandoned it. In libeling the ship, Capt. William Johnson was seeking either to condemn the ship, if it was not British, or claim salvage fees, if it was. As the ship had been abandoned, the first question for the court was whether the ship was derelict. The crew of the *Experience* knew the rule that, while allowing a privateer to fly a false flag during a chase, when firing a cannon, a ship needed to hoist its true colors. The crew of the *Experience* believed they were being attacked by a true French ship and so went ashore on the English coast. This being so, they could not have been in an act of leaving the ship permanently behind as a derelict. The court ruled instead that the ship and cargo should be returned to its owner, as it had been captured through the illegal conduct of the privateer, by firing while under false colors.

5.  *Le Bon Recontre* and *Susanna*

| Legal issues to watch for |
| --- |
| ❖  Handling multiple libelants |
| ❖  Priority of crown over other claimants |
| ❖  Fee for services provides to prize ship in distress |

With the start of the Seven Years' War, the enemy was now the French and no longer the Spanish. The British privateer *Maxwell* and American *St. Stephen* seized the French ship *Il Le Bon Recontre* (The Good Encounter) and brought the prize into New York. Neither of the two ships had letters of marque, so while in New York harbor, Capt. John Crew of the American privateer *Fox* came aboard the ship and claimed her. The commissioners of the Admiralty, knowing that they had droits for ships captured by non-commissioned privateers, initiated a libel, followed by a libel by Crew, in April 1757. The court ruled there can only be one libelant between the two, the other must be a claimant. Which of the two was properly libelant and claimant which would be determined by the facts of the case, so the court designated the earlier filer, the commissioners of the Admiralty, as the captor, for now, and designated Crew as the claimant.

On the court's order, the ship was condemned and sold. The court ruled that Crew's claim could not deprive the crown of their rights to the effects of the ship without some affirmative action, and so dismissed their claim. The more difficult issue was between the crown and the Admiralty. The court could not rule on that until inspecting the commissioners patent and inquiring as to whether they had subsequently divested themselves of the rights acquired therein. The court turned to the Admiralty in Britain for assistance in answering that question but never received an answer. In the meantime, the judge, the king, and several of the advocates had died or moved on to other roles and the case mostly died out, with its final ruling not recorded, although the crown advocate believed that the Admiralty patents from George II had died with him and so the proceeds of the sale should go to the next king, George III.

The privateer *Mary* captured the French ship *Susana*, put a prize crew onboard, and sent the ship into port. On the way, the prize was hit by a significant storm that caused the ship to lose its masts, water, and compass and sustain significant other damage. Assistance was provided by another ship led by a Capt. Stephenson, without which the *Susana* would not have made it into port. Stephenson provided masts, put up a jury mast, provided water and a compass, took several onboard of the French prisoners to give the English a numerical advantage, and took the ship in tow. The court had to determine the compensation due to Stephenson for his assistance. The court said it did not matter if this was called a salvage fee or a quantum meruit. He was awarded a fee of sixty pounds from the proceeds of the condemnation sale of the ship and cargo, and his costs, for the services performed and relief provided to a ship in distress on the sea.

6.  *La Virgen del Rosario and King v. Miller*

Legal issues to watch for

❖  Suborning perjured testimony in support of condemnation
❖  Intercession by the king for a foreign privateering victim
❖  Termination period of privateering security

In a rather complicated case in March 1757, Richard Haddon, as commander of the privateer *Peggy*, filed a libel (shown in Chapter 3), against certain foreign coins, jewelry, indigo, and arms that had sold for more than £2,400. He claimed that he had taken these from a distressed French ship, which was then sent on its way. A Greek sailor onboard the stopped ship testified that they were essentially pirates of no leader or definite nationality but there was at least one Frenchman and so this was clearly a legal prize. Upon this testimony only, the court ruled these items were a legal prize, provided that no one came forward to claim them within one year and a day, and Haddon provided security. Within that time, Phillip Y'Bannes, a Spanish resident of Havana and owner of the ship *La Virgen del Rosario y Sancto Christo de Buen Viage* appeared, claiming that Haddon had attacked him and his ship violently to steal those items.

Further, he had passes, under charter from an Englishman, to transport two Englishmen from Havana to Jamaica, but Haddon had ignored these passes. Further, all the crew were Spanish, there was no Greek sailor, and the prior testimony given was entirely fictitious. Y'Bannes was assisted by the British secretary of state of state, who directed the governor or New York to help him. He in turn had the advocate general William Kempe, in March 1758, file a claim under the king's name, for Y'Bannes, supported by the charter party documents and affidavits from one of the English passengers. Haddon and his sureties demurred, inter alia, asserting the property belonged to a Spanish subject, not the king, and a successful claim by the king would not bar a claim against Haddon's privateering bond. The court agreed and dismissed the demurrer.

Y'Bannes did not become a party to the original libel of Haddon but instead brought his own libel against the funds in September 1758. Unfortunately, this was six months after the period for finalization of Haddon's libel had occurred. The sureties for Haddon (Haddon himself could not be found) demurred to this second libel, because the court could not reverse its own judgment or if it could, the sureties had expired with the conclusion of Haddon's libel. There was a purported appeal to the lords of the Admiralty in England but the record of it was unofficial and the judge in New York ruled that they would only be overruling the condemnation in favor of Haddon, not the libel against the sureties. Y'Bannes was free to try to find Haddon and bring him to court.

Another claim was filed against the sureties, as the case continued into 1761, charging Haddon with violating the privateering rules by not bringing the ship into port and not bringing members of the captured crew with him. Witnesses in Havana were deposed, which changed the thinking of the court, that perhaps the Spanish ship had been engaged in illegal trading activities, given its lack of paperwork and any leadership but it was finally forced to rule against the sureties in July 1761, saying,

"In This view of The Evidence I should have been of Oppinion To Acquitt The Defendants, had The cause Turned barely upon The Part of The charge of Had- dons breach of The Instructions, in The Seizure of The goods of the subjects of one of his Majesty s Allies, but unfortunately for The Defendts, The Defeat of Their Defence Lays here, first There appears To be no good Reason assigned, why The Schooner was not Brought into Port; The Danger of comeing upon This coast is Not Sufficient, Even if it had been shewn clearly, That The vessel was unfitt for Such a Voyage; for she Might have been carried To one of The west India Islands, Particularly as Jamaica, which was at no great Distance from The Place where She was. Secondly The Neglect To bring in four of The Principall Persons of The Schooners Crew, is fatal... I am Therefore of Opinion That The Instructions have been Broken by cap* Haddon, and I Do accordingly Adjudge and Decree The Penalty of the Bond given by The Defendants, To be forfeited, and The Sum of fifteen Hundred pounds Sterling To be by Them Paid To his Majesty his heirs or Successors."[54]

7.   *Conception* and *Le Soleil*

| Legal issues to watch for |
|---|
| ❖   False libel and appeal to keep sale proceeds |
| ❖   Common law courts overruling Admiralty arrest |
| ❖   Salvage fee derived from ransom demand |

The Italian ship *Conception de St. Ignatio de Loyola* was captured by the privateers *Revenge* and *Hornet* and sent for libel in New York. The perishable cargo was sold, with the proceeds held by James Depeyster and Joseph Foreman, with Napthali Hart Meyers and Matthew Clarkson as sureties. Francis Koffler appealed the decision of the court in support of the *Conception's* captain, Lorenzo Ghigliano. The court had acquitted the ship and his 1/5 of the cargo and he also was to receive freight charges. No legal work was done on the appeal and the court finally discovered that the proceeds of the sale, instead of being held until the final court decision, were paid out by Depeyster and Foreman to the libelants.

The court ordered the arrest of the agents and sureties, but they were freed by a common law court on a writ of habeas corpus. So, the court decided to acquit the rest of the cargo, directing that the proceeds of the sale and the gold money found on the ship be given to Don Francisco Xavier de los Rios, a merchant of Cadiz. Koffler tried to appeal but Capt. Ghigliano had sued the four agents and sureties directly. They either had to post bail or go to jail, so they decided to settle and pay him back, in November 1758. A few months later they also settled with de los Rios. This

---

[54] Rex v Miller, Cases in the vice admiralty in the province of New York.

appeared to be a scheme where the privateer libellants got to use this prize money interest free for more than a year.

Privateers *St. George* and *Oliver Cromwell* captured French ships *Le Soleil* (the Sun) and *Le Jazon*, respectively. When capturing the prizes, there was a hostage onboard who was being held for the payment of a ransom. The prizes were libeled and condemned, with the court awarding, in November 1758, a salvage fee equal to one half of the ransom demand. *Le Soleil*, a privateer, had previously captured the British ship *Content*, and freed the ship upon receiving one hostage and a bill of exchange worth £100. It was that bill of exchange that the privateer captors were to receive one half of. It is not clear how the court intended to enforce the payment of the bill for parties outside its jurisdiction.

8.   *San Joseph* and *St. Jacques*

| Legal issues to watch for |
| --- |
| ❖  Suing privateering who violates his instructions |
| ❖  Sureties paying for privateering violations |
| ❖  Method for splitting proceeds of a prize |

The privateer *Black Snake* captured the Spanish ship *San Joseph* and initiated a libel in Rhode Island, but the ship and cargo were acquitted, as Spain was not an enemy in this war. The ship, under master Antonio de la Rosa, took on goods in Haiti, sailed for Mexico, and was stopped by the privateer *Oliver Cromwell* but with the paperwork recently checked in Rhode Island, was let go. The ship was then stopped again by the privateer *Revenge*, whose Capt. James Griffith read the same papers but decided to libel the ship. It was subsequently lost on the voyage to port. De la Rosa asked the New York government to sue Griffith's sureties for the loss of ship and cargo, on his bond of £1,500.

A libel against the sureties, Richard Sharpe and Matthew Clarkson, produced proof that the ship and its cargo were worth £3,700. The privateer instructions for this war had clearly told captains not to molest or take Spanish ships, except for any contraband they carried. The respondent's advocates, including John Morin Scott and William Livingston, argued that the inclusion of French goods from Haiti justified seizing and sending the ship in to port as a prize, and further, the ship was lost due to an act of God outside their control. The libelant's advocate, William Smith, said that the issue was one merely of Spanish ownership, which was undoubted, and Spain had the right to trade with France. The court ruled that the ship was clearly Spanish, as was the owner, and that Griffith's sureties must pay £1,500.

Two privateers, the *Oliver Cromwell* and the *Polly*, were involved in the capture of the French ship *St. Jacques*. The ship surrendered to the *Oliver Cromwell*, so the *Polly* was only a claimant in the libel. The court had to first determine whether the Polly's actions entitled that ship to a share. It ruled the ship was in sight and the actions in sailing and rowing up before the attack entitled its crew to a share. The court then devised a formula based on burthen and men aboard during boarding to calculate the relative proceeds of each ship. The *Oliver Cromwell* was 180 tons and had 60 men, while the *Polly* was 40 tons and had 30 men, so the former ship would receive 240 of 310 parts and the *Polly* 70 of 310 parts of the prize.

9.   *Catherine* and *Seahorse* and *Margretta*

| Legal issues to watch for |
| --- |
| ❖   Nationality indicated by various roles of the master |
| ❖   Paying the libelant's costs |
| ❖   Inconsistencies do not overcome the presumption |

In 1762, the ship *Catherine* was brought to libel in New York, having been captured by the privateer *Enterprise*. The ship had been sailing from New York to Haiti, sold her cargo, and loaded new cargo of sugar and indigo, heading for Connecticut. Although the nominal captain was American, the master, who also acted like the supercargo and owner, was French, M. Jerbeau. Many of the crew were French and English speakers from Jersey and Guernsey. The capture occurred in New London, based on the assertion that it was a French ship. No claim was made in the libel. And the last ship's registration was in New York. The court said that although the ship appeared nominally to be American, under British domain, given the lack of papers, the fact the captain did not testify, that there was no claim made, the testimony of the seamen that M. Jerbeau seemed to oversee everything on the voyage, and French produce onboard, led the court to believe it was a French ship, and so condemned the ship and cargo.

The ship *Seahorse*, owned by an American in Boston, had sailed to the Caribbean shortly before the war between Spain and England started in 1762. It was captured by a French privateer, which inflicted damage to it and took a hostage until a ransom was paid. Upon finally arriving in Monti Cristi, the commander of the *Seahorse*, Capt. Kirkwood, discovered that his consignee was in jail, and he was not able to trade with the local inhabitants or repair his ship. Finding another ship from the same owner in port, Kirkwood was able to do some trading, but still could not make the necessary repairs. Unable to return to Boston, the *Seahorse* instead went to a nearby French port, to trade the rotting meat in its cargo to purchase supplies, repairs, and some sugar. On the way home, it was captured by the privateer *Mars* and sent in for libel. The court said that the ownership of the *Seahorse* was clearly American, and so acquitted the ship and cargo but insisted that the libelant was correct to seize her, requiring the owner to pay the libelant's costs.

In October 1762, a libel was initiated against the ship *Margretta & Sarah*, taken by the privateer *Mars* off Cape Francois. The ship was presumedly owned by a Dutchman, but the bills of lading did not have a destination and so the cargo was also assumed to belong to the ship's owner. With the significant use of neutral ships to avoid seizure by privateers, the court's presumption was that the ship, coming from a French port with French produce, was French until proven otherwise. The court ruled that this presumption had not been overcome,

> "Examining the Documents and proofs I do not think there is Sufficient Evidence for the Claimant to Take it off. Among the Documents there are two Bills of Lading showing that the Cargoe was taken in at St. Eustatia. How that was Occasioned is not Accounted for and certainly that Suggestion is not True, the place of Destination is Left Blanck, which is unusual and it may be conjectured that it was with Design to have an Opportunity of filling them up at Sea as might best Suit the Safety of the Vessell and Cargoe. Be that as it will, they do not Agree

with some of the Other Documents, which Ought all in good Faith to Speak the Same Language.

As to the Witnesses they are Interested tho Loyall by the Statute, yet Suspicious, Fritz 's Declaration that he Carried the money to St. Kitts to pay for the Vessell, seems Inconsistant with the Paper Proving the Transferr to be at St. Eustatia where the Vessell was with her pretended Owner; the Same Document Shows that Pennistons title was Gained the 27th Feby Last, and yet Bernard Swears that the Sloop belonged to him about two years ago, for so Long he says he has Known her and that Ever since he Knew her she was Pennistons. Such weak and In consistent proofs cannot be Sufficient to Oppose to the Generall presumption which is Strengthened by that Inconsistancy; And the other Circumstance of the Sloops being so Unusually Armed with Eight Cannon, 12 Swivell a Number of Small Arms and a Crew of Different nations More than Sufficient to navigate So Small a Vessell. Her Condition Seems to Indicate Fear, and a Design to Oppose a Visitation by Vessells of Inferiour force for which a Dutch Vessell could have no Reason in those Seas."[55]

*10. America and Polly and Hester*

---

### Legal issues to watch for

❖ Seizures under the Prohibitory Act
❖ Violation of the act, even without knowledge of it
❖ Awards to re-captors of American ships

---

After the passing of the Prohibitory Act at the end of 1775, which banned all trade with the American colonies, the British were looking for such ships. The ship *America* was captured by the warship *Cruizer* and brought before the court of admiralty in North Carolina and judge James E. Bowen, in a libel initiated by the *Cruizer's* commander, Francis Parry. The accusation was that the ship imported rum and salt into the colonies, in violation of the Prohibitory Act. The commander of the *America*, Robert Cunningham, claimed that Englishmen loyal to the king owned the ship. He said his ship sailed from North Carolina with a cargo of lumber for

---

[55] The Margretta, Cases in the vice admiralty in the province of New York.

Barbados in October 1775, before the Prohibitory Act was passed. He then took on a cargo of salt and upon arriving back in North Carolina in February 1776, had his men impressed, and his papers seized.

He claimed that the two of the hogsheads of rum where owned by two of the crew and the third was for normal allowance for drinking by the crew. He asked for the ship and cargo to be acquitted. The crew testified to the normal use of rum on such voyages. The agent for the merchants testified they were friends of the government and that their agent was currently imprisoned by the rebels for supplying gunpowder to the British. Opposing this, Parry noted that some of the rum had been sold to men of another ship while in North Carolina and there was no clearance certificate. The court, in May 1776, judged this ship to be a lawful prize, condemned it, its tackle, and apparel, and ruled that it should be sold at public auction for the highest price. After the payment of wages to the seamen onboard the ship, the net proceeds were to be paid to the commander and crew of the *Cruizer*.

Americans were sometimes involved in taking back their own captured ships. The *Polly* was carrying Indian corn, staves, and heading off North Carolina when the British ship *Lilly* captured it. The owner of the ship and cargo and the master went aboard the British ship only to be told that it was being seized as a prize. Several days later, a crew in whale boats attacked the prize crew and retook the ship and cargo. As submitted to the Continental Congress, the recommendation by the appropriate committee was that the re-captors be awarded one-third of the value of the ship and cargo, with the remainder to the present owner. Congress resolved to do just that, after a public announcement and then public auction. After deducting costs, the re-captors would receive one-third of the proceeds of the auction, in lieu of salvage, and the owners two-thirds.

After the American Revolutionary War had started, British ships could be captured under the privateering acts described in the next chapter. The *Hester* was a British ship that was captured by the American privateer *Columbus* in August 1776. A prize crew was put aboard the ship but the next month, the prize was retaken by the British ship of war *Liverpool* and taken to Nova Scotia to be libeled by its commander, Capt. Henry Bellow.

The court of admiralty, following on from the request of advocate general William Nesbitt, decreed that the owners needed to pay the re-captor one-eight of the value of the prize, a significantly lower amount than was paid to the Americans for the same act of re-capture.

# Chapter 5

# PRIVATEERING – AMERICA, HANCOCK TO LINCOLN

Privateering in America began as a reflection of the wars going on in Europe. As England, France, Spain, Portugal, and the Netherlands fought with each other, the battlefields spread to their colonies across the Americas. Privateering made its way to the new world, under English royal authority delegated to the Admiralty, to issue letters of marque and reprisal to capture prizes and to set up courts to adjudicate the prizes. Governors could issue letters of marque (as shown in Chapter 4) and could set up local vice-admiralty courts. After declaring independence in 1776, the letters of marque issued by state leaders were no longer against Britain's enemies but instead against British shipping. States were also required to create courts of admiralty to deal with the large number of prize cases that came before them. Soon, the Continental Congress would also take on a role in issuing letters of marque and importantly, would create courts of appeal for prize cases initiated in state admiralty courts.

With the founding of the republic, the United States had to define again what powers would be exercised at the state and federal levels. It was decided that Congress alone would have the power to issue letters of marque and reprisal and federal courts alone would have jurisdiction over prize cases. This led to many cases in the federal courts in the early years of the republic, trying to define for a new nation what these constitutional and legislative enactments meant. As privateering arose during conflict, it was primarily during the Napoleonic Wars and the War of 1812 when prize cases from privateer captures came before the courts. The U.S. Supreme

Court spent significant time deciding prize cases on various issues. While cases continued in the 1820s during the wars of independence in South America, by the time of the American Civil War, privateering had died out.

The first section of this chapter covers powers given to itself by the Continental Congress and then later the constitutional powers given to the U.S. Congress to issue privateering commissions and create prize courts. The financial incentives were significant for privateer owners and crews, so many legal controls were put in place, including instructions to commanders, privateering commissions, and crew agreements discussed in Chapter 3. The second section deals with the admiralty law process of libeling a ship and its cargo brought in by privateers, and the many issues considered by courts in deciding whether to condemn or acquit ships and cargo, and how claimants opposed the libelants. Constantly changing geo-political considerations influenced how courts viewed the parties, during this period from the Revolutionary War to the Civil War.

The issues courts faced included whether prize appeal courts could reexamine facts, whether common law courts could mandate prize distributions, use of American courts by foreign nationals, ownership of an abandoned prize, reliance on foreign admiralty court decisions, seizing ships of former American citizens, liability for damages if there was no reason for capture, fraudulent agreement to seize a ship, loss of insurance from change in destination, retaining control over res, seizure of goods owned by British subjects with American citizenship, use of liens to defeat captors' claims, if the government or the captor received a prize, when a ship was not a prize, effect of an enemy alien as privateer commander, claimants challenging a privateer's commission, fraud in hiding a ship's papers, collusion on capture to facilitate smuggling, captors competency to testify, lack of privateering commissions for condemnation, and claims from mortgagees.

## 5.1 STATUTES

In November 1775, Gen. George Washington sent a letter to John Hancock, then the president of the Second Continental Congress, describing how Massachusetts, where he was with the fledgling American army outside Boston, had passed a statute dealing with privateering and asked Congress to consider this,

> "As the Armed Vessells fitted at the Continental expence do not Come under this Law, I woud have it Submitted to the Consideration of Congress, to point out a more Summary way of proceeding, to determine the property, & mode of Condemnation—of Such prizes as have been, or hereafter may be made, than is Specifyed in this act. Should not a Court be established by Authority of Congress to take Cognizance of Prizes made by the Continental vessells? whatever the mode is which they are pleased to adopt, there is an absolute necessity of its being Speedily determind on."[1]

The Continental Congress, realizing the desperate need of the American patriotic cause for an ocean-bound presence, but having no real navy to speak of, turned heavily to privateering. Under laws passed by Congress, the power to issue privateering commissions and letters of marque and reprisal was to reside in Congress, and not the individual states. Congress encouraged states to set up their own courts of admiralty, to replace the now defunct British courts of vice admiralty. Congress first heard and then set up special courts of capture to handle appeals of prize cases from the state admiralty courts. With the founding of the new republic, the Constitution gave only the U.S. Congress this power to grant letters of marque and reprisal, which it would subsequently delegate to the president in every major conflict up to the Civil War. The Constitution also gave the federal courts power over all cases of admiralty and maritime jurisdiction, including libels of prizes captured by privateers.

---

[1] George Washington to John Hancock (Nov. 11, 1775).

## A. 18th Century

### 1. American Revolution

Before declaring independence, the Continental Congress had called for privateering activity and for courts of admiralty to handle prize cases. In November 1775, Congress, under the presidency of John Hancock, acted on Gen. Washington's request, as proposed by a committee of seven that included six lawyers: future U.S. president John Adams, George Wythe, Edward Rutledge, William Livingston, Thomas Johnson, and future Supreme Court justice James Wilson; and Benjamin Franklin. Congress resolved[2] that privateers could take British armed ships and transport ships, assuming these privateers had received commissions from Congress or from appropriate individuals in the colonies/states. Such prizes were to be brought to the new courts of admiralty in the colonies/states, with appeals being made to Congress.

Some of the colonies/states had quickly enacted privateering legislation, including Massachusetts, perhaps the largest source of privateers during the war, where the statute both created courts for prizes brought in by privateers, and stated that the colonial council was,

> "fully impowered to commission, with letters of marque and reprisal, any person or persons within this colony, who shall, at his or their own expence, fix out and equip, for the defence of America, any vessel[l], as also any person who shall, by the owner of such vessel[l], be recommended therefor; and that all such persons so commissioned, as aforesaid, shall have full power, with such other persons as they shall engage to their assistance, to sail on the seas, attack, take and bring into any port in this colony, all vessel[l]s offending or employed by the enemy."[3]

In late March 1776, Congress passed a series of resolutions that permitted Americans to fit out armed vessels to cruise against their enemies. The vessels and their cargo, merchandize, apparel, and tackle, if

---

[2] Journals of the Continental Congress, p. 371-75 (Nov. 25, 1775).

[3] Mass., An Act for Encouraging the Fixing Out of Armed Vessels to Defend the Seacoast of America, and for Erecting a Court to Try and Condemn All Vessels that shall be Found Infesting the Same (Nov. 1775).

belonging to inhabitants of Britain, were lawful prizes when captured by a commissioned privateer.[4] The was later to be extended to,

"to all ships and other vessels, their tackle, apparel and furniture, and all goods, wares and merchandises, belonging to any subject or subjects of the King of Great Britain, except the inhabitants of the Bermudas, and Providence or Bahama islands; or to any other person or persons who adhere to him or in any wise aid or abet him in his unjust war against these states."[5]

In early April, Congress resolved to send out blank commissions for private ships of war and letters of marque and reprisal to the representatives of the various colonies, to enlist ship owners to apply for the commissions, along with sending a bond to Congress. When applying, they had to describe the ship, its armaments and ammunition, and the commander and crew. The bond required was 5,000 dollars for a ship under 100 tons and 10,000 dollars for a larger ship. The conditions for the bonds were,

"That if the above-bounden, who is Commander of the \_\_\_\_\_, called \_\_\_\_\_, belonging to \_\_\_\_, of \_\_\_\_\_, in the colony of \_\_\_\_\_, mounting \_\_\_\_\_ carriage Guns, and navigated by \_\_\_\_\_ Men, and who hath applied for a Commission, or Letters of Marque and Reprisal, to arm, equip, and set forth to Sea, the said as a private Ship of War, and to make Captures of British Vessels and Cargoes, shall not exceed or transgress the Powers and Authorities which shall be contained in the said Commission, but shall, in all Things, observe and conduct himself, and govern his Crew, by and according to the same, and certain Instructions therewith to be delivered, and such other Instructions as may hereafter be given to him; and shall make Reparation for all Damages sustained by any Misconduct or unwarrantable Proceedings of Himself, or the Officers or Crew of the said, then this Obligation shall be void, or else remain in Force."[6]

---

[4] Journals of the Continental Congress, p. 230-32 (Mar. 23, 1776).
[5] *Id.*, p. 606 (July 24, 1776).
[6] *Id.*, p. 252-53 (Apr. 3, 1776).

The instructions that these privateer commanders had to follow were also resolved by Congress the same day, as follows,

"1. You may, by force of arms, attack, subdue, and take all ships and other vessels belonging to the inhabitants of Great Britain. on the high seas, or between high water and low water mark...

2. You may, by force of arms, attack, subdue, and take all ships... carrying soldiers, arms, gunpowder, amunition, provisions, or any other contraband goods, to any of the British armies or ships of war employed against these colonies.

3. You shall bring such ships and vessels, as you shall take, with their guns, rigging, tackle, apparel, furniture, and ladings, to some convenient port or ports of the United Colonies, that proceedings may thereupon be had, in due form, before the courts...

4. You... shall bring or send the master and pilot... to the judge or judges of such court... to be examined upon oath, and make answer to the interrogatories which may be propounded, touching the interest or property of the ship or vessel, and her lading; and, at the same time, you shall deliver... to the judge or judges, all passes, sea-briefs, charter-parties, bills of lading, cockers, letters, and other documents and writings found on board...

5. You shall keep and preserve every ship or vessel, and cargo, by you taken, until they shall, by a sentence of a court properly authorized, be adjudged lawful prizes; not selling, spoiling, wasting, or diminishing the same, or breaking the bulk thereof, nor suffering any such thing to be done.

6. If you, or any of your officers or crew, shall, in cold blood, kill or maim, or by torture or otherwise, cruelly, inhumanly, and, contrary to common usage, and the practice of civilized nations in war, treat any person or persons surprized in the ship or vessel you shall take, the offender shall be severely punished.

7. You shall... send to Congress written accounts of the captures you shall make, with the number and names of the captives, copies of your journal from time to time, and intelligence of what may occur or be

discovered concerning the designs of the enemy, and the destination, motions, and operations of their fleets and armies.

8. One-third, at least, of your whole company shall he landsmen.

9. You shall not ransom any prisoners or captives, but shall dispose of them in such manner, as the Congress, or... in the colony whither they shall be brought... direct..."[7]

The commission to be given for privateers cruising on behalf of the United States was revised the following year to read,

"The delegates of the United States of New Hampshire, Massachusetts Bay, Rhode Island, Connecticut, New York, New Jersey, Pennsylvania, Delaware, Maryland, Virginia, North Carolina, South Carolina and Georgia, to all unto whom these presents shall come, send greeting. Know Ye, That we have granted, and, by these presents, do grant, licence and authority to _____, mariner, commander of the _____, called the _____, of the burthen of _____ tons or thereabouts, belonging to _____, mounting _____ carriage guns, and navigated by _____ men, to fit out and set forth the said, in a warlike manner, and by and with the said, and the crew thereof, by force of arms, to attack, subdue, and take all ships and other vessels whatsoever, carrying soldiers, arms, gun-powder, ammunition, provisions or any other contraband goods to any of the British armies or ships of war employed against these United States.

And also to attack, seize, and take all ships or other vessels belonging to the inhabitants of Great Britain, or to any subject or subjects thereof, with their tackle, apparel, furniture and ladings, on the high seas, or between high and low water marks, (the ships or vessels, together with their cargoes, belonging to any inhabitant or inhabitants of Bermuda, Providence, and the Bahama Islands, and such other ships and vessels bringing persons with intent to settle and reside within any of the United States, or bringing arms, ammunition, or warlike stores to the said states, for the use thereof; which said ships or vessels you shall suffer to pass unmolested, the commanders thereof permitting a

---

[7] *Id.* p. 253-54.

peaceable search, and giving satisfactory information of the contents of the ladings, and destination of the voyages, only excepted,) and the said ships or vessels so apprehended as aforesaid, and as prize taken, to carry into any port or harbour within the dominions of any neutral state willing to admit the same, or into any port within the said United States, in order that the courts there instituted to hear and determine causes civil and maritime, may proceed in due form to condemn the said captures, if they be adjudged lawful prize; or otherwise according to the usage in such cases at the port or in the state where the same shall be carried.

The said _____ having given bond with sufficient sureties, that nothing be done by the said _____ or any of his officers, marines, or company thereof, contrary to, or inconsistent with the usage and customs of nations; and that he shall not exceed or transgress the powers and authorities contained in this commission. And we will and require all our officers whatsoever in the service of the United States, to give succour and assistance to the said _____ in the premises. This commission shall continue in force until the Congress shall issue orders to the contrary. Dated _____ at _____. By order of the Congress."[8]

The Articles of Confederation were approved by Congress in November 1777, although not coming into force until 1781. They mentioned the use of letters of marque several times. In Article VI, states where prohibited from issuing commissions or letter of marque and reprisal to ships of war, unless the United States had issued a declaration of war, under whose regulations such ships must operate. The one exception for state issuance of commissions was if the state were "infested by pirates."[9] In Article IX, only the United States could grant letters of marque and reprisal in times of peace, which required nine states to assent, and only the United States could establish courts of appeal in prize cases.

---

[8] *Id.* p. 339-40 (May 8, 1777).
[9] Articles of Confederation and Perpetual Union, between the States of New Hampshire, Massachusetts Bay, Rhode Island and Providence Plantations, Connecticut, New York, New Jersey, Pennsylvania, Delaware, Maryland, Virginia, North Carolina, South Carolina, Georgia (Nov. 15, 1777).

Congress would continue to urge on privateers, saying,

"That it be an instruction to the captains or commanders of privateers, to annoy the enemy by all the means in their power, by land or water, taking care not to infringe or violate the laws of nations, or the laws of neutrality."[10]

Congress would later make a proclamation, stressing the importance of not attacking neutral shipping,

"A PROCLAMATION

Whereas Congress have received information and complaints, "that violences have been done by American armed vessels to neutral nations, in seizing ships belonging to their subjects and under their colours, and in making captures of those of the enemy whilst under the protection of neutral coasts, contrary to the usage and custom of nations;"

to the end, that such unjustifiable and piratical acts, which reflect dishonour upon the national character of these states, may be in future effectually prevented, the said Congress hath thought proper to direct, enjoin and command, and they do hereby direct, enjoin and command, all captains, commanders and other officers and seamen belonging to any American armed vessels, to govern themselves strictly in all things agreeably to the tenor of their commissions, and the instructions and resolutions of Congress;

particularly that they pay a sacred regard to the rights of neutral powers and the usage and custom of civilized nations, and on no pretence whatever presume to take or seize any ships or vessels belonging to the subjects of princes or powers in alliance with these United States, except they are employed in carrying contraband goods or soldiers to our enemies, and in such case that they conform to the stipulations contained in treaties subsisting between such princes or powers and these states;

---

[10] Journals of the Continental Congress, p. 196 (Feb. 26, 1778).

and that they do not capture, seize or plunder any ships or vessels of our enemies, being under the protection of neutral coasts, nations or princes, under the penalty of being condignly punished therefor, and also of being bound to make satisfaction for all matters of damage and the interest thereof by reparation, under the pain and obligation of their persons and goods.

And further, the said Congress doth hereby resolve and declare, that persons wilfully offending in any of the foregoing instances, if taken by any foreign powers in consequence thereof, will not be considered as having a right to claim protection from these states, but shall suffer such punishment as by the usage and custom of nations may be inflicted upon such offenders."[11]

The treaty of alliance[12] with France in 1778 specified that no citizen of either country could receive a commission or letter of marque to sail against the other country. Anyone receiving such a commission or letter of marque would be considered a pirate. And neither country's ports could fit out foreign privateers under commission from an enemy of either country or allow them to sell their ships, cargoes, or merchandise. After this, but before the beginning of the republic, several treaties were signed with other countries addressing privateering. For example, a 1782 agreement between the United States and the United Provinces (the Netherlands), banned the use of privateers between the two countries, under Article 8.[13]

Article 15 of the 1783 treaty between the United States and Sweden also prohibited privateering between the two countries.[14] Article 20 of the 1785 treaty between the United States and Prussia did not allow one side to issues letters of marque against the other side if it should be involved in a war. Article 21 provided specific instructions for privateering when both countries were at war against a common enemy.[15] Article 2 of the 1786

---

[11] *Id.*, p. 486 (May 9, 1778).

[12] Treaty of Amity and Commerce Between The United States and France (Feb. 1778).

[13] Treaty of Amity and Commerce, between their High Mightinesses, the States General of the united Netherlands, and the United States of America (Sept. 1782).

[14] Treaty of Amity and Commerce between his Majesty the King of Sweden and the United States of North America (Mar. 1783).

[15] Treaty of Amity and Commerce between His Majesty the King of Prussia, and the United States of America (Sept. 1785).

treaty between the United States and Morocco did not allow a party to take privateering commissions from the enemy of the other party during a conflict.[16]

## 2.   Early Republic

The Constitution, in section 8, gave Congress the power to grant letters of marque and reprisal. This power would be delegated to the president by Congress, several times, the first of which would be during the Quasi-War with France at the end of the 18th century. The power would again be delegated to the president in the War of 1812, where privateering activity would be significant, and in the Civil War nearly 50 years later, which Union side would decide not to use. Privateering would be more prominent on the Confederate side, dictated by its lack of a navy. The Judiciary Act of 1789 gave federal district courts jurisdiction over prizes captured,

> "on waters which are navigable from the sea by vessels of ten or more tons burthen, within their respective districts as well as upon the high seas."[17]

In 1794, Britain and the United States signed the so-called Jay Treaty, which stated under Article 21 that,

> "if any Subject or Citizen of the said Parties respectively shall accept any Foreign Commission or Letters of Marque for Arming any Vessel to act as a Privateer against the other party, and be taken by the other party, it is hereby declared to be lawful for the said party to treat and punish the said Subject or Citizen, having such Commission or Letters of Marque as a Pirate."[18]

It also bound privateering commanders, under Article 19, to pay for harms they caused their captives,

> "forbear doing any Damage to those of the other party, or committing any Outrage against them, and if they act to the contrary, they shall be

---

[16] Treaty of Peace and Friendship established between the Emperor of Morocco and the United States of America (July 1786).

[17] An Act to establish the Judicial Courts of the United States, c. 1, s 1, ch. 20, §§ 9.

[18] Treaty of Amity Commerce and Navigation, between His Britannick Majesty; and The United States of America (Nov. 1794).

punished, and shall also be bound in their Persons and Estates to make satisfaction and reparation for all Damages, and the interest thereof, of whatever nature the said Damages may be."[19]

The 1795 treaty with Spain prohibited each side's citizens from taking letters of marque against the other or would be considered a pirate.[20] From 1795 to 1797, the United States signed three treaties of friendship with the Barbary states which were in large part to deal with the problem of pirates attacking American merchant ships. These treaties, one of which was renewed in 1805,[21] also essentially banned privateering activities between these countries and the United States.

In June 1797, with possible war looming against Napoleonic France, Congress tried to prohibit privateering against its allies and U.S. ships or citizens.[22] Offenders could be imprisoned for up to ten years and fined up to $10,000. This was followed shortly by an act that allowed American merchant vessels to arm themselves and resist unlawful seizures by French ships.[23] A new statute authorized the president to grant and revoke commissions for privateers against armed French ships and issue regulations for their conduct. There were requirements for providing security, specifications on how to apply, and details about ship salvage.[24]

## B.   19th Century

### 1.   War of 1812

In June 1812, Congress declared war on Britain and gave the president the power to issue commissions or letters of marque and general reprisals

---

[19] Id.

[20] Treaty of Friendship, Limits, and Navigation Between Spain and The United States (Oct. 1795).

[21] Treaty of Peace and Amity between Algeria and the United States (Sept. 1795); Treaty of Peace and Amity between Tripoli and the United States (Nov. 1796); Treaty of Peace and Amity between Tunis and the United States (Aug. 1797); and Treaty of Peace and Amity between Tripoli and the United States (June 1805).

[22] An Act to prevent citizens of the United States from Privateering against nations in amity with, or against citizens of the United States, c. 5, s. 1, ch. 1.

[23] An Act to authorize the defence of the Merchant Vessels of the United States against French depredations, c. 5, s. 2, ch. 60.

[24] An Act further to protect the Commerce of the United States, c. 5, s. 2, ch. 68.

against British ships and cargoes.[25] Congress then passed another law that specified the requirements for being issued letters of marque.[26] This act first gave the president the power to revoke letters of marque he had issued under the previous act. The applicant was required to describe the ship and the crew and to post a bond of $5,000 unless the ship had more than 150 men then the bond was $10,000, as surety to obey U.S. treaties and laws, to follow instructions as to their conduct, and to satisfy damages and injuries done in violation of these requirements.

Lawfully captured prizes where to be shared wholly by the owners of the privateer and its commander and crew, based on their agreement or if no agreement, then half and half, with the crew's share settled according to navy regulations passed in 1800.[27] Recaptured American ships and cargoes taken prize were subject to a salvage fee, either mutually agreed or determined by a court. Acts onboard privateers were governed by naval regulations, prize cases were to be tried before U.S. district courts, and privateer commanders were to keep an accurate journal of their cruises. A bounty of $20 was paid for each crew member taken on enemy ships destroyed, if that ship was equal or superior to the privateer.

The president was authorized to give instructions to the privateers, which President James Madison did in August 1812, as follows:

"1. The tenor of your commission under the act of Congress, entitled, 'An act concerning letters of marque, prizes and prize goods, a copy of which is hereto annexed, will be kept constantly in your view. The high seas, referred to in your commission, you will understand generally, to refer to a low-water mark; but with the exception of the space within one league, or three miles, from the shore of countries at peace both with Great Britain and the United States. You may nevertheless execute your commission within that distance of the shore of a nation at war with Great Britain, and even on the waters within the jurisdiction of such nation, if permitted so to do.

---

[25] An Act declaring War between the United Kingdom of Great Britain and Ireland and the dependencies thereof, and the United States of America and their territories, c. 12, s. 1, ch. 102.

[26] An Act concerning Letters of Marque, Prizes, and Prize Goods, c. 12, s. 1, ch. 107.

[27] An Act for the better government of the Navy of the United States, c. 6, s. 1, ch. 33, § 6.

2. You are to pay the strictest regard to the rights of neutral powers, and the usages of civilized nations; and in all your proceedings towards neutral vessels, you are to give them as little molestation or interruption as will consist with the right of ascertaining their neutral character, and of detaining and bringing them in for regular adjudication, in the proper cases. You are particularly to avoid even the appearance of using force or seduction, with a view to deprive such vessels of their crews or of their passengers, other than persons in the military service of the enemy.

3. Towards enemy vessels and their crews, you are to proceed, in exercising the rights of war, with all the justice and humanity which characterize the nation of which you are members.

4. The master and one or more of the principal persons belonging to the captured vessels, are to be sent, as soon after the capture as may be, to the judge or judges of the proper court in the United States, to be examined upon oath, touching the interest or property of the captured vessel and her lading; and at the same time, are to be delivered to the judge or judges all passes, charter-parties, bills of lading, invoices, letters and other documents, and writings found on board; the said papers to be proved by the affidavit of the commander of the capturing vessel, or some other person present at the capture, to be produced as they were received, without fraud, addition, subduction or embezzlement."[28]

In January 1813, a further statute specified that condemned prizes were to be sold at auction in the place where they were condemned and the proceeds, after costs, were to be split between the owner and crew according to their agreement. If there was no agreement, then it would be split half for the owner and half for the commander and crew.[29] In February 1813, to further incentivize privateering, a law was enacted that addressed pensions for privateering crews wounded in engagements with

---

[28] James Madison, Instructions to commanders of private armed ships (Aug. 28, 1812).
[29] An Act in addition to the act concerning letters of marque, prizes, and prize goods, c. 12, s. 2, ch. 13.

the enemy, paying a captain $20 per month, ranging on down to an ordinary seaman, paid $6 per month.[30]

In March 1813, a statute was passed that allowed only American citizens, including those who acquired citizenship through naturalization, to work as crew members on privateers. Commanders and owners who allowed non-citizens to serve on privateers were subject to fines of $500 per non-citizen in the crew.[31] The scope of privateering activity was then widened under a statute that same month allowing anyone who did not have a commission to destroy British warships, using devices such as torpedoes, while receiving a bounty of one half the value of the ship and its cargo and tackle, paid for by the U.S. government.[32]

In July 1813, Congress released the government's share for those British ships and goods captured in America, under three statutes of neutrality[33] passed during the Napoleonic Wars, to the privateer that captured British ships which were subsequently legally condemned.[34] To further encourage privateering, in August, duties were reduced by one-third,[35] a bounty of $25 was made available to privateering owners and crews for each captured prisoner brought into port,[36] and there was further clarity on which privateer officers and seamen, wounded or disabled in the line of duty, were to receive a pension.[37] In March 1814, half-rate pensions for the widows and orphans of the crew of privateers

---

[30] An Act to regulating pensions to persons on board private armed ships, c. 12, s. 2, ch. 22.

[31] An Act for the regulation of seamen on board the public and private vessels of the United States, c. 12, s. 2 ch. 42.

[32] An Act to encourage the destruction of the armed vessels of war of the enemy, c. 12, s. 2 ch. 47.

[33] An Act to interdict the commercial intercourse between the United States and Great Britain and France, and their dependencies; and for other, c. 10, s. 2, ch. 24; An Act concerning the commercial intercourse between the United States and Great Britain and France, and their dependencies, and for other purposes, c. 11, s. 2, ch. 39; An Act supplementary to the act, entitled "An act concerning the commercial intercourse between the United States and Great Britain and France and their dependencies, and for other purposes," c. 11, s. 3, ch. 29.

[34] An Act to relinquish the claims of the United States to certain goods, wares, and merchandise, captured by private armed vessels, c. 13, s. 1, ch. 10.

[35] An Act for reducing the duties payable on prize goods captured by the private armed vessels of the United States, c. 13, s. 1, ch. 49.

[36] An Act allowing a bounty to the owners, officers, and crews of the private armed vessels of the United States, c. 13, s. 1, ch. 55.

[37] An Act to amend and explain the act regulating pensions to persons on board private armed ships, c. 13, s. 1, ch. 58.

slain in the line of duty were enacted[38] and the bounty for captured enemy crew was increased to $100.[39]

## 2.  Civil War

The United States was not engaged in a major sea-born conflict after the War of 1812 for nearly half a century, until the American Civil War. When the Civil War began, Congress was tenuous about enacting a privateering statute, as this might be viewed as recognizing the legitimacy of the Confederacy. Congress did enact a statute targeted at the suppression of piracy, but which also allowed the president to authorize, against the pirates, the use of,

> "commanders of any other armed vessels sailing under the authority of any letters of marque and reprisal granted by the Congress."[40]

In 1863, Congress finally enacted a single statute, providing powers to the president to issue letters of marque and putting a time limit on these powers of three years:

> "That in all domestic and foreign wars the President of the United States is authorized to issue to private armed vessels of the United States, commissions, or letters of marque and general reprisal in such form as he shall think proper, and under the seal of the United States, and make all needful rules and regulations for the government and conduct thereof, and for the adjudication and disposal of the prizes and salvages made by such vessels."[41]

The Union never used these powers. The Confederacy, on the other hand, had passed "An Act recognizing the existence of war between the United States and the Confederate States, and concerning letters of marque, prizes and prize goods" in May 1861. The rebel government tried to use privateers to make up for their lack of a navy, as discussed in the

---

[38] An Act giving pensions to the orphans and widows of persons slain in the public or private armed vessels of the United States, c. 13, s. 2, ch. 20.

[39] An Act in addition to an act, entitled "An act allowing a bounty to the owners, officers and crews of the private armed vessels of the United States," c. 13, s. 2, ch. 27.

[40] An Act supplementary to an Act entitled "An Act to protect the Commerce of the United States, and Punish the Crime of Piracy," c. 37, s. 1, ch. 48.

[41] An Act concerning Letters of Marque, Prizes, and Prize Goods, c. 37, s. 3, ch. 85.

trial of William Smith in Chapter 2. However, as was noted in the previous chapter, the Declaration of Paris of 1856 had called for the cessation of privateering. With the end of this war, the United States joined the other major powers in ceasing to use privateers.

## 5.2 TRIALS

Privateering in the United States began before independence, with private ship owners eager to pursue the profitable trade in capturing British vessels. Disputes started just as early, for example, when the American re-captors of the American schooner *Ranger*, in November 1775, demanded a salvage fee equal to the value of 1/4 of the ship and cargo. This was much to the annoyance of the *Ranger's* master, traveling on a barely profitable domestic voyage with only a cargo of wood. With the Continental Congress asking states to find privateers and to commission admiralty courts, there soon was significant activity in these state courts. Appeals of the state court decisions went to Congress, first to an ad hoc committee then a regular committee and finally to a separate court for capture cases. Cases before these congressional courts are described more fully in a separate book.[42]

After the Revolutionary War, the new republic, as a neutral country, had to deal with the privateers of the warring belligerents during the various French Revolutionary and Napoleonic wars, in the years from 1792 to 1815 (hereafter the "Napoleonic wars"). Some cases involved matters of treaty that could override statutory norms, such as when the property of a neutral country was found in a ship of treaty parties' enemy, becoming liable for condemnation.[43] The War of 1812 saw a massive upsurge in the use of American privateering and court activity. This fell off considerably after the wars of independence from Spain in South America, until a brief resurgence during the American Civil War, after which privateering activity ceased. Due to the large number of such cases, this section focuses primarily on those cases that came before the U.S. Supreme Court.

---

[42] THOMAS J. SHAW, THE LEGAL HISTORY OF THE REVOLUTIONARY WAR, chap. 5.
[43] Bolchos v. Darrel, 3 F. Cas. 810 (D. S.C. 1795).

## A. Revolutionary and Napoleonic Wars

### 1. *The Active* and *the Holker*

<u>Legal issues to watch for</u>

❖ Allocation of prize proceeds to mariners rising up
❖ If prize courts of appeal can reexamine facts
❖ Whether common law courts can mandate distribution of a prize

These prize cases during the Revolutionary War came before the supreme court in Pennsylvania, under chief justice Thomas McKean. In *Rittenhouse*,[44] the British ship *Active* was captured on the high seas in September 1778 and taken to Philadelphia to be libeled before the state court of admiralty. There were three parties involved in the capture, the state of Pennsylvania ship *Convention*, the privateer *Le Gerard*, and four impressed Americans (Gideon Umstead, Artemus White, Aquila Rumsdale, and David Clark) onboard the *Active*, who had risen against the ship's crew. The trial before the court of admiralty considered whether the four men had essentially ended the engagement by confining the master and some mariners to their cabins before the two other ships arrived. The jury, in November, did not and condemned the ship, allocating one-half to the *Convention*, one-fourth to the *Gerard*, and one-fourth to the four men involved in the uprising.

The case was then appealed from the state court of admiralty to Congress' committee on appeals. In December, the committee reversed the decision and found for the four men. The state admiralty judge, George Ross, refused to acknowledge the decree from Congress and paid half of the proceeds into the state treasury (for the state navy's share), taking out an indemnity bond with the state treasurer, David Rittenhouse. As a subsequent proceeding after the death of the judge, the four men succeeded in a claim against the judge's estate, which in turn sued the treasurer for payment of the indemnity bond. The case then came before the supreme court in Pennsylvania

---

[44] Ross v. Rittenhouse, 2 U.S. 160 (Penn. 1792).

That court said there were four questions to revolve: could the congressional committee on appeals investigate facts; should the court of admiralty, not a common law court, have carried out the decree; can an action be maintained on the bond; and could plaintiffs, who did not notify the defendant of the common law action, maintain this suit? The court then examined the first question of whether the court of appeals in Congress could look at reexamining the facts in an appeal. Noting the November 1775 resolution of Congress called on states to create courts of admiralty, Pennsylvania did so in September 1778, with the provision that facts could not be examined on appeals to Congress.

In creating the court of appeals in cases of capture in January 1780,[45] Congress then called on states to try these admiralty cases without a jury but that occurred after this case was reversed by the appeals committee in 1778. Therefore, the state supreme court ruled that the appeals committee could not reexamine the facts to determine that the violence had stopped before the ships arrived. It gave judgment for the defendant (against necessitating payment of the indemnity bond). Further, the court said a common law court could not involve itself in an admiralty case. Much later, the Supreme Court upheld a lower court[46] ruling that Pennsylvania had no ownership interest and the full right to the proceeds were to be paid from Rittenhouse's estate to the four men.

A suit before the supreme court of Pennsylvania was brought by the agent of 43 sailors for prize money from the wartime activities of the privateer *Holker*. The ship was owned by one of the wealthiest men in Philadelphia, Blair McClenachan. The court of admiralty had decreed this money belonged to the mariners and directed the marshal of the admiralty to give it to the agent. The defendant resisted, asserting that this was a decree of admiralty dealing with a prize that a common law court did not have jurisdiction over. The court ruled for the plaintiff saying,

> "the Courts of Common Law will not take into consideration the incidents of a prize cause, is, that they will not review or draw before them the question of prize, which ought to be determined by the law

---

[45] Journals of the Continental Congress, p. 61-62 (Jan. 15, 1780).
[46] U.S. v. Judge Peters, 9 U.S. 115 (1809).

of nations, and in the Court of Admiralty. Here, the property has been condemned; the Marshall is directed to sell it for the benefit of the captors; and the plaintiff is the agent appointed by the Judge... It is his duty to receive it. To him are intrusted the rights of the absent seamen."[47]

*2. The Betsey and Les Jumeaux and Vrouw Christiana Magdalena*

| Legal issues to watch for |
|---|
| ❖ Use of American courts for libel by foreign national |
| ❖ Foreign privateers fitting out in American ports |
| ❖ Whether American privateers can capture neutral ships |

After the start of the most recent conflict between with France and Britain, the French privateer *Citizen Genet* captured, in 1794, the ship *Betsey* and brought it into Baltimore for libel by its commander, Capt. Pierre Arcade Johannene. Instead, the neutral Swedish owner of the ship, Alexander S. Glass, and the Swedish and American owners of the cargo filed a libel in Maryland. The initial question was whether an American court has jurisdiction over a libel in a conflict in which that had no part. The other significant question was whether a foreign national could avail himself of American courts for this purpose. The Supreme Court, in an opinion by Chief Justice John Jay,[48] ruled that the American federal courts did have jurisdiction over admiralty in both prize and instance, and so could hear pleas for restitution. But it then rejected the French captain's plea as insufficient. It further ruled that without a treaty basis, admiralty jurisdiction cannot be exercised in the United States by French consuls.[49]

The French merchant ship *Les Jumeaux* (the twins), after bringing coffee and sugar from the West Indies, was transformed from a merchant ship into a privateer while in the Delaware River. The United States indicted the captain, John Etienne Guinet, for violating the U.S. neutrality laws by fitting out his ship with the intent of committing hostilities against Britain. The ship came and left port with the same four guns but later

---

[47] Henderson v. Clarkson, 2 U.S. 174 (1792).
[48] Glass v. The Betsey, 3 U.S. 6 (1794).
[49] *See* Additional Writings section for more on this case.

outside the port, added additional guns. The Court ruled, in an opinion by Justice William Patterson,

> "Nor can it be reasonably contended, that the articles thus put on board the vessel were articles of merchandize; for, if that had been the case, they would have been mentioned in her manifest, on clearing out of the port, whereas it is expressly stated, that she failed in ballast. If they were not to be used for merchandize, the inference is inevitable, that they were to be used for war."[50]

The Dutch ship *Vrouw Christiana Magdalena*, sailing from Curacoa to Amsterdam, in May 1794, was captured by the American-owned and fitted out ship *Ami de la Liberte* (friend of liberty), captained by Edward Ballard, an American citizen. He was assisted in the capture by the ship *L'Ami de la Point a Pitre*, captained by William Talbot, another American. The admiralty court in Charleston had order restitution to the master of the Dutch ship, Joost Jansen. The privateer captain appealed, and the case reached the Supreme Court.[51] The evidence showed that despite his assertions, Ballard was American, had no French commission, and the *Ami de la Liberte* was not the property of the French government but of Americans John Sinclair and Solomon Wilson.

Further, the ship had been fitted out in Virginia to sail against neutral countries, which was illegal under American law. Talbot, who had arrived an hour after the Dutch ship had already surrendered to Ballard, was a naturalized French citizen and had a privateering commission from the governor of Guadeloupe. He had helped Ballard arm his ship and they had cruised together. The admiralty court had viewed Ballard, who had put aboard a prize crew, as still being in possession of the prize when Talbot arrived. However, Ballard's capture was illegal, as he had no commission and was an American sailing on an American ship against neutral nations' shipping.

While the Netherlands and France were enemies to each other, neither were enemies to the United States and so restitution was the

---

[50] U.S. v. Guinet, 2 U.S. 32 (1795).
[51] Talbot v. Jansen, 3 U.S. 133 (1795).

obvious remedy to this illegal capture of a neutral ship. The court further did not believe that the purported owner of Talbot's ship, Samuel Redick, had truly left his American citizenship behind, due to his short residency in Guadeloupe. Even if Talbot's commission was valid, he was an American, sailing on an American-built and owned ship. The Court affirmed the restitution decree, as Ballard's capture was illegal and Talbot used an American ship, which violated the law of nations and the American treaty with the Dutch.

*3. The Mary Ford and the Grand Sachem*

| Legal issues to watch for |
|---|
| ❖  Responsibility of agents for sale of illegal prize |
| ❖  Ownership of an abandoned prize |
| ❖  Whether separate prize of privateer could be attached |

The agents of the supposed French privateers operated by William Talbot and Edward Ballard (see above), the merchant partnership of Ebenezer Hills May & Woodbridge, were libeled by one of the cargo's owners. The assertion was that the firm had sold and distributed the proceeds from the auction of an illegally captured ship and cargo to the captors, without considering the claims from the original owners. The Supreme Court reviewed the decree of the South Carolina district court, which made the agents liable for all claims of the cargo's original owner, Walter Ross. The Court noted that the agents did not own any part of the privateers, and they,

> "were not trespassers *ab initio,* and, acting only as agents, they should be made answerable for no more than actually came into their hands."[52]

In the revised decree, the agents were required to pay the net amount of the cargo sales, after deducting customs duties, plus interest from the time of the sale until the date of the court's revised decree.

In September 1794, a British merchant ship, the *Mary Ford,* was first captured by French armed ships and made a prize, with her commander

---

[52] Hills v. Ross, 3 U.S. 331 (1796).

and papers removed and a prize crew put aboard. As the prize slowed them down, the French abandoned the ship. The American ship *George*, on a voyage from Virginia to Rotterdam, next seized the ship, sending it into Boston with a prize crew. Upon the *George* filing a libel for salvage, the *Mary Ford* was claimed by the British consul, for British merchants, and the French consul, for the captors. The district court in Boston ruled that one-third of the gross value of the ship and cargo would be an appropriate salvage fee. The court did not rule on remainder, so on appeal to the circuit court, Supreme Court justice William Cushing ruled the property became the (French) captors immediately upon possession. The Supreme Court later affirmed this ruling.[53]

In August 1795, the *Grand Sachem*, commanded by Ebenezer Baldwin, was captured by the French privateer *La Montagne* (the mountain). This new prize had been involved in smuggling in the Caribbean and carried Spanish papers, flew Spanish colors, and claimed to have a Spanish owner. Upon boarding the ship, nearly $10,000 was taken and a prize crew put aboard, directed to sail to Charleston. Upon arriving near that port, the privateer was set upon by the British frigate *Terpsichore*, which captured *La Montagne* and chased the *Grand Sachem*. The latter ship was chased upon the shore, was scuttled, and then plundered. The money seized from it by the British ship was taken to Jamaica and condemned. Another ship, the *Industry*, previously made a prize by this French privateer, and its cargo, were then attached by Mr. Arnold, the owner of the *Grand Sachem*, as it lay in Charleston harbor. An agreement was reached to sell the *Industry* and its cargo, with the proceeds directed to the district court.

In the libel, the district court ruled that Mr. Arnold, as owner of the *Grand Sachem*, was owed more than $33,000 and the proceeds from sale of the *Industry* and its cargo would be used to satisfy that. Reaching the Supreme Court, on appeal from the circuit court, answered four questions. First, yes, there was sufficient reason to bring the *Grand Sachem* into port for adjudication. Second, the captors took the risk of any damage or spoliation to the prize while it was being brought into port. Third, on whether the British chasing the ship removed the privateer's liability, the

---

[53] McDonough v. Danery and Ship Mary Ford, 3 U.S. 188 (1796).

Court held that the owners were responsible through their agents, the commander and crew, "to all the world,"[54] measured by the amount of the damage. While the men could leave a sinking ship, removing money from the *Grand Sachem* was an illegal act, as was the scuttling of the ship. Fourth, on whether the *Industry* and its cargo could be attached before condemnation, the Court ruled that the agreement between the parties obviated the need to rule on the irregularity of that decision and affirmed the lower courts' rulings for Arnold.

*4. The Salmon* and *the Mount Vernon*

---

### Legal issues to watch for

❖ Whether to rely on foreign admiralty court decisions
❖ Concealment of facts from prize's underwriter
❖ Whether future sale of prize ship defeats an insurance warranty

---

The American ship *Salmon* was captured by a British privateer, on the return leg of a voyage to deliver flour to France. The ship, traveling from Port-au-Paix to Philadelphia, was carrying a few invalid French soldiers, their baggage, and furniture. It was "generally" condemned in the British admiralty court in Jamaica, based on the following allegations:

> "1st. That the vessel and cargo were French property. 2nd. That the vessel was an American transport in the French service, employed to carry flour and soldiers to and from French ports. 3rd. That the vessel had been employed in carrying dispatches for the French Government. 4th. That the vessel had been employed in trading with the enemies of Great-Britain, supplying them with the means of sustenance and of war. And, 5th. That the port from which the vessel came was in a state of blockade."[55]

This case, before the supreme court of Pennsylvania, involved two insurance policies for $28,000 that the plaintiff ship owner was demanding payment on. Jared Ingersoll and Peter Stephen Du Ponceau were counsel of the plaintiffs and William Lewis, Edward Tilghman, and William Rawle

---

[54] Del Col v. Arnold, 3 U.S. 333 (1796).
[55] Vasse v. Ball, 3 U.S. 270 (Penn. 1797).

for the defense. The insurance policy had a warranty requiring the ship and cargo to be American owned. A significant question for the court was whether to accept the reasoning of the foreign admiralty court. Because there was a general condemnation not specifying its reason, and some of the allegations were clearly contradictory (e.g. it was French property, it was American property), the court allowed evidence to show that the owner of the ship and cargo were clearly American. This meant that the warranty had not been violated. The defense asserted that facts had been concealed from the underwriter, such as the delivery of flour to France and the transporting of French soldiers, to which the court answered,

> "There can be no imputation of concealment, where each party had an equal opportunity of acquiring a knowledge of the fact; and there is strong reason to believe, if not direct evidence to shew, that the plaintiff gave the defendant that opportunity, by placing in his hands the captain's letter, reciting all the circumstances. If the defendant then refused, or neglected, to read the letter, it cannot now be assigned as a cause for vitiating the policies. Besides, if all the circumstances had been perfectly understood, there was nothing which any lawyer would have pronounced to be illicit in the trade. The cargo of flour was at the risque of the plaintiff, till it was actually delivered; and I have never heard of any law, in any civilized nation, that deemed it contraband, or unlawful, to carry a few, unarmed, invalid soldiers, to a neutral country, in pursuit of health and refreshment."[56]

The court held for the payment of the insurance policy to the ship owner, refusing to let the case turn on the soldiers' furniture, which were technically part of the cargo and French owned,

> "that the household furniture of the passengers came within the description of the cargo of the vessel; and, therefore, the warranty had not been strictly performed. I confess, that I agree in the general idea, that household furniture cannot be regarded as baggage, and must constitute a part of the cargo; but still, to admit this exception, under the peculiar circumstances of the shipment, would be too

---

[56] *Id.*

indulgent to a harsh and captious spirit of litigation; nor, throughout the history of Admiralty proceedings, can there be traced a single instance of condemnation, for such a cause."[57]

The *Mount Vernon* was an allegedly American ship, captured by a French privateer, taken to Puerto Rico, and condemned, without stating it was a British ship. In a case before the supreme court of Pennsylvania,[58] the owner sought payment under an insurance policy, which required the ship to be American owned. Mr. Duncanson, an Englishman awaiting his American citizenship, planned to do business in the East Indies, which Americans could now do based upon the new treaty of amity and commerce with Britain, but which individual Englishmen could not, due to the East India Company's monopoly. He tasked his agents with finding a ship, owned by American Thomas Murgatroyd, to sail to England. Once there, the ship would be sold to Duncanson, as his American citizenship should be finalized by then. Duncanson chose the cargo for the voyage and reimbursed Murgatroyd for the insurance premium.

The underwriter asserted that this contract for a future sale was illegal, as it violated American neutrality, and that the contract was not disclosed, which could have meant a higher premium. With evidence that this would not lead to a higher premium, and the belief that purpose of the contract was to engage in the India trade and not to aid any belligerent in violation of neutrality, the jury found for the plaintiff. Murgatroyd attempted an action in replevin to get the ship from its purchaser, McLure, but the court ruled as he had been paid for the ship by Duncanson, he had no property on which to maintain an action for replevin.[59] Duncanson then initiated an action in trover against McLure.[60] The court believed its prior decision had been wrong, as the purchase by Duncanson at a future date was fraudulent under the U.S. laws by which he acquired the ship, and so Duncanson could not maintain an action for trover.

---

[57] *Id.*
[58] Murgatroyd v. Crawford, 3 U.S. 491 (Penn. 1799).
[59] Murgatroyd v. McLure, 17 F. Cas. 1026 (D. Penn. 1800).
[60] Duncanson v. McLure, 4 U.S. 308 (Penn. 1804).

## 5. The Eliza and the Amelia and the Andrew

---

Legal issues to watch for

❖ Salvage rates based on whether state of war exists
❖ Salvage fee for recaptured neutral ships
❖ Requirements for abandonment to collect insurance

---

A French privateer had captured the American ship *Eliza*, with John Bas the master, in March 1799, which was then were re-captured by the American warship *Ganges* in April. The question during the libel of the ship before the district court involved the salvage rate. Under an act of 1798,[61] salvage allowed for a payment of one-eight the value of the ship and goods, while under another act of 1799[62] allowed for a scale of salvage values, up to one half if the recapture took place more than 96 hours after the original capture. The Court discussed whether a state of war existed or not between France and the United States and concluded that a limited war existed, allowing for the larger salvage value,

> "It is a maritime war; a war at sea as to certain purposes. The national armed vessels of France attack and capture the national armed vessels of the United States, and the national armed vessels of the United States are expressly authorized and directed to attack, subdue, and take the national armed vessels of France, and also to recapture American vessels."[63]

The *Amelia* was a German ship, sailing from Calcutta to Hamburg, captured by the French armed ship *La Diligente,* and later taken, in September 1799, by U.S. armed ship *Constitution*, led by Silas Talbot. The *Amelia* was libeled in New York, claimed by Hans Frederick Seeman. The district court awarded Talbot a one-half salvage fee, but the circuit court reversed, saying there should be no salvage fee for a neutral ship. The Supreme Court, in an opinion by John Marshall, looked through many recent U.S. statutes and found the capture to be lawful. Looking at French law, which condemned neutral ships, the Court ruled that the owner

---

[61] c. 5, s. 2, ch. 62.
[62] c. 5, s. 3, ch. 24.
[63] Bas v. Tingy, 4 U.S. 37 (1800).

received a benefit from the *Constitution's* actions. Some salvage fee was due but because Germany was not an enemy of France, it would not be one-half per the U.S. statute but one-sixth.[64]

The *Andrew* was captured, in April 1793, on a voyage from Charleston to Amsterdam, by a French privateer, sent to France, acquitted, and restored. A week later, the revolutionary government in France seized the cargo, promising to pay for it. The amounts were never paid and after years the consignee gave up and returned to America. The owner of the cargo stated that he intended to abandon the cargo. The question before the supreme court in Pennsylvania was whether the abandonment was notified in sufficient time for insurance purposes. The defendant, agent for the insurance companies, said by using equivocal language, it meant the plaintiff could still pursue the cargo, which kept the underwriters from taking action to retrieve the cargo. The court instructed the jury, which would give a verdict in favor of the plaintiff cargo owner, that,

> "no particular form of words was necessary to constitute an abandonment; that by declaring he meant to abandon, the plaintiff had made his election, and could never afterwards retract. That an abandonment must be made within a reasonable time; but that what constituted a reasonable time, was a question of fact, depending upon the relative situation of the parties, the time, and the place, after notice to the assured of the loss; and that, in the present case, there did not appear to have been any design to waive the right of abandonment."[65]

---

[64] Talbot v. Seeman, 5 U.S. 1 (1801).
[65] Bell v. Beveridge, 4 U.S. 272 (Penn. 1803).

## 6. *The Charming Betsey* and *the Flying Fish*

---

### Legal issues to watch for

❖  Intercepting ship of former American citizen
❖  Liability for damages if no reasonable suspicion to capture
❖  Liability for damages if capturing ship heading from French port

---

The *Charming Betsey* was a ship sailing out of St. Thomas (then Danish) heading to the French colony of Guadeloupe. She had come there as an American ship called the *Jane* but, on the orders of her owners, was put up for sale and was purchased by an American-born Danish citizen, Jared Shattuck. He was a merchant in St. Thomas, was a Danish burgher, owned property there, and had married there. He renamed the ship the *Charming Betsey*, loaded it with a cargo, and sent the ship to Guadeloupe, in June 1800. It had Danish papers and a Danish commander but was captured by a French privateer and sent as prize to Guadeloupe. On the way, it was intercepted by American ship of war *Constellation* in July, then sent to Martinique, the cargo sold, and the ship taken back to the United States.

In February 1800, Congress had passed an act[66] which suspended all commercial transactions between France and the United States. It was under this law that the commander of the *Constellation* had stopped the *Charming Betsey* and deemed her goods forfeit. Upon the libel being filed in Philadelphia, Shattuck made a claim for the ship, the cost of the goods lost, and his damages. The district court agreed and ordered this payment, deducting as salvage any benefit Shattuck received from being rescued from the French privateer. When the case reached the Supreme Court, the questions were whether the ship was liable for confiscation, if a salvage fee was due, and if the *Constellation* commander was liable for damages. The Court ruled that Shattuck was no longer under the protection of the United States, and as a Danish burgher was able to trade with a French island without offending the statute.

It also said that because there was little chance of the *Charming Betsey* causing any future harm, due to her lack of armaments, and it was

---

[66] An Act further to suspend the commercial intercourse between the United States and France, and the dependencies thereof, c. 6, s. 1, ch. 10.

not clear that the ship would be condemned in Guadeloupe, no salvage fee should be available for rescue from the French privateer. Regarding damages, the Court found no credible reason to interrupt the voyage and reversed that part of the lower courts' decrees, saying,

"These causes of suspicion, taken together, ought not to have been deemed sufficient to counterbalance the evidence of fairness with which they were opposed. The ship's papers appear to have been perfectly correct, and the information of the captain, uncontradicted by those belonging to the vessel who were taken with him, corroborated their verity. No circumstance existed which ought to have discredited them."[67]

In February 1799, Congress had passed an act to suspend commerce with France,[68] which authorized the seizing of U.S. ships that were sailing to a French port, to be condemned along with their cargo. Instructions were to be issued by the president to the armed vessels of the United States, but those issued by lawyer-president Thomas Jefferson were slightly different than what was stated in the act. A ship owned by Danes living in St. Thomas, the *Flying Fish*, was seized in December 1799 while on a voyage from Haiti to St. Thomas, by an American ship led by Capt. Little. Upon Little libeling the ship in Boston, it was restored, along with its Danish and neutral country cargo. Damages were not awarded in the district court but were added in the circuit court, as the ship was going from, not to, a French port. The Supreme Court, noting the difference between Jefferson's instructions to naval captains and the statute,

"Is the officer who obeys them liable for damages sustained by this misconstruction of the act, or will his orders excuse him? If his instructions afford him no protection, then the law must take its course, and he must pay such damages as are legally awarded against him; if they excuse an act not otherwise excusable, it would then be necessary to inquire whether this is a case in which the probable cause which existed to induce a suspicion that the vessel was American,

---

[67] Murray v. The Charming Betsey, 6 U.S. 64 (1804).
[68] An Act further to suspend the Commercial Intercourse between the United States and France, and the dependencies thereof, c. 5, s. 3, ch. 2.

would excuse the captor from damages when the vessel appeared in fact to be neutral."[69]

Despite this, the Court affirmed the decision of the circuit court, with Chief Justice Marshall saying,

"But I have been convinced that I was mistaken, and I have receded from this first opinion. I acquiesce in that of my brethren, which is that the instructions cannot change the nature of the transaction or legalize an act which without those instructions would have been a plain trespass."[70]

### 7. *The Mercator* and *the Dawes*

| Legal issues to watch for |
|---|
| ❖  Liability for illegal prize seizure even when later taken by force |
| ❖  Foreign condemnation not conclusive as to neutrality of prize owner |
| ❖  Fraudulent agreement to seize and condemn a ship not enforceable |

Jared Shattuck, the owner of the *Charming Betsey* discussed above, was involved in another libel, beginning in August 1804. This was for the seizure of his ship *Mercator* and its cargo by the U.S. warship *Experiment*, commanded by William Maley, in May 1800, on a merchant journey from St. Thomas to Haiti. Maley put a prize crew aboard, but the prize was subsequently taken by the British privateer *General Simcoe*. In reply to Shattuck's libel, Maley claimed the *Mercator* was a U.S. ship and that Shattuck was a U.S. citizen and so the trip to French territory violated the statutes against commerce with France. Further, that the *Mercator* was condemned in a British court of admiralty in Jamaica, as being either the property of citizens of France or Spain, both enemies to Britain at that time. If Shattuck was truly Danish, then the libel in Jamaica would not have succeeded, as Britain and Denmark (and the United States) were not enemies at that time.

Shattuck replied with his prior proof of his Danish citizenship and said he had had several of his ships seized by the British and the French

---

[69] Little v. Barreme, 6 U.S. 170 (1804).
[70] *Id.*

previously, but they had been acquitted as neutral, due to his citizenship. He noted that he had purchased the *Mercator* from an American in November 1799 and,

> "That at the time of her capture, the *Mercator* was navigated as a *bona fide* Danish vessel, and had on board every paper and document which the law required to prove her neutrality, and especially that she had, 1st, the King's passport, in the usual form; 2d, the certificate of measurement; 3d, her muster-roll, or official list of her crew; 4th, the bill of sale; 5th, the burgher's brief of her captain, Toussaint Lucas; 6th, her clearance; 7th, the invoice and bill of lading of her cargo duly attested, as to the ownership and neutrality thereof; 8th, the captain's instructions or sailing orders, and 9th, a certificate, upon oath, of several respectable merchants of the island attesting the fact of Schattuck's citizenship and residence in the island."[71]

The district court dismissed the libel, but the circuit court reversed, holding Maley liable for damages. Upon appeal to the Supreme Court, the first question was whether Shattuck owned the ship. It said the British admiralty decision did not establish any particular fact, such as Shattuck's citizenship, and neutral ships could be condemned for other reasons, such as running a blockade. This left the question of his citizenship open to inspection by the court, which found there was sufficient evidence to show he was a Danish citizen. The Court then looked at whether the ship should have been seized and found nothing suspicious enough to create a reasonable belief for capture. Because of the unjust seizure, the fact that the prize, while in American control, was seized by a British privateer using superior force did not shield Maley from liability for damages. The Court ruled against Maley, making him liable for the cost of the ship and cargo and for damages.

The British privateer/merchantman *Dawes*, which also carried cargo on a 1782 voyage from Jamaica to New York, ran into difficult weather and was forced to enter an American port. As the ship would be captured and condemned as an enemy prize, the crew agreed to seize the ship and thereby receive the proceeds of the condemnation for themselves, as per a

---

[71] Maley v. Shattuck, 7 U.S. 458 (1806).

resolution of Congress encouraging crews to do this.[72] The crew had agreed to keep some of the benefit of the owners. The ship and cargo were condemned in North Carolina and the proceeds distributed according to their agreement. Capt. Oswell Eve purchased shares from the crew and bought and sold some of the cargo, both for the benefit of the owners. After the war, the owners sued Eve in American courts, to account to and pay them their share of the proceeds. The circuit court dismissed the suit, and it came to the Supreme Court, which, noting that the condemnation itself was legal and final, ruled that it could not enforce the crew's agreement, made to defraud U.S. laws, meaning that the owners could not force Eve to account and pay.[73]

*8. The George*

---

### Legal issues to watch for

- ❖ Responsibility to condemnation proceeds never received
- ❖ Whether U.S. courts can execute decrees from prior courts
- ❖ Capture of a neutral ship is a total loss for insurance purposes

---

The *George* was captured by the privateer *Addition* in 1778 during the Revolutionary War. The ship and cargo were condemned, in October 1778, in the New Jersey court of admiralty and sold. The congressional committee of appeals reversed this decision, in December 1780, and ordered restitution but the sale by the marshal had already occurred two years previous and it was not clear where the funds went. The order of restitution was not enforced. Richard D Jennings, the owner of the *George*, in 1790, under the new U.S. Constitution, filed a libel stating he was a citizen of the Netherlands, residing in St. Eustatius and requested the arrest of Joseph Carson, part-owner of the *Addition*, to answer the decrees ordering restitution. Carson, one-third owner, was arrested and answered that the *George* was carrying British goods to the British army and navy. Further, that he never received the proceeds of the condemnation, that they remained with the marshal.

---

[72] Journals of the Continental Congress, p. 1158 (Dec. 4, 1781).
[73] Hannay v. Eve, 7 U.S. 242 (1806).

Carson also claimed that the courts in New Jersey were the ones who had jurisdiction, not those in Pennsylvania, over this matter. He soon died and his executors were made the defendants. The district court took jurisdiction but ruled in 1793 it could not compel execution of a decree from the committee of appeal. This was reversed by the Supreme Court in 1799. The district court then ruled for the libelant on the ship and cargo, the circuit court reversed, and it came to the Supreme Court. The Court said that the key question was the defendant could not give back what he did not possess. It looked to the practice of admiralty courts and said that the New Jersey court should have had possession of the ship and cargo. As such, the decree of the congressional committee ordering restoration and restitution was directed at the New Jersey court, not the privateer's owners, who had no possession.[74]

In February 1805, the American merchant ship *Manhattan* was captured by a British armed vessel but acquitted in April, as it was a neutral ship. As soon as he was informed of the capture, in late February, the owner notified the insurance company which had insured the cargo, of his abandonment. The Court ruled that when a neutral vessel is completely taken, it is a total loss, vesting in the underwriter the thing abandoned, and in the insured the amount of insurance taken out. The other question was whether the restoration of the ship and cargo changed this, but the Court believed it did not, that the total loss was vested from the time of abandonment and the insurance company was liable to pay the owner for the freight insured.[75]

---

[74] Jennings v. Carson, 8 U.S. 2 (1807).
[75] Rhinelander v. Insurance Co. of Pennsylvania, 8 U.S. 29 (1807).

*9. The Antelope and John and Henry*

| Legal issues to watch for |
|---|
| ❖ Salvage due to neutrals who overpower prize crew |
| ❖ Termination of insurance based on change in destination |
| ❖ Insurance covers a ship on a voyage, not a ship and a voyage |

The American-owned *Antelope*, with American-owned cargo, was returning from St. Thomas to Baltimore, when it was captured by a British armed vessel, in December 1806. The prize was sent to Jamaica, but the *Antelope's* remaining crew and passengers overwhelmed the prize crew and took control, sailing the ship to Charleston. The re-captors filed a libel for salvage and the owners resisted that, claiming there was no such right. The district court noted that salvage was appropriate when a ship is rescued from pirates or enemies and not typically when rescuing neutral ships from belligerents, as they should be acquitted when libeled, net of any costs incurred. The court felt it could not go against international law and practice, saying,

> "Let the libel be dismissed; but the costs must be paid by the claimants: for though I cannot give salvage as a legal right, I think the actors are entitled to liberal compensation for their zealous, though mistaken endeavours to serve the owners."[76]

The *John and Henry* was taken by a French privateer in March 1803, on a voyage from Charleston to Haiti, and sent to another port in Haiti as a prize. The military commandant there seized the cargo for his garrison but was promised payment in coffee. The ship was sent to another port in Haiti to obtain that cargo but was then seized by a British armed vessel and condemned as a legal prize by the British. The ship's owner made an insurance claim for abandonment and a total loss, based upon the seizure by the French privateer but did so after the seizure by the British. The district court ruled for the defendant insurance company and the case came to the Supreme Court. The Court said that the total loss must have existed in fact at the time the abandonment was declared by the owner.

---

[76] Waite v. The Antelope, 28 F. Cas. 1341 (D. S.C. 1807).

The Court noted that while the cargo had been taken, the ship had been restored by the French, and the insurance policy in question was on the ship, not the cargo. The key was that the insurance covered the ship's ability to make a voyage, not whether it actually did make a voyage or not. The voyage was intended to go to Haiti and so the insurance for the ship ended there. The need to obtain the replacement cargo, though, extended the voyage to take on the coffee but without the insurance cover. The Court affirmed the lower courts, concluding that,

> "The Court can find in the books no case which would justify the establishment of the principle that the loss of the cargo constitutes a technical loss of the vessel, and must therefore construe this contract according to its obvious import. It is an insurance on the ship for the voyage, not an insurance on the ship and the voyage. It is an undertaking for the ability of the ship to prosecute her voyage and to bear any damage which she may sustain during the voyage, not an undertaking that she shall in any event perform the voyage."[77]

*10. The Sarah and the Sea Flower*

| Legal issues to watch for |
| --- |
| ❖ Disregarding the decision of a foreign admiralty court |
| ❖ Seizure for violating municipal law |
| ❖ Retaining control over res despite location of court |

The *Sarah* was captured in February 1804 by a French privateer, on a voyage to the United States and taken to Cuba, where the goods were taken off the ship, condemned by the court of admiralty of St. Domingo, and sold. St. Domingo was then in rebellion against France, having been established by ex-slaves in Haiti. The purchaser of the cargo, Mr. Colt of the ship *Example*, then sailed to South Carolina, where Mr. Rose, the supercargo of the *Sarah*, filed a libel against the goods Colt purchased. The goods were arrested by the marshal, in May 1804. The articles used by the court of admiralty of St. Domingo, which was sitting in Cuba, were published nearly a week after the capture.

---

[77] Alexander v. Baltimore Insurance Co., 8 U.S. 370 (1808).

The ship was later condemned there but the district court in the United States had no knowledge of that condemnation and so ordered a restoration to the libellant. On appeal to the circuit court, the condemnation record from the court in Cuba was produced, and the circuit court reversed, dismissing the libel. The case was then appealed to the Supreme Court, which wondered if the sentence was given by a court of competent jurisdiction. Did the foreign court have jurisdiction over the subject matter, and should the Court take notice of its decision?

The *Sarah* was seized outside the two-kilometer limit, inside which vessels were liable to capture per the French municipal law. The ship was sold in Cuba, not St. Domingo. The court which condemned the ship, after it was sold, sat in Cuba, not St. Domingo. The proceedings were ex parte, without the claimants able to take part. The Court differentiated acts of war, where ships could be seized on the high seas, and those of municipal law, which only gave that right inside a nation's territory. As the ship and crew never were within the jurisdiction of the court, its jurisdiction never attached, and the sentence of the St. Domingo court could be disregarded. The Court ruled that as title never vested in the captor, due to there being no actual violation of the municipal law, the libelants should recover their property, net of appropriate expenses of the defendants.[78]

Justice William Johnson explained that there was a split in the Court's reasons for disregarding the jurisdiction of the St. Domingo court. Three of the justices felt that the property that was condemned by that court could not occur while it lay in a neutral port (in South Carolina). The following case further explains this interpretation. The other two justices believed that the seizure was undertaken for breach of a municipal regulation, while the ship was on the high seas, which would be in violation of the law of nations. Johnson disagreed with the latter belief, saying,

"The ocean is the common jurisdiction of all sovereign powers, from which it does not result that their powers upon the ocean exist in a state of suspension or equipoise, but that every power is at liberty upon the ocean to exercise its sovereign right, provided it does no act inconsistent with that general equality of nations which exists upon

---

[78] Rose v. Himeley, 8 U.S. 241 (1808).

the ocean. The seizure of a ship upon the high seas after she has committed an act of forfeiture within a territory is not inconsistent with the sovereign rights of the nation to which she belongs, because it is the law of reason and the general understanding of nations that the offending individual forfeits his claim to protection, and every nation is the legal avenger of its own wrongs. Within their jurisdictional limits, the rights of sovereignty are exclusive; upon the ocean they are concurrent. Whatever the great principle of self-defense in its reasonable and necessary exercise will sanction in an individual in a state of nature nations may lawful perform upon the ocean."

Likening the actions of St. Domingo to engaging a blockade, he would have ruled that,

"the capture of *The Sarah* was justifiable upon principles not at all dependent upon municipal regulation; that it may fairly be considered as having been made in conformity with the law of nations, and therefore, without acceding to the doctrine that a seizure contrary to the law of nations was a void seizure and that we have a right to declare that a mere marine trespass which a court of France has declared to be the act of its sovereign, I conclude that the court of St. Domingo had jurisdiction in this case, and if it had jurisdiction, it is admitted that the property was altered, and the libellant ought not to recover."

The *Sea Flower* was also captured by a French privateer, but this time within the territorial jurisdiction of St. Domingo, and then carried into a Spanish port in Cuba. The French court in Guadeloupe condemned the ship and cargo. The key issue was whether the captor and his sovereign retained power over the res during the condemnation, despite the ship being in a neutral port not under his direct control. Although the Court was split as to the reasoning and/or the final judgment, as it had been in the case of the *Sarah*, the majority felt the plaintiff had no longer had a claim,

"It is, however, the opinion of a majority of the judges that a possession thus lawfully acquired under the authority of a sovereign state could not be divested by the tribunals of that country into whose ports the captured vessel was brought -- at least that it could not be divested unless there should be such obvious delay in proceeding to a condemnation as would justify the opinion that no such measure was intended, and thus convert the seizure into a trespass."[79]

## B. War of 1812 and Civil War

### 1. *The Rapid* and *the Venus*

---
<u>Legal issues to watch for</u>

❖ Whether retrieval of goods is trading subject to condemnation
❖ Seizure of goods owned by British subjects with American citizenship
❖ Ability of Americans aboard to repatriate after learning of war

---

With the start of the War of 1812 and the significant use of privateers, many cases came to the Supreme Court. The *Rapid* was captured by the American privateer *Jefferson* on July 8, 1812, after the declaration of war. The goods aboard belonged to American Jabez Harrison, who had bought these goods from England before the war and stored them on an English held island close to the U.S.-Canada border. It was these goods that were captured by the *Jefferson*, libeled in Massachusetts, and condemned as English goods, for trading with the enemy. The Supreme Court, with Justice William Johnson writing the opinion, settled several questions while upholding the condemnation. These included whether the claimant was engaged in trading, which the Court said was to be interpreted as intercourse inconsistent with actual hostility, and whether there was a right to remove property in a foreign country after war breaks out, but ruled the claimant had no right to leave the country to retrieve goods.[80]

The *Venus* sailed from Liverpool in July 1812 and was captured by the privateer *Dolphin* in August. The goods aboard variously belonged to James Lenox of Britain, James Magee of New York, and three British subjects who gained American citizenship but then returned to live back in England: William Maitland, John Jones, and Alexander McGregor. McGregor had recently returned to the United States, Jones had remained in England, and

---

[79] Hudson v. Guestier, 8 U.S. 293 (1808).
[80] The Rapid, 12 U.S. 155 (1814).

Maitland wanted to return to the United States after notified of the capture. The Court, in an opinion by justice Bushrod Washington, first noted that the 100 casks of white lead, although listed as the property of merchants Maitland and Lenox, were actually shipped by them from London for a British subject, and therefore were rightly condemned. Goods shipped from Jones to Magee were still owned by British subject Jones, until a contract transferred the rights to Magee.

The ship, owned by Lenox and Maitland, claimed that Maitland was a resident of New York, when in fact he was then residing in Britain. For this violation of the registration requirements under a 1792 statute,[81] requiring ownership only by U.S. citizens, the ship was forfeited to the United States. The Court, after an exceedingly long opinion analyzing whether the goods of the three men who had repatriated to Britain where subject to condemnation, decided that they were and therefore reversed and affirmed parts of the lower courts' rulings, mandating condemnation to the captors for all goods owned by British subjects Lenox, Maitland, McGregor, and Jones, and for the ship, half to the United States and half to the captors.

John Marshall, in a lengthy dissent, said,

"I entirely concur in so much of the opinion delivered in this case as attaches a hostile character to the property of an American citizen continuing, after the declaration of war, to reside and trade in the country of the enemy, and I subscribe implicitly to the reasoning urged in its support. But from so much of that opinion as subjects to confiscation the property of a citizen shipped before a knowledge of the war, and which disallows the defense founded on an intention to change his domicile and to return to the United States, manifested in a sufficient manner, and within a reasonable time after knowledge of the war, although it be subsequent to the capture, I feel myself compelled to dissent...

An American citizen having merely a commercial domicile in a foreign country is not, I think, under the British authorities, concluded, by his

---

[81] An Act concerning the registration and recording of ships or vessels, c. 2, s. 2, ch. 1.

residence and trading in time of peace, from averring and proving an intention to change his domicile on the breaking out of war or from availing himself of that proof in a court of admiralty. The intrinsic evidence arising from the change in his situation, produced by war, renders it extremely probable that in this new state of things, he must intend to return home, and will aid in the construction of any overt act by which such intention is manifested. Dissolution of partnership, discontinuance of trade in the enemy country, a settlement of accounts, and other arrangements obviously preparatory to a change of residence, are, in my opinion, such overt acts as may, under circumstances showing them to be made in good faith, entitle the claimant to restitution."[82]

## 2. The Frances

| Legal issues to watch for |
| --- |
| ❖  Proof that order was placed on American's account |
| ❖  Goods on consignment still owned by consignor |
| ❖  Use of liens to defeat captors claims |

The ship *Frances*, with British goods aboard consigned to Americans, sailed from Scotland In July 1812, after the declaration of war, was captured by the privateer *Yankee* in August, and libeled in Rhode Island. The goods were claimed by Robert Thompson and William Steele, naturalized Americans living in the United States and James Thompson, another naturalized American living in Scotland. The goods of the first two were returned to them by the court but those of James Thompson were condemned by the district court, which he appealed. Another set of packages/boxes jointly owned with British subjects were also condemned. James Thompson had not tried to return to the United States until more than a year after war was declared. The Court, referring to its *Venus* judgment, affirmed the condemnation of James Thompson's share as well as any goods co-owned with British subjects or sent by them on consignment.[83]

---

[82] The Venus, 12 U.S. 253 (1814).
[83] The Frances, 12 U.S. 335 (1814).

There were six more cases related to the *Frances* that came before the Court in 1814. Three Graham brothers, naturalized citizens, had a partnership in New York (John), Philadelphia (Peter), and Glasgow (William). John Graham claimed some of the cargo on the *Frances* as his sole property, not part of the partnership with his brothers. The lower court ordered restitution of 2/3 of the cargo owned by the U.S.-based brothers but condemned 1/3 for the Glasgow-based brother. The Court believed that further proof was required, not just the later letters from the brothers and their employees but letters from John Graham showing that he ordered the shipment on his own account.[84]

Another consignee in New York was to receive goods, with the option to accept or reject the goods within 24 hours of receipt. The lower court ruled that this meant the goods were still owned by the British shipper and so rightly condemned.[85] Further proof of acceptance of a second shipment that made it through did not change the ownership, as all had to be accepted or not in both shipments.[86] Other goods were claimed by an American, Duncan Kennedy, for his merchant house. While the bills of lading stated these were at the house's risk and on their account, there were no documents showing that the goods were not still owned by the British shippers.[87] William French, another American, claimed goods were sent on his account and risk to a merchant house in New York. The court viewed his claims to ownership, as well as those of the merchant house, to not exist before the goods were consigned, therefore they were still British owned, and lawful prizes when captured.[88]

Another naturalized American from Scotland, Colin Gillespie, moved back and forth between the United States and Scotland over more than 20 years. However, he had married in Scotland, owned several businesses there, and departed Scotland more than a year after the war was declared. The Court affirmed the condemnation of his goods,[89] based on the *Venus* judgment. American Thomas Irvin claimed goods on the *Frances*, based

---

[84] The Frances, 12 U.S. 348 (1814).
[85] The Frances, 12 U.S. 354 (1814).
[86] The Frances, 13 U.S. 183 (1815).
[87] The Frances, 12 U.S. 358 (1814).
[88] The Frances, 12 U.S. 359 (1814).
[89] The Frances, 12 U.S. 363 (1814).

upon a lien that he had, arising from a partial advanced payment. The goods were shipped at the risk of and on the account of the consignor. Concerned about captors having to know the laws of many countries and possible collusion between enemy owners and neutral captors, the Court, per Chief Justice Marshall, affirmed the condemnation, saying,

> "The principal strength of the argument in favor of the claimant in this case seemed to be rested upon the position that the consignor in this case could not have countermanded the consignment after delivery of the goods to the master of the vessel, and hence it was inferred that the captor had no right to intercept the passage of the property to the consignee. This doctrine would be well founded if the goods had been sent to the claimant upon his account and risk, except in the case of insolvency. But when goods are sent upon the account and risk of the shipper, the delivery to the master is a delivery to him as agent of the shipper, not of the consignee, and it is competent to the consignor at any time before actual delivery to the consignee to countermand it, and thus to prevent his lien from attaching."[90]

*3. The Sally and the Thomas Gibbons and the Hiram*

---

**Legal issues to watch for**

❖  Whether the government or the captor receives a captured prize
❖  Whether enemy cargo was protected by presidential instructions
❖  Whether to condemn cargo shipped under license assisting an enemy

---

The *Sally* was captured, by the privateer *Jefferson*, with a suspicious cargo of salt. By witnesses produced by the libelants, they asserted that the salt was loaded at St. Andrews in Canada. The cargo was condemned by the district court, affirmed by the circuit court, and the Supreme Court, noting its decision in the *Rapid*, concluded that trading with the enemy subjects the cargo to confiscation as a prize. The issue then was who it should be condemned to, the captor or the United States. A statute of 1809[91] had forbidden commerce between the United States and the warring nations of

---

[90] The Frances, 12 U.S. 418 (1814).
[91] An Act to interdict the commercial intercourse between the United States and Great Britain and France, and their dependencies; and for other purposes, c. 10, s. 2, ch. 24.

Britain and France, allowing for the seizure of any such goods. The Court's opinion was that this municipal statute was absorbed into the operation of the law of war and that in any case, the prize act of 1812 specifically addressed this situation, giving the prize to the privateer captor.[92]

The *Thomas Gibbons* traveled from Liverpool, in August 1812, but was captured by the privateer *Atas* in October and brought into Savannah. The *Atas* was operating on a privateering commission granted in September, which attached instructions to privateers from the president. These instructions were to not interdict American ships carrying British cargo sailing from Britain. The *Thomas Gibbons* had sailed under a special license from the privy council. The only real issue was whether the instructions from the president meant American-owned cargo or also included British-owned cargo on the American ships and the Court concluded all cargo was within the instructions and thereby affirmed the lower court's dismissal of the libel.[93]

The *Hiram* was captured by the privateer the *Thorn*, in October 1812, sailing from Baltimore to Lisbon, with a cargo of flour and bread. Upon libel in Massachusetts, the claimants included the ship's owner, American Samuel G. Griffith, and various American merchants. The libelants asserted that because they sailed under a British license and the proceeds of the sales were to be sent to England, the ship and cargo should be condemned. The district and circuit courts acquitted. Upon appeal to the Supreme Court, its prior case of the *Julia* stated the principle,

"That the sailing on a voyage under the license and passport of protection of the enemy in furtherance of his views or interests constitutes such an act of illegality as subjects the ship and cargo to confiscation as prize of war."[94]

The Court found no substantial difference between that case and this one and reversed the lower courts, condemning the ship and cargo.[95]

---

[92] The Sally, 12 U.S. 382 (1814).
[93] The Thomas Gibbons, 12 U.S. 421 (1814).
[94] The Julia, 12 U.S. 181 (1814).
[95] The Hiram, 12 U.S. 444 (1814).

## 4. *The Grotius* and *the Mary* and *the Adeline*

---

### Legal issues to watch for

❖ When ship is claimed not be to a prize
❖ Whether condemnation indicates nationality
❖ Salvage rate for recapture of ship different than for cargo

---

The *Grotius* was captured after an exceptionally long voyage starting in March 1812, that included Russia, Sweden, and England, before sailing for the United States in ballast (without cargo) and being captured by the privateer *Frolic* in July 1813. Three of the crew of the *Grotius* claimed that they had never been made a prize but had merely been asked to take onboard the *Frolic's* prize master as a passenger on the *Grotius*. Conversely, the prize master, Daniel J. Very, claimed he had written prize instructions and that Capt. Odiorne of the *Grotius* had been told by Capt. Sheafe of the *Frolic* that his ship was a prize. Unusually, Odiorne was allowed to retain his papers and steer the ship into port. Without those instructions, the Court deferred a decision.[96] This came the following year, when the instructions were produced, along with an additional deposition from the surgeon of the *Frolic* and that ship's journal. The Court ruled that the ship was to be condemned to the captors.[97]

The *Mary*, an American ship, was captured by the privateer *Paul Jones* in April 1813, after a voyage delayed by embargo and severe weather requiring repairs. The ship and cargo were libeled in Rhode Island. The ship was condemned, as there was no claimant, and the cargo was acquitted in district court, but then condemned in the circuit court. The appeal went to the Supreme Court, where more information was requested, on the citizenship of those receiving the cargo and when the instructions of the president were received by the privateer captain.[98] The Court ruled that despite the ship being condemned, that did not mean it was not an American ship, which supported the claim to the cargo. The instructions sent to the privateers not to interdict American ships with British cargo meant that the cargo should be restored to the claimants. Expenses of the

---

[96] The Grotius, 12 U.S. 456 (1814).
[97] The Grotius, 13 U.S. 368 (1815).
[98] The Mary, 12 U.S. 388 (1814); 13 U.S. 126 (1815).

captors were to be deducted, as the long period since the instructions had been issued could have raised questions on their continued validity, and so justified the seizure.

The American letter of marque *Adeline* was first captured by British warships then recaptured by American privateer *Expedition*, on a voyage from France. The cargo was owned by French and American citizens situated in both countries. The re-captors claimed salvage on the ship and cargo and there were many claimants to the cargo. The court awarded 1/2 salvage on the recapture of an armed ship, 1/6 salvage on the goods, restoration of goods belonging to American citizens or residents, and condemnation of the remaining goods. The Supreme Court affirmed, as French law gave goods recaptured after one day to the re-captors. The Court had to follow reciprocity of that law for the French residents.[99]

*5. The Mary and Susan and Dos Hermanos and the Fortuna*

| Legal issues to watch for |
|---|
| ❖ Enemy alien as privateer commander |
| ❖ Claimant may not challenge privateer's commission |
| ❖ Fraud indicated by hiding of ship's papers |

In the somewhat involved case of the *Mary and Susan*, it settled for the Court the principle,

"that shipments made by merchants, actually domiciled in the enemy's country at the breaking out of a war, partake of the nature of enemy trade, and, as such, are subject to belligerent capture."[100]

The *Mary and Susan* had been captured by American privateer *Tickler* in September 1812. One of the claimants, a British born and naturalized American merchant, who had only returned to the United States after the capture, tried to invalidate the seizure, as the *Tickler's* commander was himself British, an enemy alien. The Court, though, rejected this as disqualifying the capture, saying,

---

[99] The Adeline, 13 U.S. 244 (1815).
[100] The Mary and Susan, 14 U.S. 46 (1816).

"on this point we are unanimous that it makes no difference in the case. Admitting that this circumstance should bear at all upon the decision of the Court, the utmost that could result from it would be the condemnation of his interest to the government as a *droit* of admiralty. The owners and crew of the *Tickler* are as much parties in this Court as the commander, and his national character can in nowise affect their rights. But this Court can see no reason why an alien enemy should not be commissioned as commander of a privateer. There is no positive law prohibiting it, and it has been the universal practice of nations to employ foreigners and even deserters to fight their battles. Such an individual knows his fate should he fall into the hands of the enemy, and the right to punish in such case is acquiesced in by all nations. But, unrestrained by positive law, we can see no reason why this government should be incapacitated to delegate the exercise of the rights of war to any individual who may command its confidence, whatever may be his national character."[101]

In the case of the *Dos Hermanos*, the Court ruled that claimants had no right to litigate the question of whether the captors had a valid commission. Justice Joseph Story, noting great irregularities in the lower courts' proceedings, reminded them of the procedures for a libel,

"It is the established rule in courts of prize that the evidence to acquit or condemn must in the first instance come from the papers and crew of the captured ship. On this account it is the duty of the captors, as soon as practicable, to bring the ship's papers into the registry of the district court and to have the examinations of the principal officers and seamen of the captured ship taken before the district judge, or commissioners appointed by him, upon the standing interrogatories. It is exclusively upon these papers and the examinations, taken *in preparatorio,* that the cause is to be heard before the district court. If, from the whole evidence, the property clearly appear to be hostile or neutral, condemnation or acquittal immediately follows.

If, on the other hand, the property appear doubtful, or the case be clouded with suspicions or inconsistencies, it then becomes a case of

---

[101] *Id.*

further proof, which the court will direct or deny according to the rules which govern its legal discretion on this subject. Further proof is not a matter of course. It is granted in cases of honest mistake or ignorance or to clear away any doubts or defects consistent with good faith. But if the parties have been guilty of gross fraud or misconduct or illegality, further proof is not allowed, and under such circumstances the parties are visited with all the fatal consequences of an original hostile character. It is essential, therefore, to the correct administration of prize law that the regular modes of proceeding should be observed with the utmost strictness, and it is a great mistake to allow common law notions in respect to evidence or practice to prevail in proceedings which have very little analogy to those at common law."[102]

The *Fortuna* was captured by the privateer *Roger* in April 1814 and brought for libel to North Carolina. The ship's journey started in Riga and included stops in England, Barbados, Jamaica, and Cuba, and time sailing within British convoys. The cargo's primary claimant was Martin Krause of Riga, a neutral. However, parts of the ship's papers were discovered at different times in different places, the last were concealed in the ship's frame. The ship and cargo were condemned and on appeal, came to the Supreme Court, which asked for further proofs. On re-hearing, the Court affirmed, saying this voyage was done under the auspices of a London merchant house, noting,

"there is a general shade of suspicion cast over the whole case by the fact that all the material papers relating to the transaction were mysteriously concealed in a billet of wood. Had there been nothing fraudulent intended, these papers ought to have been delivered along with the documentary evidence. But they were not discovered until betrayed by one of the crew. It is upon the investigation of these papers principally that the circumstances occur which discover the true character of this voyage."[103]

---

[102] The Dos Hermanos, 15 U.S. 76 (1817).
[103] The Fortuna, 15 U.S. 161 (1817); 16 U.S. 236 (1818).

*6. The Bothnea and the George and the Anna Maria*

| Legal issues to watch for |
|---|
| ❖  Collusion on capture to facilitate smuggling |
| ❖  Collusion proved by actions of prize crew and fitting out |
| ❖  Privateer liable for damages caused after capture |

The *Bothnea* was captured by the privateer *Washington* in November 1813, after departing Halifax on a smuggling voyage to the United States, and then libeled in Massachusetts. There was suspicion that there was collusion, as the privateer mounted only a single gun, had a small crew, and had dropped the captured crews off before bringing the ship in for condemnation. The Court ruled for condemnation to the captors, after the government raised questions on the suspicious nature of this seizure,

> "Was it not the usual custom during the late war for the owners of privateers to stipulate with the officers and crew that the latter should receive one moiety or some other definite proportion of the proceeds of all prizes? Were there any cases where the crews were engaged to serve on monthly wages without participating in the prizes? Was it not usual for privateers to bring in the prisoners captured by them? What was the usual and adequate crew and armament of a privateer of about 25 tons burthen, intended for a cruise from the eastern ports, in the Bay of Fundy and along the coasts of Nova Scotia?"[104]

In another case of suspected collusion, the *George* was captured by the privateer *Fly*. The Court asked the following questions concerning collusion,

> "1st, the force of the *Fly;* 2d, the shipping articles; 3d, the cargo of the *George;* 4th, the number of her crew; 5th, the place and other circumstances of her capture; 6th, the sending the mariners on shore instead of bringing them into the United States."[105]

The Court ruled the capture to be collusive and affirmed the condemnation of the ship and cargo to the United States. This was based

---

[104] The Bothnea, 15 U.S. 169 (1817).
[105] The George, 14 U.S. 408 (1816); 15 U.S. 278 (1817).

upon the ship was not fitted out for a long voyage, the commander was only 21 years old, the ship had voluntarily exposed itself to a known privateer area, the privateer captain was the owner, the seamen were on wages and not sharing in the prize proceeds, the prize master took instructions on where to go to port in case the seizure was seen as fraudulent, and the supercargo had agreed to take on a small additional cargo for the voyage to the United States.

The American ship *Anna Maria* was captured by the privateer *Nonsuch*, which was flying British colors, in October 1812, apparently traveling to a British port. The whole crew was taken off and put in irons, but the prize crew sold some of the cargo for provisions and the prize was subsequently run aground in Cuba, where the ship and the remaining cargo were sold off. The owners of the *Anna Maria* initiated a libel against the owners of the *Nonsuch* for the damages they incurred. The libel was dismissed in the district court and was appealed to the Supreme Court, which looked at whether the ship might have been trying to enter a British port. Finding that the ship had no license to protect it from capture in an enemy's port, the Court said the initial stop and search was reasonable but what followed was not. Ordering the lower costs to determine compensation for the libelants, the Court said

> "However meritorious may have been the services of the private armed vessels of the United States in the aggregate, those individuals who have acted with this culpable disregard to the rights of others ought not to escape the animadversion of the law. The conduct of the officers of the *Nonsuch* on board the *Anna Maria* was unjustifiably licentious. Breaking open trunks when keys were offered them, taking out the crew and putting them in irons, and leaving her in this situation were acts not to be excused. The honor and the character of the nation are concerned in repressing such irregular ties, and the justice of the Court requires that compensation should be made for the injury which the libellants have sustained."[106]

---

[106] The Anna Maria, 15 U.S. 327 (1817).

*7. The Nereide and the Star and the Anne*

---

<u>Legal issues to watch for</u>

❖ Enemy nature of ship does not condemn neutral cargo
❖ Condemnation removes salvage right from original owner
❖ Captors not incompetent to testify for further proof

---

The *Nereide* was captured by the privateer *Governor Tompkins* in December 1813, on a voyage from London to Buenos Aires and back. The ship and cargo were libeled in New York and condemned, specifically the cargo belonging to British and Spanish subjects. In a long analysis, the Court determined that just because neutral cargo was carried in an enemy-owned and armed ship, as the *Nereide* carried ten guns, did not make the cargo subject to condemnation. The Court reversed the condemnation of the cargo owned by residents of Buenos Aires. This was a majority decision, with other justices not concurring, as the *Nereide* was armed, had sailed in a British convoy, and fought a short battle before surrendering, demonstrating sufficient hostility to require condemnation of the goods.[107]

The *Star*, a British merchantman sailing from the East Indies to Britain, was captured by the American privateer *Surprise* in January 1815. The ship had previously been an American ship condemned in the Halifax vice admiralty court. In the 1815 libel in New York, the testator of the former American owner entered a claim for the ship, net of salvage. This was rejected by the lower courts, with the ship condemned to the captors. The claimants asserted that the prize act of 1812 had overridden the salvage act of 1800,[108] which had specified that upon condemnation by a competent authority, there were no rights of restoration to the original owners. The Supreme Court did not agree, ruling merely that the 1812 prize act had not mentioned that law but had said "agreeably to the provisions heretofore established by law."[109] The Court affirmed the lower courts' condemnation to the captors, as the prior owner's rights had previously been extinguished in the Halifax condemnation.

---

[107] The Nereide, 13 U.S. 388 (1815).
[108] An Act providing for Salvage in cases of Recapture, c. 6, s. 1, ch. 14.
[109] The Star, 16 U.S. 78 (1818).

The British ship *Anne* was captured by privateer *Ultor* in March 1815, off Santa Domingo. Spain's consul protested that the capture happened inside Spanish territory, but the captors testified that it happened outside their territory. The Court dismissed the Spanish protest as not being authorized by the Spanish government and noted that the captured ship had started the battle, thereby giving up any right to claim neutrality, affirming the lower courts' condemnation. Against the claimants' objection to use of the captors' testimony, the Court said,

> "that captors, are in no cases admissible witnesses in prize causes being rendered incompetent by reason of their interest. It is certainly true, that, upon the original hearing, no other evidence is admissible than that of the ship's papers, and the preparatory examinations of the captured crew. But upon an order for further proof, where the benefit of it is allowed to the captors, their attestations are clearly admissible evidence. This is the ordinary course of prize courts, especially where it becomes material to ascertain the circumstances of the capture, for in such cases the facts lie as much within the knowledge of the captors as the captured, and the objection of interest generally applies as strongly to the one party as to the other. It is a mistake to suppose that the common law doctrine as to competency is applicable to prize proceedings. In courts of prize, no person is incompetent merely on the ground of interest. His testimony is admissible, subject to all exceptions as to its credibility."[110]

### 8. *The Amiable Nancy* and *the Divina Pastora* and *the Josefa Segunda*

| Legal issues to watch for |
| --- |
| ❖ No damages for lost profits for due to privateer misconduct |
| ❖ American court involvement as neutral in libels |
| ❖ Condemnation proceeds when violations of U.S. law |

The *Amiable Nancy* was captured by American privateer *Scourge* off Haiti in October 1814 and then libeled in New York by the *Amiable Nancy's* supercargo Frederick Roux. He claimed that the privateer stole personal items and money from his crew and sailing items off the ship, in addition to

---

[110] The Anne, 16 U.S. 435 (1818).

the ship's papers. The ship was released but subsequently captured by the Royal Navy and condemned, due to a lack of papers. The owner had to pay to retrieve his ship and cargo. Testimony from the captain of the marines on the *Scourge* agreed that the lieutenant of the boarding party had let his men plunder, after it was discovered that the ship was a neutral. The district court found for the libelants, who included the owner, supercargo, mate, and others, who had sought damages of $15,000. The only issue upon appeal was the specific damages. The circuit court rejected the awarding of lost profits on the voyage, which the Supreme Court concurred with, as being too difficult to estimate with certainty.[111]

The Spanish *Divina Pastora*, on a voyage to Spain, was captured by the Argentine privateer *Mangoree*, in October 1816, and sent into Massachusetts to be libeled, during the wars of independence in South America. The district court ordered restitution of the ship and cargo. Reversing and sending the case back to the circuit court for further findings, the Supreme Court laid out its analysis as to the involvement of American courts,

"Unless the neutral rights of the United States, as ascertained by the law of nations, the acts of Congress, and treaties with foreign powers, are violated by the cruisers sailing under commissions from those governments, captures by them are to be regarded by us as other captures *jure belli* are regarded, the legality of which cannot be determined in the courts of a neutral country. If, therefore, it appeared in this case that the capture was made under a regular commission from the government established at Buenos Ayres by a vessel which had not committed any violation of our neutrality, the captured property must be restored to the possession of the captors. But if, on the other hand, it was shown that the capture was made in violation of our neutral rights and duties, restitution would be decreed to the original owners."[112]

The *Josefa Segunda* from Havana was captured by a Venezuelan privateer *The General Arismendi* in February 1818, with a cargo of enslaved

---

[111] The Amiable Nancy, 16 U.S. 546 (1818).
[112] The Divina Pastora, 17 U.S. 52 (1819).

persons onboard. Heading towards the United States, the prize ship was finally seized by customs officials in Louisiana. The ship was libeled and condemned for the benefit of the United States. The Supreme Court said that the only important consideration was a violation of the U.S. statute prohibiting the important of enslaved people into the United States.[113] The claimants said the visit to the United States was out of necessity, but this was rejected, as there were many other ports bypassed to get there. They also claimed the taking was piratical, but the Court rejected this, finding that there was a valid commission from Venezuela.[114] The ship was condemned and sold and then the "cargo," the human beings taken from Africa to the United States, were also sold, the proceeds of which became the dispute in a later Supreme Court case.[115]

*9. La Amistad de Rues and the Amiable Isabella*

| Legal issues to watch for |
|---|
| ❖ Awarding damages to neutral libelant |
| ❖ Requirement of libelant to clearly demonstrate violation of neutrality |
| ❖ Lack of privateering commission does not impact condemnation |

*La Amistad de Rues* was captured by a Venezuelan privateer *La Guerriere*, in November 1817, and later captured by an American armed vessel and brought into New Orleans. The original Spanish owners libeled the ship and goods and asked for restitution and damages. The original captors asked for restoration of their prize ship and cargo. The district court awarded the original Spanish owners the ship, cargo, and damages against the original captors. On appeal, the Supreme Court ruled that the violation of neutrality was not clearly made out, which was up to the libelant asserting it to do, so reversed and condemned the ship and cargo to the original privateer captors. The Court also declined to provide any damages to a neutral libelant in its courts, saying,

---

[113] An Act to prohibit the importation of Slaves into any port or place within the jurisdiction of the United States, from and after the first day of January, in the year of our Lord one thousand eight hundred and eight, c. 9, s. 2, ch. 22.

[114] The Josefa Segunda, 18 U.S. 338 (1820).

[115] The Josefa Segunda, 23 U.S. 312 (1825).

"a more general objection is to the allowance of any damages in cases of this sort as between the belligerents. The doctrine heretofore asserted in this Court is that whenever a capture is made by any belligerent in violation of our neutrality, if the prize come voluntarily within our jurisdiction, it shall be restored to the original owners. This is done upon the footing of the general law of nations, and the doctrine is fully recognized by the Act of Congress of 1794. But this Court has never yet been understood to carry their jurisdiction, in cases of violation of neutrality, beyond the authority to decree restitution of the specific property, with the costs and expenses during the pending of the judicial proceedings.

We are now called upon to give general damages for plunderage, and if the particular circumstances of any case shall hereafter require it, we may be called upon to inflict exemplary damages to the same extent as in the ordinary cases of marine torts. We entirely disclaim any right to inflict such damages, and consider it no part of the duty of a neutral nation to interpose, upon the mere footing of the law of nations, to settle all the rights and wrongs which may grow out of a capture between belligerents. Strictly speaking, there can be no such thing as a marine tort between the belligerents. Each has an undoubted right to exercise all the rights of war against the other, and it cannot be a matter of judicial complaint that they are exercised with severity, even if the parties do transcend those rules which the customary laws of war justify. At least they have never been held within the cognizance of the prize tribunals of neutral nations.

The captors are amenable to their own government exclusively for any excess or irregularity in their proceedings, and a neutral nation ought no otherwise to interfere than to prevent captors from obtaining any unjust advantage by a violation of its neutral jurisdiction. Neutral nations may indeed inflict pecuniary, or other penalties on the parties for any such violation, but it then does it professedly in vindication of its own rights, and not by way of compensation to the captured. When called upon by either of the belligerents to act in such cases, all that justice seems to require is that the neutral nation should fairly execute its own laws and give no asylum to the property unjustly captured. It is bound therefore to restore the property if found within its own ports; but beyond this it is not obliged to interpose between the belligerents.

If indeed it were otherwise, there would be no end to the difficulties and embarrassments of neutral prize tribunals. They would be compelled to decide in every variety of shape upon marine trespasses *in rem* and *in personam* between belligerents without possessing adequate means of ascertaining the real facts or of compelling the attendance of foreign witnesses, and thus they would draw within their jurisdiction almost every incident of prize. Such a course of things would necessarily create irritations and animosities, and very soon embark neutral nations in all the controversies and hostilities of the conflicting parties."[116]

*The Amiable Isabella* was captured by the privateer *Roger* in December 1814, on a voyage from Havana to London, although purportedly to Hamburg. The prize was taken to North Carolina to be libeled, where the district court condemned the ship and cargo. Some of the ship's papers were found hidden on board, others were on the person of the supercargo, some papers were mutilated, and still other papers had been thrown overboard and spoliated. On appeal, the Supreme Court first rejected the claim that a privateer sailing without a commission was a reason for not condemning the ship, saying,

"A preliminary question was raised at the original argument that the libel ought to be dismissed because the capture was made without public authority and by a noncommissioned vessel. Whether this be so or not we do not think it material now to inquire. It is a question between the government and the captors, with which the claimant has nothing to do. If the ship and cargo be enemy's property, it cannot be restored to the claimant. If the captors made the capture without any legal commission and it is decreed good prize, the condemnation must, under such circumstances, be to the government itself. If with a commission, then it may be to the captors. But in any view the question is matter of subsequent inquiry after the principal question of prize is disposed of, and the government may, if it chooses, contest

---

[116] La Amistad de Rues, 18 U.S. 385 (1820).

the right of the captors by an interlocutory application after a decree of condemnation has passed and before distribution is decreed. The claimant can have no just interest in that question, and cannot be permitted to moot it before this Court."[117]

The Court affirmed the condemnation of the ship and cargo, believing that there was fraud, which agreed with the captor's claim that the scheme of the voyage was founded in a London merchant house, thereby disproving the claims of neutrality,

"that the voyage had its origin in London and was to terminate there and that the usual frauds of false papers, false destination, and suppression of evidence have been resorted to for the purpose of giving a neutral character to hostile interests... It is to be recollected that by the settled rule of prize courts, the *onus probandi* of a neutral interest rests on the claimant. This rule is tempered by another, whose liberality will not be denied, that the evidence to acquit or condemn shall in the first instance come from the ship's papers and persons on board, and where these are not satisfactory, if the claimant has not violated good faith, he shall be admitted to maintain his claim by further proof. But if, in the event, after full time and opportunity to adduce proofs, the claim is still left in uncertainty and the neutrality of the property is not established beyond reasonable doubt, it is the invariable rule of prize courts to reject the claim, and to decree condemnation of the property. There is another rule too, founded in the most salutary and benign principles of justice, that the assertion of a false claim, in whole or in part by an agent of, or in connivance with the real owners, is a substantive cause of forfeiture, leading to condemnation of the property."[118]

---

[117] The Amiable Isabella, 19 U.S. 1 (1821).
[118] *Id.*

*10. The Hiawatha (Prize Cases)* and *the Springbok* and *the Hampton*

Legal issues to watch for

❖ Ships in port assumed to have notice of establishment of blockade
❖ Ships using blockade transshipment port not always condemned
❖ Refusal to consider a claim from mortgagee

In the American Civil War, privateers were not deployed on the Union side. The use of privateers on the Confederate side was discussed in the *Smith* case in Chapter 2, so the prize cases presented here all involved captures by Union armed warships.

In the *Prize Cases*,[119] the Union had created a blockade of Southern ports, based on a proclamation by the president, in April 1861. Several ships were captured and condemned for trying to evade the blockade, all claiming ignorance of the blockade. Ships in blockaded ports had 15 days to depart after the establishment of the blockade (on April 30) and were presumed to have notice of this. One of the cases involved the *Hiawatha*, which was captured on May 20, after spending many days taking on new cargo and getting a tug to take the ship out. This exceeded the allowed period, so the Court ruled that the ship and cargo were properly seized.

The *Circassian* was a British ship captured for running the blockade in May 1862 and condemned. The Court laid down the rule that,

> "It is a well established principle of prize law, as administered by the courts both of the United States and Great Britain, that sailing from a neutral port with intent to enter a blockaded port and with knowledge of the existence of the blockade subjects the vessel and in most cases its cargo to capture and condemnation."[120]

The *Cheshire* was captured in December 1861 outside Savannah, taken to New York, and condemned. This was despite its papers claiming that the ship was destined for either Halifax or Nassau and claims that the ship was only intended to inquire whether the blockade was still in existence. The Court articulated the rule that even an approach to a port known to be

---

[119] Prize Cases, 67 U.S. 635 (1862).
[120] The Circassian, 69 U.S. 135 (1864).

blockaded was itself a violation of blockade, subjecting the ship and cargo to condemnation. The reason for this was,

"If approach for inquiry were permissible it will be readily seen that the greatest facilities would be afforded to elude the blockade, the liberty of inquiry would be a license to attempt to enter the blockaded port, and that information was sought would be the plea in every case of seizure. With a liberty of this kind, the difficulty of enforcing an efficient blockade would be greatly augmented."[121]

The Court also ruled that property belonging to a commercial house situated inside Confederate enemy territory was rightly condemned, despite some partners being established in the neutral country of Britain.

The *Springbok* was captured, in February 1863, off Nassau, a well-known blockade running transshipment port, and condemned. The Court ruled that while the cargo should be condemned, this ship should not be,

"where goods destined ultimately for a belligerent port are being conveyed between two neutral ports by a neutral ship, under a charter made in good faith for that voyage, and without any fraudulent connection on the part of her owners with the ulterior destination of the goods, that the ship, though liable to seizure in order to the confiscation of the goods, is not liable to condemnation as prize."[122]

The *Hampton* was captured in January 1863 and condemned, with the only claim from a mortgagee, which the Court refused to consider in a prize case,

"because an obvious principle of necessity must forbid a prize court from recognizing the doctrine here contended for. If it were once admitted in these courts, there would be an end of all prize condemnation. As soon as a war was threatened, the owners of vessels and cargoes which might be so situated as to be subject to capture would only have to raise a sufficient sum of money on them, by *bona fide* mortgages, to indemnify them in case of such capture.

[121] The Cheshire, 70 U.S. 231 (1865).
[122] The Springbok, 72 U.S. 1 (1866).

If the vessel or cargo was seized, the owner need not appear, because he would be indifferent, having the value of his property in his hands already. The mortgagee, having an honest mortgage which he could establish in a court of prize, would either have the property restored to him or get the amount of his mortgage out of the proceeds of the sale. The only risk run by enemy vessels or cargoes on the high seas, or by neutrals engaged in an effort to break a blockade, would be the costs and expenses of capture and condemnation, a risk too unimportant to be of any value to a belligerent in reducing his opponent to terms."[123]

The *Marshall* was seized by a Confederate ship in May 1861, and later, a claim was made against the owner's insurance policy. The policy would pay if the ship were taken by pirates but not if captured otherwise. The issue before the Court was whether a ship of the Confederacy should be considered a pirate, or whether it was legally commissioned by an enemy government in a declared war, such that the seizure should be deemed a lawful capture. The Court ruled the Confederacy a de facto government, meaning the seizure was a capture and therefore the loss was not covered under the insurance policy.[124]

The *Diana* was captured in November 1862 off the Texas coast, and libeled but restitution was granted by the district court, due to the ship allegedly entering a blockaded port due to necessity. The Court did not find the argument compelling and reversed, saying,

"It is undoubtedly true that a vessel may be in such distress as to justify her in attempting to enter a blockaded port. She may be out of provisions or water, or she may be in a leaking condition, and no other port be of easy access. The case, however, must be one of absolute and uncontrollable necessity, and this must be established beyond reasonable doubt. "Nothing less," says Sir William Scott, "than an uncontrollable necessity, which admits of no compromise, and cannot be resisted," will be held a justification of the offense. Any rule less stringent than this would open the door to all sorts of fraud.

---

[123] The Hampton, 72 U.S. 372 (1866).
[124] Mauran v. Insurance Company, 73 U.S. 1 (1867).

Attempted evasions of the blockade would be excused upon pretenses of distress and danger, not warranted by the facts, but the falsity of which it would be difficult to expose."[125]

The *Andromeda* was captured off Cuba, in May 1862, on a voyage from Texas to Havana, was libeled, and condemned, as a prize of war. The Supreme Court ruled the master clearly still owned the ship, despite his attempt to transfer it to a British citizen, and its enemy nature was evidenced by the spoliation of the ship's papers when boarded. The Court held that,

> "The enemy character of the vessel is quite as clearly proved... the condemnation both of vessel and cargo seem to us, therefore, well warranted... We think the proof that the *Andromeda* and her cargo were liable to capture and condemnation for breach of blockade equally clear... It would be enough to say that the libel shows a case of prize, and that is sufficient for jurisdiction... The rule is that a libel in prize must allege generally the fact of capture as prize of war, and the libel in the record is in conformity with this rule."[126]

---

[125] The Diana, 74 U.S. 354 (1868).
[126] The Andromeda, 69 U.S. 481 (1874).

# *Afterword*

As described in Chapter 5, privateering was authorized but not used by the U.S. government in the American Civil War, although the navy-poor Confederacy did employ it. This was despite, unlike all the other maritime powers, the U.S. government declining to ratify the 1856 provision in the Paris Declaration banning the use of privateers (discussed in Chapter 4). Consequently, four decades later, in the last conflict with American involvement of the 19th century, the Spanish-American War, privateering was again raised as a possibility. In a letter from the U.S. ambassador to Britain, John Hay, to the U.S. secretary of state, John Sherman, in the days just preceding the declaration of war, the possible use of privateers was broached, along with the divergent British positions, based upon their nation's experiences since banning privateering,

> "There is a good deal of discussion here, both in public and in private, in relation to the effect upon the rights and interests of neutrals at sea of hostilities between the United States and Spain... a prominent representative of the shipping interests of England in the House of Commons... proposed, in the event of either belligerent employing privateers, to treat such vessels as pirates.... [A] member of Parliament, who is greatly interested in matters of maritime law, who most earnestly expressed the hope that the United States would not, in the present juncture, adhere to the treaty of Paris and thus tie their hands permanently from the employment of privateers, a step which he thought was a great mistake on the part of Great Britain in 1856. We might of course, for sufficient reasons, waive our right to fit out privateers, and our equally undoubted rights of visitation and search without entering into any engagement which should make such waiver binding against us in the future."[1]

---

[1] John Hay to John Sherman (Apr. 18, 1898).

Sherman's reply, discounting the potential use of privateers but supporting the other three provisions of the Paris Declaration[2] with which the United States agreed, said,

> "In the event of hostilities between United States and Spain, the policy of this Government will be not to resort to privateering, but to adhere to the following recognized rules of international law: First, the neutral flag covers enemy's goods, with the exception of contraband of war; second, neutral goods, with the exception of contraband of war, are not liable to capture under the enemy's flag; and, third, blockades in order to be binding must be effective."[3]

Although official use of privateering ceased, and was eventually legally banned,[4] illegal pirating did not die out completely. The main piratical activity in the Americas, which began with the War of Spanish Succession, materially reduced in the early 18th century but pirating carried on sporadically through the American Civil War and continued to occasionally be a menace to the U.S. global commercial affairs. The actions of the Barbary pirates, who had been preying on American shipping since the founding of the republic and loss of Royal Navy protection, led to two small wars against those North African states in the 19th century. The wars, ending in treaties, did not permanently solve the pirate problem.

With conflicts and tensions in the Middle East and Africa rising in the early 21st century, pirates appeared in the troubled nation of Somalia. In April 2010, several Somali pirates attempted to capture a U.S. Navy ship, lighted to look like a merchant vessel. Their attack was expected and was repulsed, and the men were captured, tried, and convicted of several crimes, including piracy. They challenged their convictions, inter alia, based on upon the definition of piracy, claiming they never robbed anyone. Under modern U.S. statutes, piracy is defined and punished as,

---

[2] Declaration Respecting Maritime Law, Paris (Apr. 16, 1856).
[3] John Sherman to John Hay (Apr. 23, 1898).
[4] 18 U.S.C. §§ 1654.

"Whoever, on the high seas, commits the crime of piracy as defined by the law of nations, and is after-wards brought into or found in the United States, shall be imprisoned for life."[5]

The court of appeals[6] relied almost entirely upon the reasoning from the opinion of the district court, which they affirmed, but noted that another district court in a separate trial had allowed the dismissal of the piracy conviction, because Justice Story in *Smith* in 1820 (see Chapter 2) had said the law of nations had limited piracy's definition to robbery on the sea. The district court in this case came to a different conclusion. It began by stating that the Constitution gave Congress the power to define and punish three separate offenses:

"(1) "Piracies ... committed on the high Seas," (2) "Felonies committed on the high Seas," and (3) "Offenses against the Law of Nations.""[7]

The district court had broken piracy into two types: municipal piracy, definable under the laws of the United States, which had to have a nexus with one of the United States to exert jurisdiction, and general piracy, defined under the law of nations, which had universal jurisdiction allowing any nation to try defendants for the crime. To be able to try anyone under general piracy, because there is no federal common law, a statute had to be enacted by Congress that brought the law of nations into U.S. law.

As the act of 1819 (see Chapter 2) had done so, the key question was how the law of nations defined piracy. Based on the *Smith* case, that Court in 1820 viewed that definition as being limited to the act of robbery on the high seas. For the district court, the question then became whether the law of nations was static or whether it evolved, concluding,

"In view of the statutory language chosen by Congress in enacting the general piracy statute at issue in this case, and the Supreme Court case law examining the meaning of the "law of nations," the Court concludes that the phrase "law of nations," as used in 18 U.S.C § 1651, requires application of the modern international consensus definition

---

[5] 18 U.S.C. §§ 1651.
[6] U.S. v Dire, No. 11-4310 (4th Cir. June 2013).
[7] U.S. v. Hasan, No. 2:10cr56 (E.D. Va. Oct. 2010).

of general piracy. Doing so, however, does not mean that courts are somehow creating law. Instead, it means only that courts are recognizing that which has already been accepted by an overwhelming majority of countries as the definition of general piracy, and courts must be careful to do so only when it is, in fact, clear that an overwhelming majority of countries have definitively accepted such a definition. In exercising such care, courts assuage concerns about the clarity of the definition of proscribed conduct for defendants facing prosecution."[8]

Looking to the 1958 Convention on High Seas and the 1982 United Nations Convention on the Law of the Sea, and considering the significant number of nations who had signed or ratified these agreements, the district court used these definitions to find the current definition of piracy, under the law of nations (i.e. customary international law), to be:

"(A) (1) any illegal act of violence or detention, or any act of depredation; (2) committed for private ends; (3) on the high seas or a place outside the jurisdiction of any state; (4) by the crew or the passengers of a private ship or a private aircraft; (5) and directed against another ship or aircraft, or against persons or property on board such ship or aircraft; or

(B) (1) any act of voluntary participation in the operation of a ship or an aircraft; (2) with knowledge of the facts making it a pirate ship; or

(C) (1) any act of inciting or of intentionally facilitating (2) an act described in subparagraph (A) or (B)."[9]

---

[8] *Id.* at 629-30.
[9] *Id.* at 640-41.

The court also said that use of the modern definition of piracy under the law of nations, as opposed to the one used in 1820, was not in violation of Due Process. This was because any expanded definition would take a significant amount of time to be accepted as part of customary international law. This long gestation period should provide sufficient notice, as was fully described in *Smith*, where,

> "The Court found that, by incorporating the definition of piracy under the law of nations, Congress had proscribed general piracy as clearly as if it had enumerated the elements of the offense in the legislation itself."[10]

---

[10] *Id.* at 639.

# Appendix – Legal Issues to Watch For

This listing summaries all the legal issues which were noted across the many trials presented in the chapters on piracy and privateering.


## Chapter 1

- ❖ Scope of the crime of piracy
- ❖ Importance of the intention to turn pirate
- ❖ Extraterritorial jurisdiction of English law
- ❖ Pleading without benefit of counsel
- ❖ Use of fellow defendants as witnesses
- ❖ Implied malice
- ❖ Qualifying for a royal pardon
- ❖ Acting under color of a privateering commission
- ❖ Withholding evidence
- ❖ Choosing common law instead of civil law
- ❖ Joining a pirate crew after being marooned
- ❖ Crew member who was constrained
- ❖ Aiding and abetting in a murder on the high seas
- ❖ Proving revolt on a ship from pirate's articles
- ❖ Piracy when only receiving pirated goods
- ❖ Use of common or civil law in colonial piracy trials
- ❖ Accomplice testimony
- ❖ Cross-examining witnesses
- ❖ Charged with conspiracy to commit piracy
- ❖ Special proofs needed for women pirates

- ❖ Charged with piracy for socializing with pirates
- ❖ Piracy by attacking a warship believing it was a merchant ship
- ❖ Proof against a physician pirate
- ❖ Various reasons for excusing those found on pirate ships
- ❖ Accusing all men on a pirate ship to find the actual pirates
- ❖ Convicting and condemning minors for piracy
- ❖ Allowing piracy if the victims are enemies
- ❖ Use of circumstantial evidence to prove piracy
- ❖ Using piracy as a front for a murder charge
- ❖ Colonies' ability to prosecute murder on the high seas

## Chapter 2

- ❖ Piracy on non-U.S. ships by non-U.S. nationals tried in U.S. courts
- ❖ Prosecutorial discretion to not try piracy and murder
- ❖ Concurrent jurisdiction for crimes on the high seas
- ❖ Convicting a pirate on testimony of a single witness
- ❖ Differentiating piracy from larceny in feloniously running away
- ❖ Whether violence is necessary for piracy
- ❖ Statutory definition of piratical robbery
- ❖ Whether commissioned privateers can be charged with piracy
- ❖ If privateering statutes shield privateers from civil courts
- ❖ Identifying pirates at trial
- ❖ Trying an indigent, non-citizen for piracy
- ❖ Double jeopardy in dismissing hung jury in piracy trial
- ❖ Requesting a jury of moiety
- ❖ Delaying a trial for character witnesses
- ❖ Planning a piracy with fraudulent currency and forged papers
- ❖ Excluding juror who would not consider capital punishment
- ❖ Differential treatment for Black pirates

- ❖ Whether to granting part of prize to non-commissioned privateer
- ❖ General carriers making general claims to prize cargo
- ❖ Claimants must take risk of cargo
- ❖ Destination port and lack of documents indicating smuggling
- ❖ Return of ships to neutral masters
- ❖ Payment for consuming cargo
- ❖ Condemnation of enemy laders, consigners, or exporters
- ❖ Claim for recapture of ship by former owner
- ❖ Evidence needed to prove national ownership
- ❖ Evidence of loyalist expulsion beyond reject loyalty oaths
- ❖ Determining captor when same prize taken twice by British ships
- ❖ Allocating prize between captor and re-captor
- ❖ When military cargo is contraband
- ❖ Need to inspect passport of neutral ship
- ❖ Current residence proves nationality
- ❖ Privilege afforded to enemy residing in neutral country
- ❖ Use of neutral nationality to mask ownership of vessel
- ❖ Taking prize to a port with an admiralty judge with a commission
- ❖ Cargo not on vessel condemned
- ❖ Use of false passes and neutral colors
- ❖ Seizing a ship under a flag of truce
- ❖ Intervention in libel by a government official
- ❖ Actions necessary for onlookers to share in a prize
- ❖ Recapture periods and locations under a peace proclamation
- ❖ Salvage fee due if recapture outside allowed period
- ❖ Entitlement to additions made to a recapture
- ❖ Fraud during a libel re-addressed in later proceedings
- ❖ Flying false colors during an attack
- ❖ Handling multiple libelants

❖ Priority of crown over other claimants

❖ Fee for services provides to prize ship in distress

❖ Suborning perjured testimony in support of condemnation

❖ Intercession by the king for a foreign privateering victim

❖ Termination period of privateering security

❖ False libel and appeal to keep sale proceeds

❖ Common law courts overruling Admiralty arrest

❖ Salvage fee derived from ransom demand

❖ Suing privateering who violates his instructions

❖ Sureties paying for privateering violations

❖ Method for splitting proceeds of a prize

❖ Nationality indicated by various roles of the master

❖ Paying the libelant's costs

❖ Inconsistencies do not overcome the presumption

❖ Seizures under the Prohibitory Act

❖ Violation of the act, even without knowledge of it

❖ Awards to re-captors of American ships

## Chapter 5

❖ Allocation of prize proceeds to mariners rising up

❖ If prize courts of appeal can reexamine facts

❖ Whether common law courts can mandate distribution of a prize

❖ Use of American courts for libel by foreign national

❖ Foreign privateers fitting out in American ports

❖ Whether American privateers can capture neutral ships

❖ Responsibility of agents for sale of illegal prize

❖ Ownership of an abandoned prize

❖ Whether separate prize of privateer could be attached

❖ Whether to rely on foreign admiralty court decisions

- ❖ Concealment of facts from prize's underwriter
- ❖ Whether future sale of prize ship defeats an insurance warranty
- ❖ Salvage rates based on whether state of war exists
- ❖ Salvage fee for recaptured neutral ships
- ❖ Requirements for abandonment to collect insurance
- ❖ Intercepting ship of former American citizen
- ❖ Liability for damages if no reasonable suspicion to capture
- ❖ Liability for damages if capturing ship heading from French port
- ❖ Liability for illegal prize seizure even when later taken by force
- ❖ Foreign condemnation not conclusive as to neutrality of prize owner
- ❖ Fraudulent agreement to seize and condemn a ship not enforceable
- ❖ Responsibility to condemnation proceeds never received
- ❖ Whether U.S. courts can execute decrees from prior courts
- ❖ Capture of a neutral ship is a total loss for insurance purposes
- ❖ Salvage due to neutrals who overpower prize crew
- ❖ Termination of insurance based on change in destination
- ❖ Insurance covers a ship on a voyage, not a ship and a voyage
- ❖ Disregarding the decision of a foreign admiralty court
- ❖ Seizure for violating municipal law
- ❖ Retaining control over res despite location of court
- ❖ Whether retrieval of goods is trading subject to condemnation
- ❖ Seizure of goods owned by British subjects with American citizenship
- ❖ Ability of Americans aboard to repatriate after learning of war
- ❖ Proof that order was placed on American's account
- ❖ Goods on consignment still owned by consignor
- ❖ Use of liens to defeat captors claims
- ❖ Whether the government or the captor receives a captured prize
- ❖ Whether enemy cargo was protected by presidential instructions
- ❖ Whether to condemn cargo shipped under license assisting an enemy

❖ When ship is claimed not be to a prize

❖ Whether condemnation indicates nationality

❖ Salvage rate for recapture of ship different than for cargo

❖ Enemy alien as privateer commander

❖ Claimant may not challenge privateer's commission

❖ Fraud indicated by hiding of ship's papers

❖ Collusion on capture to facilitate smuggling

❖ Collusion proved by actions of prize crew and fitting out

❖ Privateer liable for damages caused after capture

❖ Enemy nature of ship does not condemn neutral cargo

❖ Condemnation removes salvage right from original owner

❖ Captors not incompetent to testify for further proof

❖ No damages for lost profits for due to privateer misconduct

❖ American court involvement as neutral in libels

❖ Condemnation proceeds when violations of U.S. law

❖ Awarding damages to neutral libelant

❖ Requirement of libelant to clearly demonstrate violation of neutrality

❖ Lack of privateering commission does not impact condemnation

❖ Ships in port assumed to have notice of establishment of blockade

❖ Ships using blockade transshipment port not always condemned

❖ Refusal to consider a claim from mortgagee

# ADDITIONAL WRITINGS

## *USE OF U.S. COURTS BY FOREIGNERS*

Two sets of historic cases address the use of the U.S. courts by foreign nationals, involving the varied legal theories of prize and legal fictions.

**Prize**

The first case was a prize court case, the *Betsey*, which originally came before the district court in Maryland. The Swedish owner of the ship, and part-owner of the cargo, believed that the district court had jurisdiction. The French privateer captain believed U.S. courts did not have jurisdiction, and the French consul was the appropriate forum, despite the ship and cargo landing in Baltimore. Although being given the power over all cases involving admiralty under the U.S. Constitution, the district court ruled for the privateer, agreeing that it did not have jurisdiction over a prize case. The circuit court affirmed, so the case came to the U.S. Supreme Court.

The Swedish appellant's argument was that this was a civil case of admiralty, for restitution. That was an important point, as the Judiciary Act of 1789 had expressly only given district courts power over civil matters in admiralty. Adjudication of admiralty law was typically split between courts of prize and courts of instance, with the latter dealing with all non-prize matters, such a maritime contracts and torts. The French appellee asserted that the question whether it was a valid prize had to precede the matter of restitution. By definition, a prize only could only be taken in times of war, and the United States was not at war with either Sweden or France. Therefore, Judiciary Act limited the district court from hearing prize cases.

The Supreme Court, in a final opinion by the original chief justice, John Jay, held that every district court in the United States had the full powers of a court of admiralty, either in instance or in prize, thereby overturning the decisions of the lower courts. The court directed the district court to determine the claim for restitution for libel by the varied owners of the ship and cargo. The Court also held that no foreign power could erect any court within the jurisdiction of the United States, including those of admiralty, unless so created under a treaty.

## Legal fictions

The second set of cases involves the ability of a foreigner to bring a claim within the United States for an act that occurred outside the United States against a foreign national. In late 2019, a young Englishman on a motorbike was struck and killed by a car driven on the wrong side of the road by an American. The driver left the UK under purported diplomatic immunity. The U.S. government refused the UK's formal request for extradition, and she would not return voluntarily. The UK family had to resort to suing in U.S. courts, based upon cases three centuries' old, the first decided in Britain and the latter two within the United States.

## Assault

In 1773, the case of *Fabrigas v Mostyn* was brought in the English court of common pleas, for actions that happened on the British-controlled island of Minorca. The plaintiff was Anthony Fabrigas, a citizen of Minorca, and the defendant was John Mostyn, an English member of Parliament and governor of Minorca. Fabrigas alleged that, in September 1771, Mostyn had him assaulted and falsely imprisoned, incommunicado, in a filthy dungeon without trial or probable cause, and then forcibly banished him to Cartagena, Spain.

This affair had started when Fabrigas was refused permission to sell his inventory of wine by the governor-appointed local administrator. The governor said that a majority of the island's residents disagreed with Fabrigas' proposal to allow sales of wine at any time, preferring sales only be allowed on certain dates, as determined by drawn lots. Fabrigas claimed that the local administrator had sold his own wine, for a profit, and he, Fabrigas, could produce 150 men involved in wine making who supported his petition. He was arrested, kept in the dungeon for days, and deported to the Spanish mainland.

The charges, produced only when Fabrigas was being banished, were for:

"your seditious, mutinous, and insolent behaviour to me the governor, and for having dared most dangerously and seditiously to raise doubts and suspicions amongst the inhabitants..., and to excite them to dispute my authority, and disobey my orders; and for having further presumed most dangerously to insinuate, that his majesty's troops under my command, without any authority from them for such false and scandalous insinuations, were imposed upon."

Mostyn insisted that as governor of Minorca, he has the power to do what he did. The English jury did not agree, deliberating for only an hour before awarding the plaintiff damages of £3,000 and costs. Defendant Mostyn appealed (by filing a writ of error), asserting, inter alia, that the case could not be tried in England for overseas acts. The high court, in an opinion by Lord Mansfield, said that these types of cases could properly be tried in England:

"So all actions of a transitory nature that arise abroad may be laid as happening in an English county... But the law has in that case invented a fiction; and has said, the party shall first set out the description truly, and then give a venue only for form, and for the sake of trial, by a videlicet, in the county of Middlesex, or any other county. But no judge ever thought that when the declaration said in Fort St. George [in India], viz. in Cheapside [in England], that the plaintiff meant it was in Cheapside. It is a fiction of form; every country has its forms, which fictions of are invented for the furtherance of justice; and it is a certain law shall never be contradicted so as to defeat the end for which it was invented."

He concluded by applying that analysis to the harms alleged and locale in this case,

"as to transitory actions, there is not a colour of doubt but that every action that is transitory may be laid in any county in England, though the matter arises beyond the seas; and when it is absolutely necessary to lay the truth of the case in the declaration, there is a fiction of law to assist you, and you shall not make use of the truth of the case against that fiction."

## Litigation

*Fabrigas* was citied in an 1811 U.S. case, *Livingston v. Jefferson*. Future U.S. secretary of state Edward Livingston sued former U.S. president (and former U.S. secretary of state and lawyer) Thomas Jefferson. Livingston claimed that Jefferson interfered, in 1807, with his title to some property in New Orleans, by asserting federal ownership of the land. Livingston had acquired the land as payment for legal fees. The case was brought in the federal circuit court of Virginia, where Jefferson resided, which included Supreme Court chief justice John Marshall, riding circuit.

In his concurring opinion supporting dismissal, Marshall explained that, in England, all actions were originally local, as juries were expected to have knowledge of the matter being tried, instead of having to rely upon witnesses or experts to provide such knowledge. He further explained that English superior courts could direct juries to sit on a case in any county in the nation. This was not a matter of jurisdiction but of venue (i.e., a place people come to). This judge-made rule allowed a plaintiff to aver, for a contract which on its face names the place it was made, that place could be in any county in England. So, it was a legal fiction used to create the venue needed for calling a jury and conducting a trial. Marshall said that this legal fiction applied to all personal torts and to contracts, including contracts for land. He then noted the limits of this judge-made rule:

> "The distinction taken is that actions are deemed transitory where the transactions on which they are founded might have taken place any where; but are local where their cause is in its nature necessarily local... & an action of trespass *quare clausum fregit* [upon land] is a local action."

Marshall noted the problem of a right without a remedy, where a court had jurisdiction over a trespasser but who never appeared in the district where property was located to establish venue. He approvingly noted Mansfield's comments in *Fabrigas* categorizing actions as in rem and in personum, instead of as local and transitory. But as *Fabrigas* concerned assault and not trespass to property, this was to be considered obiter dictum, and in any event the original dichotomy of local and transitory was re-affirmed by later English caselaw.

## Seizure

The result in *Fabrigas* was fully recognized in American law in 1843 through the Supreme Court case of *McKenna v. Fisk*. Charles B. Fisk was accused of breaking into the storehouse of Bernard McKenna, in 1839, in Alleghany County, Maryland, and both taking and destroying goods, chattels, and the storehouse itself. The damages alleged were for the loss of the temporary storehouse, not affixed to real property, and for

> "one thousand gallons of spiritous liquors of different kinds; a large quantity of coffee and of tea; various clothing ready made for sale; two hundred bushels of Indian corn; all the promissory notes and accounts of sundry persons due to [McKenna];... at least $400; all the furniture, articles, and other articles in said storehouse."

The key point raised was whether the circuit court for the District of Columbia could adjudicate a case arising from actions that occurred in Maryland. The plaintiff asserted the three counts consisted of trespass to real property and damage to two kinds of personal property. While the trespass to real property was local, the damage to personal property (the goods and chattels) was transitory and could be tried before a court anywhere the defendant was.

The defendant, on the other hand, insisted that all the three counts were *quare clausum fregit*, having to do with trespass upon real property and so were local charges only triable before a court in Maryland. Confusingly, the charges listed in the plaintiff's declaration, specifying the counts, were said to have occurred in Washington County, District of Columbia, even though they actually occurred in Alleghany County, in the state of Maryland. The Court ruled against the defendant's claim that venue, even for transitory causes of action, must be where the trespass took place and clarified the confusing situs of the trespasses by saying:

> "The venue for trial is a legal fiction, devised for the furtherance of justice, and cannot be traversed. So that, if A becomes indebted to B, or commits a tort upon his person or upon his personal property in Paris, an action in either case may be maintained against A in England, if he is there found, upon a declaration alleging a cause of action to have occurred in an English county, in which the action is laid, without taking notice of the foreign place."

Printed in Great Britain
by Amazon